W9-DCJ-030

Ibamba

Books by Wynant Davis Hubbard

IBAMBA

WILD ANIMAL HUNTER

WILD ANIMALS

THE THOUSANDTH FROG

FIASCO IN ETHIOPIA

BONG'KWE

Ibamba

WYNANT DAVIS HUBBARD

New York Graphic Society
Publishers, Ltd.
Greenwich, Connecticut
1962

LIBRARY OF CONGRESS CATALOG NO. 62-19239

The publisher gratefully acknowledges permission
to reprint portions of this book which were originally
published in condensed versions under the following titles:
Chiquiqui, © 1934, The Curtis Publishing Company;
The Mighty Lion, © 1955, Fawcett Publications, Inc.;
Curse of Ibamba, © 1957, Fawcett Publications, Inc.;
The Lion Turned Green, Courtesy of STAG Magazine.

Published simultaneously in Canada by
Longmans Canada, Limited, Toronto

Printed in the United States of America by
The Book Press

To Iz, without whose gay and courageous companionship this would have been a very different story. Also to Sandy, without whose cooperation and encouragement this book might never have been written.

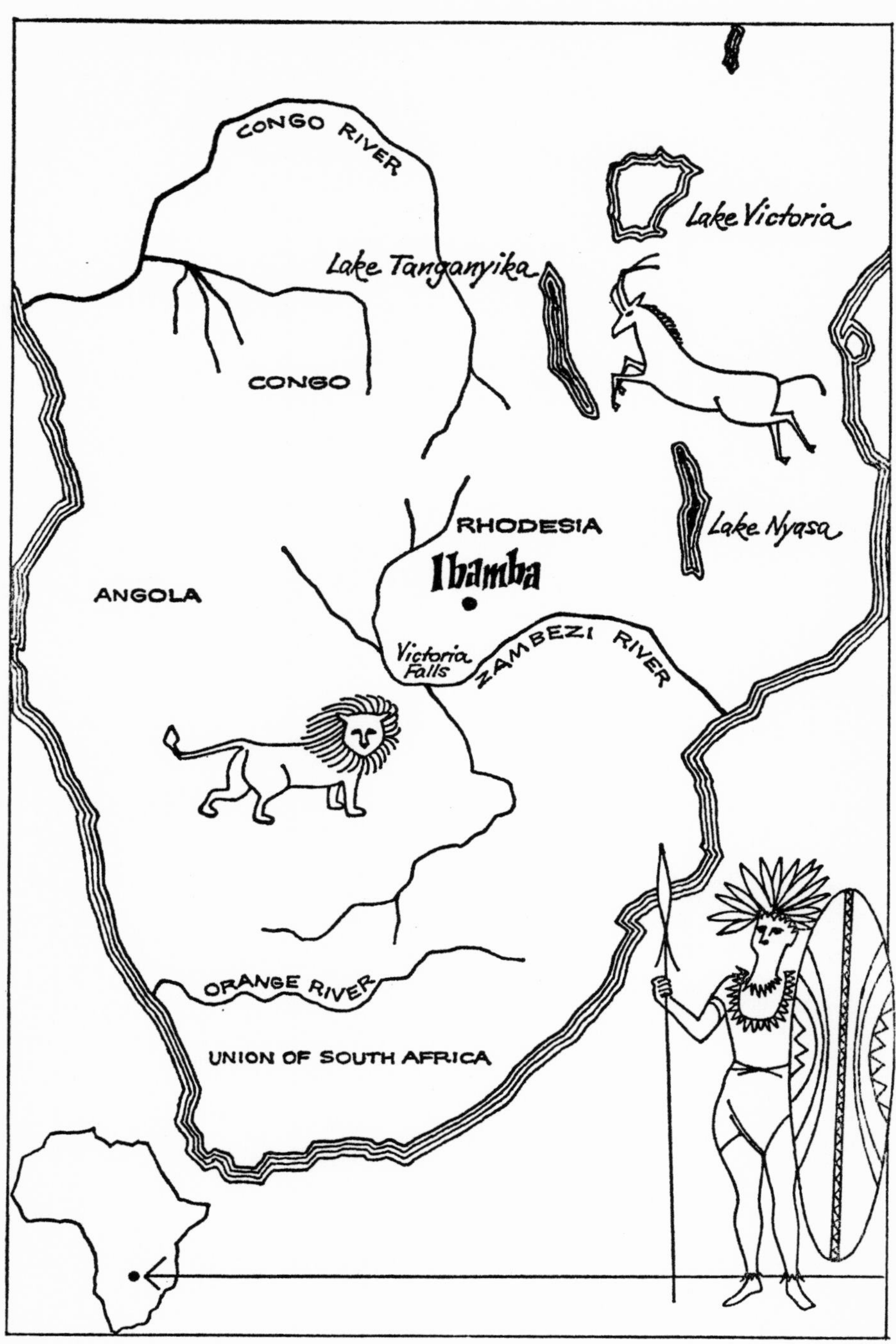
CONGO RIVER
Lake Victoria
Lake Tanganyika
CONGO
RHODESIA
Lake Nyasa
Ibamba
ANGOLA
Victoria Falls
ZAMBEZI RIVER
ORANGE RIVER
UNION OF SOUTH AFRICA

A NOTE FROM THE PUBLISHER

IT will doubtless seem curious—and possibly even outrageous—to the interested reader of this volume that the publisher chose to issue it without any photographs of the beguiling animals who are so important a part of the narrative. Actually, neither publisher nor author had any choice in the matter. The events described in IBAMBA took place some thirty years ago, and thirty years can take a terrible toll on personal possessions, particularly if one constantly moves about the world as the Hubbards did. During World War II while they lived in the West Indies, a tropical wind and rain storm destroyed all the negatives and most of the prints recording this African adventure. What came through the storm were impossible to reproduce with any clarity. But in the few blurry, faded snapshots that survived one caught the assertive individuality of each of the Hubbards' "foster children": the bright-eyed intelligence of Mr. Thomas, the civet cat; the vast good humor of Paddy, the lioness; the finicky elegance of Jane Emmeline John, the crested crane, to mention only a few. So it was decided that to include photographs of just any civet cat, or any crane, would be as unthinkable as using stand-ins for Mijbil the Otter or Elsa the Lioness. The reader, then, must "see" these delightful creatures without pictorial assistance. In any case, they emerge as fully dimensional characters from the text itself and are listed below in order of their importance, rather than appearance in the story:

MR. THOMAS .... *a civet cat*

PADDY .... *a lioness*

FWIFWI .... *an oribi (antelope)*

JANE EMMELINE JOHN .... *a crested crane*

GARBAGE .... *a ground hornbill*

POPEYE .... *a wildebeest*

FLAGS .... *a reedbuck*

TWEETIE .... *a pigeon*

(Plus two unnamed duiker antelopes, a lechwe antelope and two spotted genets.)

chapter one

OUR adventure began to take concrete form in 1928–29 in an apartment on West Ninth Street in New York.

I was newly married. Which is why I say *our* adventure. Isabella was a beautiful mite of a girl with true black hair which shone with glints of an illusive red; her lovely face dimpled when she smiled and laughed, which was often, and her nose was flecked with little freckles. She could cook, and cook well, which was unusual for a girl whose experience had been mainly dancing in musical comedy. Isabella—Iz, of course, to all her friends—was also one of the finest horsewomen I have ever known. Petite as she was—and she perhaps seemed tinier to me than to others because I hulked over six feet two and weighed in at around two hundred and twenty-five—there was not a horse in her father's riding academy that she could not handle. Iz was eighteen, going on nineteen, when we began to talk seriously of going to Africa. I was ten years older.

I had long wanted to establish a research station in Northern Rhodesia, in British Central Africa, for the study of the apparent immunity exhibited by wild animals to many of the diseases which decimate flocks and herds of domestic animals throughout the Dark Continent, as well as elsewhere in the tropics.

The thought had begun to form in my mind during my first trip to Central Africa, which began in 1922 and lasted through 1925. On my return to America I discussed my thoughts in detail with my old friends, irascible, kindly Dr. William T. Hornaday, then director of the New York Zoological Society's Bronx Zoo; Carl Akeley; and Dr. Theobald Smith, then director of the Princeton School of Veterinary Research. These men encouraged and guided me, and attempted to help raise the money necessary to finance such a station.

About this time my first book, *Wild Animals,* was published. First National Pictures Company called me to ask if I would be interested in leading an expedition to Africa to produce a wild-animal film. I jumped like a trout at the opportunity. The terms of the contract were such that I thought I could earn enough—provided, of course, that the picture was successful; and who at the age of twenty-six could think otherwise?—to finance the research station.

I made two pictures, and they were eventually released successfully under the titles *Adventures in Africa* and *Untamed Africa.* I, however, lost out financially. I was badly hurt toward the end of the expedition while tying up a wild lion we had caught to act in the picture, and when I finally recovered after months in a hospital, my rights to a cut in any profits had been lost in a tangle of legalities.

During my long convalescence I wrote my second book, *Bong'kwe,* which was the fictional life story of a great African bull buffalo. The book was based upon the knowledge I had accumulated hunting the tremendous animals and capturing fifty-two—bulls and cows, calves and adults. More, I believe, than any man has taken alive. As a writer of African adventure stories and articles I was moderately successful and lived well, although, as with all free-lancers, precariously at times. Still, I did not have, and it appeared remote that I would ever have, enough to finance the building of a research station to study wild animals.

Then, in 1928–29, along with two sisters and a younger brother, I inherited what was then a considerable fortune. My share was ample to take up land in Rhodesia and begin building the station.

Ever since I had made my first trip into the part of Northern Rhodesia inhabited by a tribe known as the Mashakulumbwe, or Ba'Ila—an area which stretches for two hundred miles to the west of the railway on both sides of the Kafue River—and seen the permanent water of the river and the lagoons and camped on a piece of land called Ibamba, I had wanted to own that piece of land.

Ibamba, which is a native word meaning "lagoon," was beautiful. On the wooded part stood giant fig, mahogany, and bloodwood trees. Surrounding the higher tree-covered strip lay acres and acres, square miles, actually, of gently rolling grasslands in which lagoons and water pans lay hidden. It was superb cattle country.

The property—it had once been surveyed—was more than a hundred miles from the railway line. Too great a distance, in the early days before the advent of motorized vehicles, to be commercially profitable. For this very reason the country surrounding Ibamba abounded in game of many species, and the property was ideal on which to build a wild-animal study station.

Except for one thing. Ibamba had been cursed by a great native chief, and since then no man had succeeded in living on the land for any length of time.

The legend told of the chief of the great village which had once stood on Ibamba, among the giant fig trees and near the edge of the treeless flatland bordering the Kafue River. Feeling that death was approaching, the chief had eaten of a special medicine which would ensure his resurrection and afterlife in the form of a great maned lion.

That a person swallowing the proper potion can ensure the transmigration, or transmutation, of his soul, or spirit, into another form after death is a belief widely and firmly held among native peoples.

Because the chief was old and jealous of life and, some said, foresaw that foreigners with white skins would someday conquer his people, he cursed the place of his dying, which was Ibamba.

The night he was buried beneath the door of his hut lions roared mightily on the flatlands and others roared in the bushveld. A fortnight later, when the funeral dance was held and many of the chief's wives and slaves were slain so that he would have attendants in the world of spirits—as was the custom before the white man came—and more than a hundred cattle were speared, the lions came again. They prowled around the spreading glow of light from the fires and the flaming torches, there on the edge of those brooding flats and, as had never happened before, rushed in among the drunken, howling dancers and seized whole carcasses of cattle and carried them away.

Then the people of the village knew that the chief had spoken truly when he had said he would become a lion and that his spirit would live forever in the body of a great tawny black-maned animal. Following the counsel of their elders, the villagers gathered their belongings and brought together their herds of cattle and flocks of goats and fat-tailed sheep and made ready to move to another place. As the women and children and the aged walked away, the young warriors ran from hut to hut with flaming torches and fired the thatch of every dwelling and every storage bin. When they were gone, nothing remained except heaps of smoldering, smoking ashes.

Regardless of Ibamba's reputation, Iz and I decided that was where we wanted to settle, and we began planning in earnest. Despite our comparative affluence, it soon became apparent that if we were to carry through our ambitious plans, we would need help. It takes time to liquidate an estate—particularly one involving extensive real-estate holdings—and only a limited amount of cash was available to us to cover initial expenses. We decided to try and persuade various companies to contribute equipment or supplies.

I wrote or dictated the originals and Iz typed the letters. We pored over *Thomas' Register* and studied the pages of the newspapers in which used trucks and tractors and other equipment were offered. Soon after the requests for donations went out, we began to receive offers to supply beds and mattresses, biologicals, chemicals and laboratory apparatus, carpenters' and mechanics' and agricultural tools; canned and preserved foods; paints, gasoline and oil; plumbing supplies and bottled gas to fire the Bunsen burners, sterilizers and other laboratory machines.

The offerings were so generous that we were forced to rent storage space in which to receive, inspect, and in some cases repack the equipment which flooded in. With every donation our hopes and enthusiasm mounted, and we worked at fever pitch, swept along with the magnitude of our dream.

Iz had never been to Africa. That she did not have the faintest conception of what life in a remote area of such a newly opened territory as Northern Rhodesia would be like did not affect her at all. Or if she did have qualms, she successfully concealed them from me. We were swept up in the excitement and promise and glamour which always surrounds the organization and departure of an expedition to a faraway country.

For me, going to Africa was almost like going home. I had many friends and relatives in America. But I had lost my heart to the wild rolling country of the bushveld, the unbelievable herds of animals, and the laughing, fighting, nearly naked natives. In my nostrils was the sour-sweet smell of burning cattle dung and the smoke-impregnated thatch; of hot dust, and the clinging odor of sweating working cattle. The snorts of hippos rising in the river to draw fresh breaths, the cough of a hunting leopard, the lyrical tinkle of "an *m'pira,*" and the roaring of a great maned lion sounded in my ears.

Iz did not have these memories. She had done the final typing of many of my manuscripts and listened to my stories about Mangineera, Charlie Portuguese, Jam, and Charlie Matabele. She had heard about the cautious cleverness of lions and the wild excitement of catching elephant calves with one's hands. Stories too often repeated, but to which she always attended.

I never knew, I never thought to ask, because I was so full of my knowledge and hopes, what Isabella expected Africa to be like or to give or to take away from her. It never occurred to me what a profound change it would be for her to live where there was no telephone or radio, and where mail came only once a week. We would be fortunate to see another white person during the dry season, and would see none at all during the six months of rain. It was selfish of me. My only excuse is that I was so accustomed to that manner of living that these things seemed unimportant.

So, one damp, misty morning we sailed out of New York aboard a freighter of the South African Line bound for Beira, Mozambique, via the Cape Verde Islands, Cape Town, Durban, and Lourenço Marques. On board were dozens of crates and huge cases and boxes stenciled with our name; a small crawler tractor which we had bought secondhand; a stake body ton-and-a-half Ford truck; our personal belongings, including all our china, silverware, and books and eleven cases of fine bathtub gin.

The ship discharged our cargo at Beira. We had a last dinner with the skipper in the English Club; arranged for our goods to be passed through the port in bond to Livingstone, Northern Rhodesia, and booked a compartment on the thrice-weekly train for ourselves.

Except for the occasional half-naked native leaning on a spear to watch the train go by, and the tiny settlements along the line which served trading posts and scattered farms and ranches hidden from us deep in the blue of the veld, the land looked lifeless and of almost unbearable monotony. I knew that great herds of sable and roan and eland antelope roamed the country; that kudu and klipspringers and baboons lived on and around the frowning *kopjes,* that only a few miles from the steel ribbon of the railway elephants and rhinos browsed and bred and lived out their lives; and that hippos bathed and honked in the pools of the rivers. I told Iz of these things, and that where she looked, lions might have walked while she and I and the land slept away the night. It was hard for her to believe because none of these animals were visible from our window.

We steamed toward Salisbury, through that capital city, and on to Bulawayo (or, translated from the native, the "place of the killing"), the bustling commercial center of both Southern and Northern Rhodesia. There we changed to another train, one which ran to the west and then to the north, to terminate nearly a thousand miles away on the bank of the Upper Congo River in Belgian territory. Before resuming our journey, we stayed a few days in the town, for Bulawayo was the last real shopping center we would see for a long time. After we had established ourselves on our ranch, it would be mainly from Bulawayo that we would order most of our needs, after studying the slim mail-order catalogues and leaflets which would be sent us.

On again by rail northward to Wankie, where the coke ovens smoked and flared, across the ages-old elephant trail which traversed the tracks and along which the monstrous animals journey from the region of the Shangani River westward toward Lake N'gami and the borders of the Khalahari Desert, only to return months later.

Then Victoria Falls and the "thunder which smokes." The train crosses the gorge so close to the cascading torrents that when the wind is right, spray wets the cars and windows. Then Livingstone, the hot, dusty, malaria-ridden capital of Northern Rhodesia.

We stayed there several days. There was so much to be done. The first thing, of course, was to deposit our letter of credit and travelers' checks in the Standard Bank. Then we walked to the Zambezi Trading Company office and store to talk with the founder and owner, Mopani Clarke and to complete the details for the purchase of the ranch, Ibamba, which he owned.

Fred J. Clarke was in his late sixties. He was one of the earliest arrivals in Northern Rhodesia, and had built a fortune trading cattle from the Barotse to the west and then driving his herds to the railway which was pushing north toward the Congo. He sold the animals, at very respectable profits, to feed the thousands of men hacking a way through the bush, fighting and boozing, laying the steel sleepers and the long rails so that the copper could be carried from Katanga and coal for the smelters brought up from Wankie.

Mopani is the name of one of the hardest woods which grow in the Rhodesias. Fred had not come by his nickname just by chance. But we found him fine and easy to deal with, and we paid down a large sum as earnest of our intention to buy Ibamba and signed notes for the balance in an atmosphere of mutual respect and friendship. A friendship and confidence which, even in the rough years which were to follow, never slackened. Mopani remained always a true and understanding friend. He was a wealthy and influential man, owning a flourishing business and many farms and ranches. He helped us greatly with the government, the customs people, and at the bank.

Old friends rallied around, and evenings at the hotel were convivial with reminiscences and tall tales of hunting and experiences. Iz listened wide-eyed and quiet to the tanned men in khaki shorts and open shirts as they spoke of elephants slain; of charging buffalo; of men blotted by charging animals or mauled to death by lions. The scratches and scars on the men's bare legs and arms from the thorns and catnail vines of the bush were fresh and newly scabbed. This was different from the talk in some elegant New York apartment. Those who spoke would be our neighbors; they would, when occasion offered, drop in to visit us. The men were real and the life they described was real. For the first time Iz began to realize what life in Rhodesia was going to be like.

There was one point on which everyone was in agreement: I was crazy, insane, stupid, to buy Ibamba. No one could keep cattle on those eighty-two hundred acres. The lions would run us off. No place in either of the Rhodesias supported so many lions.

It was admitted that I had caught more lions alive than any other hunter in the territory. But that was just more proof of how crazy I was; who could do anything with a full-grown wild lion? Just because I had been lucky enough to get away with making the lions act in motion pictures didn't mean I could control or escape the depredations and attacks of the lions on Ibamba. Earnestly they pleaded and argued with Isabella to give up the idea of Ibamba; to use her influence with me to have me change my mind. They were truly and honestly concerned.

In the late twenties Northern Rhodesia was a very young country so far as occupation by whites was concerned. Opened up around 1900, the territory was first governed by the British South Africa Company, and had only been transferred to the British Crown in April, 1924, two years after my first visit and five years before Iz and I arrived. There were approximately ten thousand whites scattered over the 287,950 square miles, concentrated mainly in the mining towns and the settlements along the railway line. There were a million and a half natives, thousands of whom had never seen a white person.

Dependent upon natives for help in accomplishing the daily tasks of washing, cooking, plowing, delivering the mails, firing the locomotives, herding cattle, transporting goods, and caring for children, the whites lived apart yet in close intimacy with the indigenous inhabitants. The majority of the whites spoke one or more of the tribal languages fluently, and everyone spoke a bastard *lingua franca* known as Kaffir, which was based largely on the Zulu and Matabele languages and had originated in South Africa.

It was natural that everything the natives did—their beliefs and customs, their ceremonies and systems of tribal government—were of vital interest and the subject of constant discussion and debate.

Reading this as you sit in a comfortable chair, with the soft light of an electric lamp adjusted to your need and surrounded by the safety and comfort of a modern home or apartment in some bustling city, it may be difficult for you to comprehend how deeply immersed the early settlers became in the native life, the lore and legends, in such a territory as Northern Rhodesia in those days.

Many of us, particularly those on ranches and farms, the hunters and traders, never saw another white person for months at a time. The greater part of our daily conversation was in a native language. Our children, if we had any, learned to speak native sooner and more proficiently than English. Our talk was about witch doctors, great chiefs, hunting, the weather and, always, about the great herds of game which thronged the land; of raids on fields of corn and pumpkins by elephants and bush pigs and baboons; the cattle, goat, and sheep killing by lions and dog stealing by leopards. We debated the spread of rinderpest, hoof-and-mouth disease, of blackleg and Texas fever and pleuropneumonia by herds of buffalo and antelope and discussed the danger from the dread tsetse fly, whose bite brings slow death to all domestic animals.

So it was natural, while we talked in the bar or on the veranda of the hotel in Livingstone in the evenings after the great heat had passed, that Iz was told not once but many times of the legend of the curse which was reputed to lie like a deadly miasma over the flatlands and the bushveld of Ibamba.

chapter two

WITH delivery of the manifests, railway bills, and other documents pertaining to the loads of equipment following us by goods train, our business in Livingstone was completed. We entrained once again, our destination the small railway settlement of Choma, another two hundred and fifty miles to the north.

I was nervous as the powerful locomotives snarled and belched great clouds of steam and smoke in their steady effort to haul the long train up out of the Zambezi Valley onto the highlands. I felt like a bridegroom on the eve of his wedding night. If, up to that time, I could ever have been said to have had a home in Africa, the location would have been Choma. It was near Choma, at a place called Tara, that seven years before I had started my life as an African hunter and catcher of wild animals. There I had hired my first natives and had begun to speak and understand the native languages. Men of all sizes and of all shades from deep black to brown came to apply for work. A few were dressed in white men's cast-off clothing, and these I learned quickly to avoid. Others wore torn khaki shorts, simple breechclouts of tanned soft antelope skin, and one or two, just nothing at all. Some carried worn pass books in which former employers had scribbled recommendations, but the majority didn't have such things. All were armed with long, wickedly barbed throwing spears and shorter long-bladed stabbing spears.

I find it a great tribute to the native of Africa that out of my inexperienced and haphazard choice of employees so large a proportion turned out to be loyal, skillful, and devoted workers. In those days we paid our natives practically nothing. Seven shillings and sixpence, $1.85, a month for the average worker, with something more for the cook, the washboys and houseboys, wagon drivers, sawboys, gunbearers and trackers. In addition we fed our natives two and a half pounds of whole corn per day and a pound of coarse salt a week. If there was meat, secured by hunting or from the killing of a cattlebeast, the meat was divided among all. The womenfolk and children of the men, all of whom lived in a village which they built not too far from the house of their employer and which was called the compound, soaked and skinned and pounded the grain to flour while the menfolk worked. Ruling the compound, instead of a chief, was the *capitao,* a sort of general foreman chosen by the employer. It was a simple, workable, and satisfactory arrangement to all.

During that first year I gradually sorted out the men into those I thought would make the best workers for particular jobs. These men stayed with me during my first three years, a number of them traveling with me on what developed into a very hard and dangerous journey, lasting almost twelve months, into a remote region of Portuguese East Africa. The same men—with, of course, many new ones—worked with me during the motion-picture-making expedition. These were the extraordinarily courageous, skillful, wise, and patient men without whose help I could never have captured the full-grown lions, the leopards, the buffalo, and hundreds of other wild animals which passed through my hands.

It was while I was learning to be a hunter at Tara that I acquired my native names. While I was learning to speak native, I was called Misterrela, "The Silent One," for the simple reason that I lacked sufficient vocabulary to talk freely. Then I was tagged with Karisiangoma, "The Man Who Loves the Tom-toms," because I so enjoyed watching the natives dance and tried to learn drum language. Later, when I bought a whole freightcar full of hawks and eagles, I acquired the name of Sibyunni'byunni, which means "The Father of Birds." This name stuck, and I was known by it ever after.

As Iz and I sat in our compartment on the train, watching the dry, drear, and endless bushveld roll by, I grew more and more anxious as to whether word had been spread that Sibyunni'byunni was returning. Weeks before I had written to my old friend, Hugh K. McKee, who owned the small hotel and the one store in Choma, requesting him to send out the news through the villages that I was coming. I could not explain to Isabella the anticipation and the anxiety which swelled in me as we rattled nearer and nearer to Choma. Would the natives to whom I was bound by deep and moving experiences be waiting to greet me, or had some died, or might they have been too far away to hear the news, or be working for some other man? I had been away more than two years.

The engineer pulled a cord in his cab and the ridiculous piping whistle of a British locomotive sounded above the rumble and clackety-clack of the train. The coaches lurched and banged ends as brakes were applied. As our movement slowed, I leaned far out the window, staring at the crowd of natives which always gathers to watch the arrival of a train. My gaze leaped from one dark smiling face to another.

Then I saw him, Mangineera, the most skillful tracker and most devoted gunbearer I had ever known; the man I called my little bulldog. There he stood, all five feet of him proud and straight in a spotless khaki shirt and shorts so freshly ironed, I was sure whoever had done the pressing had finished less than an hour before. His round, deeply pock-marked face split in a wide grin as he saw me. The remains of his nose, which had been clawed by a leopard when he was young, wrinkled upward above his flashing smile of welcome, and his teeth, filed to points, gleamed white behind his lips.

Beside Mangineera, standing even more erect and towering above him, because Mangineera was more than half pygmy from the Congo, was Jam, Barotse hunter, gunbearer, and leader among men. On the clean dark wool of his old askari jersey were pinned the ribbons he had won fighting with the army against the Germans. He was smiling, too; his shorts had been pressed until the khaki shone, and he had wound puttees about his legs above his bare feet.

With a lump clutching at my throat and through eyes misted with a great happiness, I saw that almost all my boys, all my reckless, hunting, catching men were there. The tall, debonair, sardonic Charlie Matabele; small yellow-skinned Charlie Portuguese, who was my *capitao;* Lavison, the table boy who doubled as valet when I was out in the bush and who came from Nyasaland; Shafumu and

Shaluma, the Mashakulumbwe men; Shamakembie, whose name means hatchet man and who could trot fifty miles a day, day after day, carrying the mail, and Tickie, a young man yearning to become someday a hunter like Jam.

McKee had walked the hundred yards from the store, and when I leaped from the train, neglecting Iz in my excitement, I greeted him effusively and then rushed toward Mangineera. The others gathered quickly round as my hand and that of my gunbearer clasped together firmly and for a second longer than was usual. As I shook hands with each, the men turned their heads, embarrassed by their emotion, and shuffled their feet and wriggled their bodies as children do when they line up before a teacher.

Iz, of course, had heard the names of all these men. By name they had appeared in stories I had told or written, for each of them had sweated and hunted, carried and walked shoulder to shoulder with me across thousands of miles of the bushveld and valleys and the mountains of Central Africa. As I brought the natives forward and named them for her, Iz flashed her wonderful smile. Right then she was given the native name which was to be always hers, Masec-casecca, "the smiling one."

The "boys" flooded onto the train. Any native who works for you, regardless of his age, became your boy in those days, and no offense was intended or felt. Our luggage was passed quickly out the window and that in the van collected. With 'Kee we walked to the hotel, followed by a laden procession of natives balancing suitcases and bundles and parcels on their heads and shoulders.

Mrs. McKee was a small, wiry, intensely Scottish woman. She welcomed us graciously, rolling her r's in the best Highland tradi-tion, and showed us to our room. While Iz was unpacking and freshening up after the dusty, cindery train ride, I went out to talk for a while with my boys. When they learned that I was buying Ibamba and intended to settle, they were very happy. There was no mention of my hiring them or of wages. The important part was that, once again, we were together.

When I inquired how so many had been able to meet me, the

answer, voiced by Charlie Portuguese, made me very proud and at the same time very humble.

"When you went away," said Charlie, "we took the money you had given us and we went to our villages. We have not worked for any other man. It was a long time, but we knew that you would come back again."

While we waited for our freight to arrive, I completed arrangements with McKee to handle and store the perishables against the day when I could truck them out to Ibamba, and we purchased further necessities. We talked of the weather; the new and old government officials; about traders and missionaries and farmers and ranchers, but always about Ibamba.

The ranch—it was not in any sense a ranch at all, but rather just an uninhabited piece of the veld which had been surveyed once, years before—fascinated everyone. In the evenings, perched on a tall stool at the bar or relaxed in a chair in the lounge, Iz listened to more of the legends about Ibamba.

It was in the years just before the outbreak of World War I, so the tales went, that the curse which the old chief had placed on Ibamba began to take realistic form. It was then that Dobson, the first magistrate of the Namwala District, completed his years of duty, and deciding to retire, picked the eighty-two hundred acres of land which he named Ibamba as the most beautiful spot he knew, and bought it from the government.

Northern Rhodesia was a very young country in those days. There were scarcely twenty-five hundred whites in the whole enormous territory, many parts of which were still unexplored and unknown. The *boma* of Namwala was, and still is, the seat of government for the district and for the Mashakulumbwe, or to be more formal, the Ba'Ila tribe, which was one of the last to submit to the white man. The Mashakulumbwe men wore no clothes; they built a tall cone of their own hair mixed with beeswax toward the back of their heads, shaved the front of their skulls, and were known as great warriors, cattlemen, hunters, and some of the most licentious of natives. After World War I the Mashakulumbwe region was declared a native reserve. Except for Ibamba, no white person could own land within the reserve. Ibamba remained available to whites so that there would be one place to which natives could come for work and to which they might sell their produce.

The greater part of the Mashakulumbwe country consists of the wide, long, and level Kafue River flats which, eons ago, were probably the bottom of a great lake or inland sea. The flats are a region of dark rich soil on which grows a dense carpet of rank tall grass, each stalk as thick as a lead pencil and from six to twelve feet tall. Trees are conspicuous by their absence.

Winding through the flats is the Kafue River, one of the main affluents of the Zambezi, having water the year around. It is a slow stream of clear water, about fifty yards wide, in which there are many hippos and uncounted thousands of crocodiles. Each rainy season the river overflows its banks, flooding the flats sometimes to a depth of only a foot or so, and sometimes, when the rains are heavy, burying the land under six feet or more of water. Grass manages to grow above the water's surface, and millions of red, blue, and yellow water lilies.

Over the centuries the river has changed its course many times, with the result that lagoons abound. Hundreds of thousands of sitatunga, lechwe, wildebeest, and puku antelope fed in the tall grass along the edges of the lagoons and on the shorter grass where the land rises gently to merge into the bush country which borders the flats on all sides. Enormous herds of buffalo roamed the flats and wallowed in the mud. Along the fringes of the flats, particularly toward the end of the dry season, when water was scarce elsewhere, herds of zebra, blue wildebeest, roan, sable, kudu, and eland antelope were found in large numbers. There were wart hogs and bush pigs, bushbuck, reedbuck, impala, duiker, and tiny grysbok.

As in all such magnificent game regions, Carnivora abounded. Leopards hunted cane rats and puku in the papyrus by the river and the lagoons. Cheetahs and bush cats, servals and lynx, roamed the drier parts. And everywhere there were lions, but nowhere in greater numbers than on Ibamba.

Ibamba has four and a half miles of river frontage. Most of the ranch is flat grassland, but there is a long broad piece of higher well-timbered land running at right angles to the river and, in one place, ending only some two hundred yards from the water. It was there, on an ironstone outcropping, that Dobson built the first small two-room stone house. It enjoyed a wonderful view out across the flats and the winding river to a low range of mountains far in the distance.

At the opposite end from the river and the house on the timbered piece is a dense broad *saka*. A *saka* is a particularly tangled growth of vines, trees, bushes, and creepers, usually dim and dark, with little or no grass on the ground, and in which a man, hunting, has to travel mainly on his hands and knees. Lions love *sakas*, and it is to *sakas* that buffalo, kudu, and other antelope retire to drop their calves or to hide when wounded.

The great *saka* on Ibamba, some two miles long and a quarter of a mile wide, was notorious as a breeding ground and haunt of lions. There was an abundance of game, and water was always close.

The permanent water of the Kafue made the whole region, and particularly Ibamba, fine cattle country. Dobson, after he had built the house, bought cattle and settled down to live out his days as a rancher. This, however, was not to be. When war broke out, Dobson volunteered and was accepted. He arranged with Tommy Dugan, a well-known hunter and settler, to take over during his absence, and went off to the war.

Tommy did his best to keep up the place and increase the herds of cattle. It was an uphill task. The lions and the crocodiles got so many of the cattle that there was little total increase, and no profit.

No one ever knew how many lions Tommy killed in one way and another. Even he lost count. Tommy trapped them, he shot at them at every opportunity, and lay awake many nights in a machan built in a tree close to the cattle kraals. After he moved the kraals close to the house, he shot at the lions from the windows. In desperation he even poisoned lions, which no self-respecting man would do except in emergencies. Still the lions kept the upper hand. Young lions were taught to kill by using the Ibamba herds of cattle as practice animals. A self-respecting lion usually kills only once or twice a week, and he or she does this cleanly. Young lions, however, are clumsy at first, and they raise havoc striking and clawing at any and all animals within reach. These ripped and torn cattle generally have to be destroyed, so the damage can be very high.

Tommy stuck this out for some three years. Then one night he shot a lion from his bedroom window. The lioness, as so often happens when her mate has been killed, went berserk. She uttered a terrible heart-rending moan of grief and started prowling around the house, seeking the man who had killed her mate. Tommy could hear her circling, circling, brushing against the flimsy screened bit of veranda and sniffing at the ground. He had only a Bulala head lamp—an acetylene gas flame which burns in front of a round mirror and is fed through a flexible tube from a small generator carried in a pocket—and couldn't easily pick out the moving animal. Anyway, the lioness was too close, most of the time, for him to be able to spot her with the lamp from a window without opening it and leaning out, which he had no intention of doing.

While he was in the living-dining room, Tommy heard a noise from the bedroom. Kicking open the door and directing his light into the room, he saw the lioness raised against the window and clawing at the stone sill to get in. He fired, but missed, and the lioness disappeared. Tommy spent the rest of that night sitting in a chair beside the window and listening. Although he heard the lioness for some time after firing at her, she made off as daylight began to show across the flats.

That was the night Tommy decided he had had enough, and that the lions could have Ibamba if they felt they needed it that badly. The next morning he had the natives herd all the cattle together, packed up his belongings, closed the house up, and started on the one-hundred-and-twenty-five mile trek to the railroad.

There he got in touch with Dobson's bank, sold the cattle, and sent in the money.

Not many months after that word reached Northern Rhodesia that Dobson had lost a leg in the fighting, been operated upon, and had subsequently died. His estate was wound up and Ibamba put up for sale.

For more than a year the land lay vacant, and reverted to the wild again. No natives lived on the ranch. In the brooding silence which lay over the far-flung flats and the great *saka*, only the lions and the antelope and zebras came and went their ways. Hippos fed in what had been the little vegetable garden close by the river, and many of the crocodiles migrated to more well-stocked areas.

Then in 1919, Lord Roundsley, looking around for a place to buy for his nephew, Montague Smith, heard of Ibamba and bought it. Smith was very happy about the idea, and decided to make something of a party of his taking over the property.

Smith gathered several of his friends, both male and female, and loaded up two trek wagons, each pulled by eighteen oxen, and set out for Ibamba.

They made quite a party of the trip, moving slowly and taking time out for hunting along the way. Then the day came when they camped not far from the big native village of Marla, which lay only some six miles from Ibamba.

After camp was set, Smith went off with a native to shoot something for the pot. It was quite late when he returned, and he was very excited. They had run into a lion, and Smith had fired at it, wounding it, he was sure, quite badly. It being too late to go after the lion, he had come back, but he was going after it the first thing in the morning. His friends tried to dissuade him. None of them were experienced hunters, and a wounded lion can be extremely dangerous. But Smith was determined, and when his friends woke up, he was gone. What was worse, he had gone alone, without even a native to help him. His friends were frantic, and quickly rallied natives. With Smith's former hunter to guide them, they went to the spot where he had seen and shot at the lion the evening before.

They called and hollered and fired shots and tried to track him, but all to no avail, and eventually they could only return to camp to wait.

An hour went by. Everyone was getting more and more worried. The sun was well up and hot. Smith had no water with him as far as anyone knew, and he might be lost. Another half hour dragged by. Then there was a shout from the natives. Smith was coming. But as his friends leaped up to run to him, they saw that something was terribly wrong. Smith was weaving on his feet like a drunken man. He was covered with dust, and his hat was pulled far down on his head. His rifle was gone!

They rushed to him. He was covered with blood, and could barely speak. All he could mutter was, "Don't take off my hat, don't take off my hat."

Nobody ever found out exactly what happened that early morning out in the bush, although it was only too obvious that Smith had found his lion. He was badly bitten and clawed. His friends tried their best to cut his clothes off and sponge him and clean the wounds. During all of this Smith clung firmly to his hat with clenched hands. But it had to come off. Holes in the felt showed that the lion had bitten Smith in the head. When his friends finally got the hat off, Smith gave a sigh and died. His skull had been punctured by four large deep holes, and the bones of the head had been crushed. It was only by keeping his hat pulled tight that he had managed to make his way back to camp.

The party went no farther, but turned sadly back to the railway line. Ibamba remained uninhabited and still, brooding through the changing days and nights and alternately drying out and flooding with the coming of the dry season and the rains. As the years went by and the lions multiplied, the malevolent reputation of the ranch increased rather than decreased as stories were told and retold. Every night when the roaring of the lions could be heard thundering and reverberating from Ibamba, the native children in the Kasenga Mission compound three miles away cowered in the huts and pressed close to their mothers, and the fathers cursed that piece of bush as the home of devils.

The next man to try and break the curse of Ibamba was Pete Cavadia. Pete was one of the early traders of Northern Rhodesia. He and his brother had long maintained a very successful grain and cattle-trading store at the Namwala *boma.* But once the Mashakulumbwe country, except for Ibamba, had been declared a native reserve, the Cavadias could not run their cattle on it without paying high taxes to the government for grazing and kraal privileges. So they rented the grazing rights to Ibamba and put many of their cattle on the ranch, each herd guarded by two natives; because of Ibamba's reputation one of them was allowed to carry an old rifle.

The lions took a heavy toll. But with the prices at which the Cavadias traded the cattle, they could afford to take the losses. Every week the lions got one to three cattle, and the crocodiles got another one or two.

Then I came along and bought Ibamba. To explain this piece of seeming madness I must go back a bit in time.

When I had first come to Northern Rhodesia, it was during the early years of development and settlement of the territory. Life was wild and free, game was abundant, and professional hunting, a respectable occupation. I hunted elephants, tangled with rhinos, buffalo, lions, leopards, and wart hogs, and handled hundreds of birds, snakes, and four-footed creatures at the base camp-ranch. We had young leopards, wild dogs, wart hogs, and bush pigs, sable and duiker antelope, mongooses and civet cats, mambas, cobras, puff adders and pythons, monkeys and baboons, a pangolin, cane rats, blue jays, eagles, vultures, hawks, finches, cranes and spur-winged geese, cheetahs, bush cats, reedbuck, kudu, and so on and on.

I went up into the Mashakulumbwe country and fell in love with its beauty; after camping on Ibamba, I went on farther to the village of Sheasongo, near Nanzilla. Making friends with Sheasongo, one of the most powerful of the independent chiefs, I took hunters from his village and pushed westward into the unknown country called the Home of the Lion. Here the number and variety of the game was fantastic, and I hunted more lions and impala, waterbuck, wildebeest, zebra, roan, sable, and buffalo. At Kaiingu I hunted hippos and crocodiles, killing one of the latter which measured twenty-two feet five inches, and whose stomach contained a number of ivory bangles, head shells, and brass armlets which had once bedecked the people it had eaten.

In the course of these years I studied with native doctors to learn what I could of their medical practices. Sheasongo and I became friends, and I passed through the exciting and gory blood-brothership ceremony and became his *mulangumu.* As a result, everything which belonged to him belonged to me, and vice versa. That is, if either of us could get it from the other. This ceremony also made me the heir apparent to Sheasongo's chieftainship. As an acknowledged chief I had my own *olimba,* or xylophone players, and could always call upon the village and the people of the tribe for labor, hunters, or other help.

On my second trip to Rhodesia, to be sure that we would have lions to act in the motion picture and because, so far as I knew, no one had ever captured full-grown wild lions, I bought seven circus and zoo lions in Johannesburg and brought them in great crates into Rhodesia. When we hauled these out along the track toward Namwala, natives thronged about the wagons to stare in wonder and shout and sing. At night the lions roared in their cages and the sound thundered across the veld and through the villages. Later we caught nine wild lions and turned them loose in kraals and sets to act and then released them, which was something wondrous and puzzling to the natives. Because of the number of lions I trapped, and also shot, I achieved a reputation among the natives as a lion man.

Through this work with lions I grew to understand them and to respect and admire them above all other animals. And in the villages and the compounds it was whispered that Sibyunni'byunni could, and did, talk with lions, that he was a *matakatsi,* a witch doctor.

My purpose and reasons for choosing Ibamba as the place on which to build my dream of a research station were not based wholly upon the number of lions inhabiting the property. Certainly they were a great attraction, but if I was even to begin to accomplish the tasks I had set myself, I would need a variety of other animals.

Enormous areas in Africa and in other tropical countries were closed to pastoral development because of the tsetse fly or other disease-producing organisms. I was convinced that one way in which these regions might be opened up and made productive was through utilization of certain wild creatures. Many of these animals served as hosts during various stages of the development of the germs of diseases which were fatal or crippling to domestic stock. But the wild ones lived and thrived where domestic species wasted and died. Perhaps I was starry-eyed or too much of a dreamer, but it seemed to me that before all the magnificent wild animals were exterminated by the onrush of what we so complacently call civilization, some attempt should be made to discover whether or not their apparent immunity could be made available to men.

Particularly, I had in mind the possible development, by cross-breeding of selected and like species of wild and domestic animals, of new, stronger, larger, and more disease-resistant breeds.

Especially, I wanted to experiment with the cross-breeding of buffalo and cattle. The huge, truculent Cape buffalo is considered by many to be the most dangerous of all big-game animals. Buffalo have killed many dozens of white and native hunters. Wounded, they are awesome in their cunning, their speed and strength, and their vindictiveness.

Captured young, however, and raised with kindness and in the company of domestic calves, buffalo were no more dangerous, at their worst, than Brahman bulls. I knew because I had handled and raised buffalo calves. In addition to their capacity to resist disease, buffalo are equipped to forage and thrive on the harsh, rough, low-nutriment-value herbage of the plains and bush of Africa. They are large animals, and from a butchering point of view their meat is distributed over their carcasses in the right places. The buffalo's broad splay hooves support it in the mud of the rainy seasons, and its legs are short and powerful. The hides are thick and of good quality.

Why, I kept asking myself, shoot or kill off all the buffalo before their possible economic value has been determined?

Across the Kafue River and only a few miles to the north and east of Ibamba was the Banga area. Here, toward the end of the dry season, were concentrated some of the greatest herds of buffalo in Rhodesia, perhaps even in Africa. It was at Banga that I caught thirty-seven in the short period of six weeks.

To the west lay the Home of the Lion and vast herds of antelope, zebra, and buffalo. There were more animals to the north, but that region was closed to hunting.

Only a few men like Dr. Hornaday and Carl Akeley shared my enthusiasm and dreams. The majority considered me lacking in my upper story. No one, so they said, could tame or handle Cape buffalo. That I had done so made no difference. For some reason my often announced theory—that at birth no animal is, by human definition, either wild or domestic by reason of inherited characteristics—provoked skepticism and derision. I was nuts, a crackpot, a wholly impractical dreamer. When I tried to explain that I believed that, at birth, any animal, human or other, was only an animal, and that what it developed into as it grew was determined by its physical structure, its environment, and the teaching of its parents, few would listen.

Now, thirty years later, it is almost too late. Most of the great herds of wild animals have been destroyed, although very large sums are being spent and many hours of effort are being devoted to studies to determine the "commercial" and economic possibilities of such remnants of the herds as remain.

chapter three

OUR freight came, and the railway cars—which are much smaller than those used in America—were shunted onto the siding. With my boys I tackled the job of unloading and sorting out.

The truck and tractor arrived on an open flatcar and were inches deep in dust and cinders. We cleaned them and put in oil and fuel and new batteries, but they were reluctant to start. When the engines finally caught, it was a precarious business to maneuver the heavy machines onto the ramp, from which the flatcar was separated by several feet. I managed it with much shouting of directions from the excited natives. We used the truck to move the cases and crates to the back room of McKee's store for safekeeping.

There were huge and very heavy rolls of nine-gauge wire stock fencing; barrels of flour; a huge case containing a kerosene-burning refrigerator with a large water-cooling tank on the top; steel cylinders of compressed gas; a bathtub, toilet, and washbasin contributed by the Crane Plumbing Company; mattresses, box springs and steel bed frames and bedroom furniture donated by Simmons; cases of glassware and laboratory apparatus; an autoclave to sterilize instruments; boxes and packages of carpenters', mechanics', masons', and agricultural tools; bundles and bales of shovels, picks, mattocks, and spare handles; ten-foot-long whipsaws with which to saw logs by hand into planks and boards; great coils of rope, cases and cases of food; toilet paper, bedding, china, books, a typewriter, stationery supplies, and medical equipment; an enormous box of hams and sides of bacon packed in fine salt; a portable forge and blacksmith's tools and an anvil; lanterns, lamps, cooking pots and pans; a tremendously heavy stove from Kalamazoo and our trunks of clothes.

It was now that the careful, detailed planning which we had done in New York began to pay off. Every box and crate had been numbered and the contents listed. In anticipation of the first trip from Choma to Ibamba a number of boxes had been packed with the food and equipment we would need when we set up our first camp. Only these needed to be opened to get us started.

As we unloaded the railway cars and trucked the loads to the store, Iz checked the numbers of the parcels against a list, and those marked for immediate use were set aside. I viewed the mounting pile with dismay and wondered if it could all be loaded aboard the truck.

Transport of this mountain of equipment over the rutty, sandy trail winding a hundred and twenty-five miles across the veld—in which hard hidden stumps, ant-bear holes, and treacherous mud lay in wait for the unwary—presented a fearsome task. The track—it could not be called a road—to Ibamba and on to Namwala had originally been made by wagons drawn by eighteen straining oxen. Of necessity it wound around anthills, turned and twisted to avoid large trees and soft ground near waterholes and pans. Because the oxen required grazing every day, the track sought areas where grass was available; it led from village to village so that the drivers and the traders could barter for food, grain, hides, and skins. There was no place where gasoline or oil or tires or tubes could be obtained, nor were there any mechanics.

On every trip by truck or car one had to carry extra gasoline and oil, water for the radiator and to drink, a full box of tools, a tire and tube-repair kit, and a few spare parts. The experienced carried food and bedding, too, because in the event of a major breakdown it often took days to make repairs or for help to come.

Other materials would be needed in addition to the equipment and supplies we had brought from the United States and purchased in Cape Town, Durban, Bulawayo, and Livingstone. But first we would have to construct buildings for their storage and protection. A tremendous amount of work confronted us. Most of our tasks had to be completed in the four or five months before the coming of the rains, when travel and out-of-doors construction would become impossible.

Once on Ibamba, we would be starting from scratch. If we needed planks, boards, or beams, we had either to buy expensive imported pine, fir, or spruce—because Africa lacks softwood timber—and transport it from the railway line, or find mahogany, bloodwood, mopani, and other trees of suitable size on Ibamba, cut them down, drag them to saw pits behind teams of oxen, and there mark the logs off and saw them into suitable lumber by hand. Bricks for building had to be made on the spot from suitable clay and sand, by hand, be sun dried, and then piled in great kilns and burned to a firm redness. The kilns, burning night and day, would have voracious appetites, and just supplying firewood would be a major operation. Gravel would have to be washed to make concrete for floors, tons of sand collected for cement, and hundreds of sixteen- to twenty-foot poles cut and carried in to build kraals for the cattle.

While all this work was going on, a compound for our natives would have to be built, and for this hundreds of bundles of long dry grass for thatching, poles for the walls, and pounds and pounds of mud for plastering would be needed.

To roof our projected house and some other buildings we would need bundles and bundles of corrugated iron sheets, which are very heavy. We needed casement windows and doors, mosquito wire, bags and bags of cement and lime, and lead and iron piping. To feed the natives—because we could not possibly prepare land, plant, and reap before the end of the rains—we would have to buy and store several hundred two-hundred-pound bags of whole corn and many bags of coarse salt. And always there were the awkward, four-hundred-pound fifty-gallon drums of vital gasoline and kerosene and drums of oil and grease.

The day of our departure for Ibamba, so long anticipated, finally came. 'Kee and Mrs. 'Kee were up to see us off as dawn began to lighten the eastern sky. The air was cool and crisp as, bundled in sweaters, we drank the tea and crunched the toast our hostess thoughtfully provided. When we walked from the hotel, a bluish haze hung in the air. It was light smoke wafting through the thatched roofs of the huts in the compound, scenting the faint breeze with the acrid odor of smoldering hardwood.

Mrs. McKee saw to it that our scoff box was filled, and put in a few meat sandwiches and a ripe tomato or two. A scoff box is one of the essentials without which travel was impossible. *Scoff,* in Rhodesia, meant either "eat" or "food." The scoff box is a light wooden box, generally one in which fifty pounds of laundry soap in bars had originally been packed. It is fitted with a hinged lid and with compartments to hold, as snugly as possible, jars of tea, sugar, peanut butter, or jam; cups and saucers, a few items of cutlery, and a can opener; a tin of milk, can of bully beef, and small enamel teapot. There is room for a small loaf of bread, which should be wrapped in a damp cloth; a hundred-tablet bottle of quinine and another of aspirin.

Nobody would think of going on even a short trip without a scoff box and one or more canvas water bags. Water bags hold about a gallon, are made of dense, tightly woven material, and should be washed periodically. As the water seeps slowly through the fabric and the passing air evaporates the moisture, the water inside cools a few degrees.

The boys, wrapped in blankets against the cold, were waiting beside the truck. They would ride on top of the load wherever they could find a perch. They were grinning with anticipation, and I saw that their throwing and stabbing spears, their sleeping mats and other belongings, had been festooned all over the load. They climbed aboard, seeking places where they could crouch and dodge the branches which we knew would hang over the track. There was much good-natured banter between them and the hotel natives who had gathered to see them off.

We shook hands with the 'Kees. Iz took her seat in the cab and I climbed behind the wheel. The engine caught and I let it warm up. Tramping on the lever which brought the auxiliary Ruckstel gears into operation—these gave us three additional very low and powerful speeds—I let out the clutch. Smoothly, with only minor shudderings of protest, the heavily laden truck rolled forward, gaining speed as I opened the throttle. A final wave, and with a toot on the horn we headed onto the road to the west and the beginning of our great adventure. A Mauser 9.3 rifle and a 12-gauge shotgun, both loaded, rested on the floor and the seat between Iz and myself.

For the first twenty miles the route could be classed as a road. We were still within the area of the outlying farms which lay scattered over the bushveld surrounding the railway nucleus at Choma. The farms were hidden from us by the stands of crooked trees whose growth had been impeded and tortured by the hot fierce grass fires which annually swept the land. We passed roads which branched off to serve the farms, and as these became fewer and fewer, the track worsened.

The bush pressed in closer from each side. Low-hanging branches and bushes beat against the fenders and sides of the cab and banged against the windshield. The rains had cut steep-walled gullies along the sides and across the rutted way. Progress was slow and twisting and careful. Occasional logs lay across the road, and we had to stop while the boys hopped off and removed them. Already they were covered with the fine red dust churned by our wheels to float behind us as a high plumed tail. Ant bears, seeking the ants which are their food, had dug slanting burrows, eighteen inches in diameter and to a depth of many feet, in numerous places. If a wheel dropped into one of these, we could easily break an axle.

We saw few animals. A troop of vervet monkeys scampered across the road and, chattering, took to the trees. A mongoose with a long white tail scurried for safety. They are nocturnal animals, and this one should have been curled up in a burrow or the bole of a tree long before. A small flock of cackling guinea fowl hurried excitedly through the bushes as we chugged around a bend. Guineas are excellent eating, but before I could stop and tumble from the cab with the shotgun, they had run too far for me to follow. Francolins, which are somewhat like partridge, only longer of leg and neck and more often called by their native name of *quale,* were the most common birds. Like guineas, they are good eating, but they run like the wind and dodge and twist among the bushes. Usually the birds are seen singly or in pairs.

The fauna made a poor showing. Although Iz said nothing, I am sure she wondered where were all the wonderful antelope and zebras and lions I had so vividly described as thronging the bush. As we huffed and rattled along, I explained that we were traveling through veld where water was very scarce. That was why there were no villages and no game. Indeed, this kind of African country is both depressing and monotonous. With the cessation of the rains the trees and bush drop their leaves and rise stark and bare. The coarse grass stands sear and yellow, waiting for the fires which the natives light to rid the land of the dry harsh stalks their cattle cannot eat and which impede their hunting by concealing the game. For miles and miles the veld on either side of us stretched endlessly uninhabited, forlorn in its emptiness and baking in the heat which poured down from the cloudless sky and caused us to shed our warm clothing.

The track led north and then swung toward the east. Perceptibly it descended, and the sandy soil became heavier and more mixed with clay. Flowering syringa trees appeared here and there beside the track. The white and purple blossoms brought a touch of incongruous gaiety and color to the somber, silent land.

A few scattered bottle palms appeared along the side, and taller ones raised their plumed heads above the more lowly trees, the graceful fronds spreading fanwise against the vault of the sky. Long bunches of round, shiny brown nuts hung in clusters below the fronds. Iz remarked on these, and I told her the nuts were called vegetable ivory because of the hard milk-white hollow kernels which could be dried and polished something like elephant ivory. The husks are covered with a short fibrous growth which the natives eat, gnawing it off with their teeth.

I stopped and sent the boys to fetch some of the fallen nuts, and they showed Iz how they ate them. She tried, and reported the fibers tasted like a dry breakfast food eaten without milk or sugar.

I could not repress a grin when, after two bites, she surreptitiously dropped her nut over the side.

The color of the earth changed from red to black. The track became more rutty and bumpy. During the rains it had been soggy mud, and it had dried out only recently. A line of green trees appeared, marking the bed of a river. The river, except for an occasional pool, would be dry and sandy, I knew, but life-giving moisture remained beneath the surface. There were herds of cattle now, and flocks of goats and sheep and frequent villages. Palms and syringas became more numerous, and the country leveled off. We were, I told Iz, driving beside the M'beza River. Soon we would turn north again and cross the river, but first we would stop for lunch with bearded Tommy Dugan, who had a small trading station near the crossing and who was the last and only man to have lived on Ibamba.

As we came within sight of Iz's first glimpse of the grass-covered treeless arm of the Kafue flats, at the head of which Tommy had built his home and store, the establishment was far from impressive. Amid a large area stamped to dust and bare of grass by the hooves of countless cattle brought to the store for sale stood a low thatched rectangular mud hut, the front eave of which had been extended to form the roof of a veranda. Resting in the shade from the thatch above were a couple of ancient deck chairs, the canvases spotted with dried mildew and the stains of age, and a square-topped table fashioned from the remains of a packing case by someone whose talents most obviously did not qualify him as a carpenter. The door into the establishment hung not too squarely in its frame; it had been made of planks, the edges of which had not been sawn square, so that there were long cracks between the boards.

Beyond this building, which was home to Dugan, stood another, very similar but smaller. To one side of this were a few round conical-roofed mud huts similar to those we had seen in the villages we had passed.

A row of ancient but still fruitful papaya trees stood in a line a few yards from the store. Their gray sickly-looking trunks, scarred by the heart-shaped marks left when the leafy branches turned yellow, dried, and fell, reared skyward fifteen and twenty feet. All about the buildings and the immediate vicinity the ground was dotted with fresh and old patty-cakes of dung dropped by cattle, and the earth was a mixture of trodden, pulverized manure and sand mixed with the raisinlike droppings of sheep and goats and the blotchy excreta of innumerable chickens.

At the sound of our motor Tommy came to the door of the store, and then strode to meet us as I pulled to a shuddering stop. He let out a whoop of surprise and pleasure when he saw that it was Sibyunni'byunni who was driving. Nimbly avoiding the jets of steam hissing from the radiator, within seconds Tommy had thrust his gnarled, tanned hand into the cab and was pumping my arm off my shoulder.

Tommy had not changed a bit since I had seen him nearly three years before on my last trip out of the Mashakulumbwe country at the conclusion of the motion-picture expedition. Tall and slender, his full beard was trim and black, without a trace of gray. He bowed to Iz, and in a voice tuned with the clipped precision of the British collegian or public-school graduate, made her welcome and invited us to lunch.

Inside Tommy's house, a surprisingly extensive book case filled with worm-eaten and mildewed volumes stood at one side of the room. There was almost a whole set of an encyclopedia, novels, a history or two, some adventure tales and books on veterinary medicine, hunting, economics, and the folklore of the natives. I was pleased to see my book *Wild Animals* among these. On a homemade table under a window, covered with mosquito netting but without glass, stood a kerosene lamp with a shade and a pile of magazines and newspapers. The few passers-by always saved whatever periodicals and papers came to them and dropped them off at M'beza for Dugan.

Lunch was our sandwiches, washed down with hot tea from the kitchen and topped off with generous slices of ripe papaya. I think this was the first time Iz had tasted this delicious melonlike fruit.

Naturally, Tommy had to tell Iz about the night at Ibamba when the lioness tried to climb through the window to get at him after he had shot her mate. He was sure that the deep marks of her claws could still be seen in the soft sandstone of the window sill. Iz's eyes widened a bit when Tommy persisted in telling her exactly where to look among the tumbled remains of the house walls to find the marks.

It would have been fun to sit and gossip the remainder of the day, but we still had seventy miles to go. Tommy understood, promised to visit us, and waved us on our way to the river crossing and forward to Ibamba.

As soon as we had churned through the deep dry sand of the crossing and ground up the sloping riverbank, the country surrounding us changed. The track often crossed long stretches of fine sand where the engine labored mightily and we crawled in our lowest gear, for the secret of successfully crossing sand is to keep moving, however slowly. Palms became numerous. The forbidding dry bushveld lay behind us. On either side of the track the veld opened, and we could see for hundreds of yards.

There were pans of water near the road where lovely stately cranes waded, seeking frogs and small fish among the lily pads. In comparison with the land behind us the country through which we drove was green and fresh and alive. The veld was dotted with small low-growing flowers, mostly of a blue or violet color, and torrents of a crimson climbing vine tumbled from some of the thorn and mimosa trees. Herds of cattle, tended by friendly naked youths who waved and called to us, appeared frequently near the track. Villages were more frequent and much larger. Every so often we drove up shoulders of higher land, projecting into the flats from the tree-covered veld bordering the rolling prairie. From these minor elevations Iz could look out across the tremendous grassy sweep of the flats and learn the immensity of the old lake bottom.

Until we had come to M'beza, Isabella had sat very quietly in the cab. Glancing at her, I could see that her face was thoughtful, and her expression, speculative. First impressions are important, but I was not greatly worried because I knew that once we reached the country bordering the flats, the change from the dreary empty bushveld would be all the more welcome and surprising.

And so it was. The graceful palms, the water, the greenness and the flowers, the natives, and the weird baobab trees—some with trunks fifteen feet in diameter—delighted Iz. Her interest quickened and questions flew.

At the villages our boys, riding proudly atop the swaying load, shouted the news that Sibyunni'byunni was returning and was driving the truck. Men and women raced from the huts and from their tasks to shout words of welcome. Though Iz could not understand the language, there was no mistaking the friendliness and joy of the people. They were so pleased that I had come that our journey became something of a triumphal tour. The excitement was contagious. I drove with a grin on my face and felt somewhat like a minor king.

At the large village of Kabulamwanda, Chinda, the youngish chief, insisted upon stopping the truck. Each of his forearms were covered from wrist to elbow with eight broad ivory bracelets, or bangles. The forepart of his head was shaved smooth and shone with oil. From the back of his scalp rose a cone of hair and beeswax eighteen inches high, studded with brass and aluminum upholstery tacks. The golden feathers and downy black nob which had once adorned the head of a crested crane waved in the fore of the cone. The weight of this heavy permanent headdress had pulled his scalp tight and drawn his eyebrows unnaturally high above his piercing eyes. His facial appearance, despite his grin of welcome, was fearsome and cruel. Like all the Mashakulumbwe, who worship their cattle and want to look like them and will not kill a beast except for a funeral, no matter what its suffering, Chinda had had his upper front teeth knocked out. This was a tribal custom performed in the belief that the removals made the people look like cattle. It did nothing to enhance their appearance.

A hundred, two hundred natives crowded about us. The women wore short skirts made of the tanned skin of the red lechwe antelope which abounded on the nearby flats. This was their tribal dress. Some of the older men, elders and counselors of the village, had lengths of gaily printed cotton goods wound around their waists and hanging below their knees. Most of the other men wore skin breechclouts or, like the youths and children, nothing at all. The majority of the males carried several long, wickedly barbed throwing spears on their shoulders or heavy knobkerries, or native axes. They smelled of ashes and castor oil, sweat and cattle, and the fumes filled the cab and enveloped us.

All were fascinated with Isabella, and smiled and waved and called to her. When she flashed her own smile back at them, they howled and cried with glee and approval. However, the afternoon was wearing on. I did not want to be rude, but we still had thirty or more miles to go. Reluctantly the natives stepped back, and as I tramped on the starter button, formed a corridor through which we drove. With shouts of *hambla gushi,* "go in peace," and cries to return, we headed down a slope and resumed our journey.

Some game appeared now that the great heat of the day was slackening. A small herd of lovely impala stood for a moment, watching our approach, and then dashed across in front, leaping the track in tremendous bounds. Iz exclaimed with delight at the antelope's wondrous agility and beauty.

We saw several little duiker antelope; mousy grayish-brown in color. When full grown, the largest weighs barely forty pounds. Solitary creatures, they stood rigid beside the bushes or in the open, their petal ears thrust forward, and watched us pass with large liquid eyes. The boys behind banged on the top of the cab, the signal for me to stop, and when I did, they begged me to shoot. But this was not a time for killing, and we went on.

In every village—there were several between Kabulamwanda and Marla—the women screamed and trilled a welcome and the men shouted and dashed beside us, yelling questions to the boys behind. Chickens and wild doves scuttled and flew from our path.

Marla is one of the larger of the Mashakulumbwe villages. There were perhaps five hundred inhabitants, and the chief was a powerful ruler, owning many hundreds of cattle. It was not uncommon for a great chief to possess a thousand cattle, worth, on an average, at least five pounds, or twenty-five dollars, a head.

Pete Cavadia, the Greek trader whose main trading stores were at the Namwala *boma* and at Pemba on the railway line, maintained a branch store at Marla. Of the usual mud and thatch construction, it was built on a small elevation. The storekeeper, a Greek and probably a relative of Pete's, for the Greeks have strong family ties, came to the door and waved. We waved back, but did not stop. The brilliant sun, the heat rays from which were striking almost flat across the land, was sinking close to the tops of the palms which formed the distant horizon. We had only a few more miles to go to reach the Kasenga Mission, four miles this side of Ibamba.

Raising a great cloud of dust, we swept through the village and then onto an arm of the flats where the grass, still too moist to burn, rose to the top of the cab on either side. A mile ahead, rising from the sea of grass, we could see a long tree-covered island of high dry ground.

It was well after five, and we had been on the road nearly twelve hours, with time out for visiting, when I drove our heavily loaded swaying truck up the sandy rise on which the mission stood. The track, which swung to the left to lead on to Namwala, fanned out on the slope in a myriad of ruts as others, breasting the rise, had sought passage through the sand. The grass had been burned off the higher ground, leaving only the hard dry crowns and exposing the soil to the fierce sun and the drying winds. The engine growled and knocked protestingly, and the radiator boiled and steam flew from under the hood, but we successfully attained the summit.

To our right, partially hidden by avenues of tall gum trees and rows of silver-leaf pine, lay the buildings of the Kasenga Mission, one of the oldest in Northern Rhodesia. It had been built, and was still headed, by the Reverend John Price, my old friend and a minister of the First Primitive Baptist Mission to the Ba'Ila nation, and his devoted partner and wife, Florence.

We sat for a long time, looking at the scene which had opened before and a little below us when we had reached the crest of the rise of land. Beyond the flat, which was some three miles wide, the veld rose again. The high land, which stretched for two miles, was covered thickly with a dark growth of trees. In the fast-approaching twilight they cast long shadows, joining and melting together to throw a protective mantle of dimness and uncertainty, through which it was difficult to see. The wooded land floated like an island in an ocean of undulating grass. To the east a few hundred yards of the Kafue River glimmered, silvery in the dying sunlight, its banks lined with thick green growths of tall papyrus.

The island of trees and the grass which flowed in endless waves against its shore and stretched away to the barrier of the river challenged us with a brooding defiance. It was as if that land at which we gazed so hungrily and for so long and which we had come so far to see was challenging us to make it ours. It was Isabella's first look at the thirteen square miles which was Ibamba.

Many thoughts passed through our heads as we sat in the cab, surrounded with waves of oily heat from the engine: our dream and intention of building a wild-animal research and study station on Ibamba; of creating a home on that wild, untamed bit of Africa; the repeated warnings we had been given that we were doomed to fail because of the number of lions. We thought of that long sandy mucky track behind us, and of the fact that all our supplies would have to be hauled over it; and of the fact that, aside from the mission and the magistrate's *boma,* fourteen miles on beyond, our nearest neighbors would be seventy miles away. During the rainy season we knew that we would be isolated, our home surrounded by miles upon miles of flooded flats, and that travel, in the event of emergency, could only be by dugout or canoe.

Although we had everything we needed on the truck, it was too late to drive over to Ibamba and set up a camp. I stepped on the starter, and turning, drove off the track onto the mission and to the side of the main house, where we were cordially welcomed by John and Florence.

John Price was a tall, powerful man in his early sixties. With his square, rugged face, tanned the color of old walnut from years of exposure to the sun and wind, prominent chin, and strong work-hardened hands, he looked more like a prize fighter than a missionary. Florence was a cheerful motherly woman with a flair for cooking and baking and gardening. She hovered about Isabella like a hen with a new chick, and served us with a sumptuous and delicious dinner.

Later, as Iz and I lay on hard beds in the mission guest room, waiting for the sleep which always comes tardily when one is overtired and excited, we heard lions roaring on Ibamba. The majestic booming sound was faint, but there was no mistaking the rumble and power of the deep voices. I smiled in the dark. The roaring was a welcome and familiar sound. In my mind's eye, before I fell asleep, I imagined a great maned lion stalking proudly across my property. I liked the thought. Lions on my property. That would make them my lions.

chapter four

THE next morning, after a leisurely breakfast—there was no hurry now that we could step off the Prices' veranda and actually see our ranch—we assembled our natives and drove across the flat and up the rise where I remembered Dobson had built the original house.

The remains were there. Crumbled and fallen red stone walls; the dark circular patches of rotten manure which showed where the kraals had stood, the poles long eaten away by the white ants; the line of nine mulberry trees, and the cracked dipping tank. We drove under a huge spreading wild-fig tree and prepared to unload and set up camp. The bole of the tree was nearly seven feet in diameter, and some of the branches, two feet thick.

A small group of a dozen or so natives awaited us, for the word had gone forth from the villages we had passed that Sibyunni'byunni was returning. I hired them at once because we would need many hands.

By evening camp was up. There was a bedroom shelter consisting of grass walls and a roof tied to a wooden framework with bark. In this was the fine steel bed with the box springs. It looked a trifle out of place, but comfort was the important thing. Each of the legs stood in a tin filled with water and kerosene to prevent ants and bugs from climbing. While campmaking was in progress, Iz and I examined the ruins of the small house and found the marks of the lioness' claws where Tommy had said they were. Tentatively, we began plans for our own new house.

As the night closed in and the stars suddenly became brilliant—there is little twilight in the tropics—we settled in our chairs by the table and broke open a bottle of Scotch. Not far away the cook was busy with his pots and pans over an open fire and Lavison was polishing the silver preparatory to setting the table.

The soft breeze and the chattering of the natives about their fires was comforting and restful. This was my wife's first experience of camp life in Africa, and I watched to see how she reacted. Africa is not the kind of country one can just tolerate. One either loves it fiercely or one hates it.

I need not have worried. When a hippo honked a short way up the river and I explained that it was probably a bull coming onto the land to feed and calling his harem, Iz listened interestedly.

It wasn't necessary to explain that hippos are harmless and feed on grass. She knew that. We listened to the calls of the night birds, to a flock of guinea fowl settling noisily for the night in a tall tree not far away. Neither did the vastness of the dark, stretching mile upon mile around us, frighten her. I thought of how some neurotic movie queen would be depicted with her hair tousled and awry, clutching the nearest male as the terrifying sounds of the birds, or of some small animal, drifted into camp. I smiled to myself. Iz would do.

It was quite a bit after dinner that the serenity was suddenly shattered. I was pouring a nightcap when a shot rang out on the still air. It came from the cattle kraal down by the river. We ran to the top of the rise where the remains of the old house stood and looked down to see grass torches flaring in the night and to hear the boom of another shot. The bawling of cattle drifted to us faintly, and the growling roars of lions. Pete Cavadia's cattle, which had been allowed to graze on Ibamba up to our arrival, were being attacked. Mangineera, who had run up with us, after stopping to seize one of my rifles, yelled a question. The answer came faintly that lions had broken into the kraal and killed a beast. There wasn't much we could do; we were half a mile away, so we waited for daylight.

In the morning we found that the lions—there had been three—had succeeded in stampeding the cattle out of the flimsy kraal, killing one and eating a good part of it.

Grimly Mangineera, Jam, Charlie Portuguese, Charlie Matabele, and Shaluma pointed out that this was just a beginning, and that when we had our own cattle on the ranch, the lions would have such a feast that we would have to leave. They even hinted darkly that they thought I was crazy to build a house. We wouldn't be able to stay, so why go to all that trouble? The matter went even a little further than that. Witchcraft and centuries-old beliefs had surrounded them all their lives. I sensed a very definite feeling of fear and uneasiness among the boys. They had caught lions with me, had stood with me when we had faced angry lions afoot and killed them. We had caught buffalo together and chased elephants. But nevertheless, the curse which they believed to be on Ibamba preyed on their minds and emotions. They were certain that our present effort was foredoomed to failure.

Realizing this, I called all our boys together and made a little speech. I reviewed our hunting experiences and pointed out that they themselves were the ones who said I was a *matakatsi;* that I was a man who spoke with lions in the night. I grew a little boastful and stated my belief that even though lions might kill Pete's cattle while they were on Ibamba, no lion would hurt a beast of *mine*. They shook their heads dubiously and then went about their tasks for the day.

One of these was to build a machan, or tree platform, down by and above the kraal where the lions had killed the previous night. It is not considered sporting to kill lions from a machan, but it is an eminently practical method and one which, considering Isabella's inexperience, was the safest. Inasmuch as the lions had not finished the beast they had killed, it seemed reasonable that they would return that night and feed again. This seemed like a good opportunity to begin Iz's education, so I told Mangineera to make the machan more comfortable than he usually did.

With Charlie Portuguese and Charlie Matabele and some others, Iz and I examined the ruins of the old house more closely. The original building had been about forty-two feet long and twenty-five feet wide, divided into two rooms of equal size. Each room had opened onto what Dobson or Dugan intended to be a long veranda, facing to the southeast. The veranda commanded a magnificent view of the river a quarter of a mile away, the sweep of the flats stretching for miles and miles, and the mountains beyond, looming bluish and hazy through the dancing waves of heat.

The veranda floor, like that of the house, had been planned to lie eighteen inches or so above the level of the ground for the sake of dryness. Now it was just a heap of rubble, covered with many large blocks of red sandstone fallen from the house wall. The builders had used clay chopped from a nearby anthill as mortar, but years of rain, pouring down after the roof had been removed, had dissolved it and washed it away, and the once thick stout walls had crumbled. One of our first tasks was to clear away the tumbled material, sort out the usable stones, and carry away the debris.

Behind and adjoining the two square rooms, and facing to the northwest and the tree-covered portion of Ibamba, there had once been two smaller rooms at each corner of the building, separated by another veranda much shorter than that in front of the house. One of these small rooms, which had a single window, had served as the kitchen. The opposite one, about fifteen feet by ten, had been either a bathroom of sorts or a room for storage.

Two very nicely shaped wild mabunga, or bloodwood, trees grew thirty feet apart and some fifty feet beyond the front of the building. A great purple-flowered bougainvillaea had been planted near the base of one tree, and the vine, reaching up, had grown and entwined itself in the branches and spread to the second tree to form a canopy over the ground between. On the west grew the nine mulberry trees, and to the east and north rose five of the giant fig trees and a few mimosa which had been badly hacked and chopped by someone wanting fuel and too lazy to walk away from the house to fetch it.

Standing on the remains of the front veranda, there was no doubt in either Iz's mind or mine that Dobson had chosen the most advantageous and beautiful location on which to build.

We decided to rebuild the walls of the house, using cement instead of clay, and the stones available. The two square rooms would be bedrooms, and we would complete the long veranda and screen it with mosquito wire. The former storeroom would become a bathroom, and both bedrooms would have doors and windows opening onto the front veranda and doors to the back veranda. There would be casement windows opening to the east and west, and the master bedroom would have a Dutch-type fireplace in one corner.

That we were ambitious, perhaps even a bit lavish, in our planning is probable. But if our plans and hopes materialized, we expected to have frequent guests come to the station to study and work with the animals we would have and to carry forward experimental and scientific studies in the laboratory. We wanted to have adequate quarters for accommodating our expected visitors; a living room in which people could congregate to discuss the day's work and problems; a large enough dining room; a kitchen of sufficient size.

Mulling over ideas, we agreed to knock out the eastern wall of what had been the kitchen. Then, if we constructed a wall at right angles to the old house to form the front of a new building, we could build a long ell running northward, the windows of which would open eastward onto the wonderful view of the flats and river and westward over the arm of the flats which lay between Ibamba and the Kasenga Mission.

The new building would have cement and concrete floors only a little higher than the level of the ground. Steps would lead down from the former kitchen into the new living room to give us a split-level house. There would be a parapet instead of a wall between the living room and the old house, and the square room which had once sounded to the rattle of pots and pans would become a conservatory filled with plants and flowers.

This much accomplished, we marched from the ruins and with help from the boys began measuring and laying out designs for the new building. We had plenty of string and lots of stakes, and gradually an outline took shape.

The living room, which would also contain a fireplace and our library of over two thousand volumes, was to be forty-five feet long by twenty-five wide. Next to this was the dining room, twenty-five by twenty, and then a sort of butler's pantry to house the refrigerator, sink, and shelves and cabinets for china and glass.

We wanted the kitchen, which adjoined the pantry, to be as cool and comfortable as possible because, although we had a cook, we both enjoyed preparing food and surprising each other with different and often exotic dishes. So we laid the kitchen out to be thirty feet long, twenty-five wide, with two windows on the west and two on the east, separated by a door to open onto a small roofed but not screened service veranda.

The last room was for storage and was the same size as the kitchen. There was an entrance at the end through which supplies could be carried and to which a truck could be backed up. There was also a door to the kitchen.

As we surveyed the lines of tightly drawn strings which I had carefully squared at each angle and which had been strung in parallel lines to indicate the widths of the foundations, we were mightily pleased with ourselves. Charlie Portuguese and I were slightly perturbed, however, when we considered the huge number of bricks we would have to manufacture. Mangineera, when he returned to tell me that the machan was completed, raised his eyebrows at the plan. In addition to his main and real work as my gunbearer and tracker, Magineera was also a master brickmaker. The magnitude of the job he knew he was going to have to do appalled him somewhat.

We had supper early, then walked down to the kraal, the boys following with our guns, a big electric searchlight, blankets, pillows, and water bottles.

Mangineera had done a good job. He had even made a flimsy sort of ladder for my wife to climb to reach the machan, which was perched in a fork of a tree about eighteen feet above the ground. From it we could look right into the kraal onto the cattle, and I could see the bait, not far away, where it had been chained to a heavy stake driven deep into the soil.

The sun had gone as our carriers walked back toward the camp and we climbed to the machan. We smoked a last cigarette, adjusted the blanket over the poles and grass on which we lay, tried the light to see if it was aimed at the bait, gave our rifles a last look-see, and settled down to wait in the deepening darkness. Behind us Mangineera squatted with his back against the trunk of the tree. Jam sort of sprawled on the other corner.

Night is the time when the veld comes alive. The game is afoot and feeding. Small cats and mongooses start on their rounds, looking for beetles, mice, unwary birds, and frogs. Leopards begin their nightly prowl through the papyrus in search of a juicy cane rat. Upriver a half mile, a bull hippo honked and blew through its nose. Fifty yards away, half hanging over the river by their swaying nests, a flock of egrets chattered sleepily. Straight above us, in the top of the tree, a pigeon cooed once as a last farewell to light.

From her gentle and regular breathing I could tell that Iz had fallen asleep. Even though I dozed, too, I heard a plover cry out. The abrupt yelp was sharp and carried a warning. Mangineera stirred behind me. We lay waiting. Within minutes another plover cried, and Mangineera's bare foot pressed on my leg. The lions were coming! Despite the many times I had lain and listened to their approach across country through the blanket of the night, my throat tightened a bit and I swallowed. Gently I awoke Iz as still another bird cried out, nearer this time, and more distinct. In my mind I could picture the magnificent beasts striding slowly and confidently through the darkness, their tails switching and their heavy broad heads slowly nodding with the motion of their powerful shoulders.

It is nights like this that bring one into communion with the heart of wild Africa. Lying in the darkness, listening to the many sounds and interpreting these to follow the movements of the night birds and the animals, brings a person close to the wild life which moves constantly about him. Night is the time when young animals gambol in the cool and the baby antelope take their first bite of grass and their first drink of water. It is also the time when growing youngsters first sniff the stench of lions and learn that alertness and fear must be a constant part of their lives. It is the time when low-slung civet cats stretch their heads forth with lightning speed to seize a luscious beetle and crunch it between their sharp needlelike teeth.

A plover cried again, this time scarcely two hundred yards away, and in the open land across which we had walked down from our camp. The machan shook gently as both Jam and Mangineera shifted their weight to more flexible positions. I ran my hand over the two heavy rifles lying between my wife and myself, with their muzzles over the front edge of the platform.

The minutes dragged by as we lay tense and expectant. There was not a sound to indicate the whereabouts of the lions which we were certain were not far away. Probably they were standing in the darkness, sniffing the faint breeze and studying the situation. The carcass had been moved from where they had left it the night before, but they could smell it. Lions are extremely cautious animals and seldom rush into any situation. They have a tremendous curiosity, and will lie for hours just watching a camp of humans. Then we heard the cattle getting to their feet and moving about in the kraal below. It was too dark to see them even from fifty feet or so. Mangineera's foot again pressed against me. He had heard something which had escaped my civilization-hardened ears. Then a low bird-like whistle sounded in the long grass; few people seem to know that lions whistle. Then there was a low growl below. A moment of silence. The chain with which the bait was tied down rattled. The lions were on the kill. We waited, listening, to give them time to settle down. The horrid sounds of ripping meat and hide, breaking bones, and the gurgling, swallowing noises of big animals gulping food rose to us.

I took Isabella's hand—it was damp with perspiration—and put it on the switch for the light. Slowly, trying to make no sound nor sudden movement which could be seen from below as we lay silhouetted against the stars and sky, I eased my rifle up and aimed toward the sound below. I pressed against my wife, and with a click the light went on and flooded the scene.

Two lions lay behind the carcass, staring up at us. I glimpsed another off to the side. One of the two was a male, about three or four years old, with a nice mane. As they tensed to leap out of the light, I shot the male in the throat. He rose straight up in the air, so high as to almost go out of the light, then, falling, stumbled and rushed off into the night. At the sound of the shot the two others vanished.

Mangineera and Jam let out wild yells of triumph. Then they shouted down to the herdsmen to stay in their hut. From our camp we could hear yells and shouts and see the fires blaze up. We played the beam of the searchlight into the grass and all about beneath the trees, but failed to pick up any eyes or to see where the lion I had shot had gone.

Lighting cigarettes, we settled down and discussed the affair, then made ourselves as comfortable as possible against the rest of the night.

Not long after we had ceased talking, a dreadful heart-rending moan rose from the long grass. There was a choking sort of roar. I thought for a moment that we were listening to the dying agonies of the lion I had shot. Again the moan rose into the night. The sound moved in a circle about the machan and the kraal, ending in another roar. It was one of the lionesses, calling her grief. We knew then that the lion was dead, but the lioness below could be terribly dangerous. Round and round she prowled. Once I caught her eyes with the light, but she either turned her head quickly or moved behind some grass before I had time to shoot.

Our two boys called instructions to the men in the hut below not to make a sound. Not to move. If they drew attention to their presence or annoyed the angry, grief-stricken lioness, she might charge the flimsy hut and tear it down. It would be dangerous for us to try to shoot if such a melee started.

I do not know how long the lioness continued her vigil and her prowling. Once she rushed right beneath us, knocking against the ladder and shaking the machan. One loses all sense of time in the night, and under such conditions. A great pity welled up in my heart for the lioness as she poured forth her grief. It was frightening and terrible to hear. There was a menace and rage in her voice which boded ill for any human who might cross her path. I thought of Tommy Dugan, alone in the house which was now a heap of ruins on the rise behind us, while another lioness prowled, moaning and roaring, just as the one below. At that moment my sympathies were all with Tommy and his decision to abandon Ibamba.

Lions mate for life, and families are very devoted to one another. But—and I say this with some shame as a man—male lions do not exhibit the grief and pain and rage when their mate is killed which lionesses pour forth.

Sometime toward morning the lioness went off. We dozed uneasily on the poles and grass which became flatter and harder with each passing half hour. Then the false dawn threw a faint light across the veld. I awakened to hear voices, and peered sleepily below to see the natives from our camp crowding about. Mangineera and Jam climbed down, carrying the rifles, and Iz and I followed. After a quick recount of what had happened, natives swarmed up to bring down the paraphernalia in the machan and others scattered to search for the lion, which we felt certain must have died nearby.

It was nearly a half hour before we found it. After taking the shot, it had dashed off, blindly probably, and dived into and under a great clump of grass, where it had died immediately. The bullet, as I had thought, had hit the lion in the throat as it had started rearing upward, and plowed its devastating path through its body. We later recovered the bullet from near the base of the tail. At such short range the 500/450 which I always use is a terrifically powerful weapon. A 480 soft-nosed bullet propelled by eighty grains of cordite, or norite, strikes with an awful wallop.

Quickly the boys fashioned a litter from poles, and carrying the lion, they escorted us back to camp. The native women, who had quickly crowded around with their children, greeted us with their high keening and shouts of joy. Another lion was dead. Another cattle-killer gone. Long live the king. The skin, after the boys tanned it with ashes, brains, and fat and worked it soft with their hands, would end as a rug beside our bed in the house we were building.

We settled down to work. Trenches were dug for the foundation for the new house. Mangineera sought for and found clay suitable for brickmaking, and a gang was set to work digging the clay, wetting it, mixing it with sand, and trampling it smooth and consistent with their bare feet. The mixture was then slapped and pressed into forms, and the soft clay bricks were set out carefully, row upon row in the sun to harden so that we could pile them in kilns and burn them. Standing naked in a hole in the ground with a short plank before him as a table, Mangineera turned out a thousand bricks a day. Other natives gathered huge piles of wood for the brick burning, and still others dug pits for the sawyers; chipped stones for building; cleared land near the river for the vegetable garden; carried up water, and did the hundred and one tasks necessary to running a camp and getting the construction under way. While this was going on, we concentrated on getting the walls of the old house up and a roof on so that we could get under cover and be more comfortable.

Near the old dip tank which Tommy Dugan had originally built we set up a rather flimsy kraal for cattle. It was only a hundred yards from our temporary camp, so we didn't bother to make it strong. Instead of the usual construction of poles set upright in the ground in a circle, and standing like a great basket, we put a few poles in upright, then lashed others to them horizontally. We felt this would serve until we located a position for more permanent kraals.

At the end of the first week I made a trip in to the railway and saw Pete Cavadia and arranged to buy a hundred head of cows and young stock with a couple of bulls, and brought out more materials. On my return I selected the cattle I wanted from those Pete had running on Ibamba, herded them with my own boys, and kraaled them at night in our new kraal.

It was about ten days after we had shot the lion that we awoke one morning to find that three lions had swum the river, come across the flat, and lain on an anthill not far from camp for a long time, watching what went on. Later, after the camp had fallen asleep, the lions had descended the anthill, walked to the cattle kraal, and lain there watching the cattle for some time. The impressions of their bodies were sharp and deep in the dust. One lion had lain so close that its forepaws actually lay inside the kraal, underneath the lowest horizontal pole. We hadn't heard the cattle get up and move about, and never knew why the dogs which were all about camp had not raised a ruckus.

After watching the cattle for some time, the lions had risen and walked up to where we were digging the foundations for the house. They had walked all around, just as if they were inspecting the work. From there they had gone to the sawpits and inspected them. Having seen all they wanted, they had left, walking down the beginnings of a road along which we dragged logs from the bush to the sawyers.

This gave me my chance to boast a little. "You see," I told my natives, "the lions come. But they know that I, Sibyunni'byunni, am here, and that these cattle belong to *me*." The boys gaped at me. "You see for yourselves that the lions, although they were nearly into the kraal, touched nothing."

They could not but admit the truth of this, but there were dubious shakings of heads, and I heard uneasy murmurs. These were happenings beyond their comprehension which they didn't like at all.

Two weeks passed. During this period, starting at two in the morning so as to make a round trip in one day, I made additional journeys to the railway. We had added some goats and a few fat-tailed sheep to our stock, and these we kraaled in a small enclosure a bit farther away from camp than the cattle. Sheep and goats smell. During this time we had heard lions roaring on several nights, but they had not come closer than a half-mile or so. One night they did raid one of Pete's kraals and killed two cattle. But we did nothing about this, as we were too busy with our building program.

Two weeks to the day of their first visit, the three lions returned. Again they swam the river, and again lay on the anthill. When all was quiet, they inspected the cattle for a time, then walked about the foundations, looked at the pile of boards and timbers rising by the sawpits, then inspected the goats and sheep. As on their first visit, they awakened no one and touched nothing. That is, they touched nothing of ours, but in the early morning hours, around three o'clock, they attacked Pete's kraal down by the river and succeeded in killing one young animal.

I discussed this with my hunters. They argued that the lions were afraid to tackle our cattle, which were so near the camp, and that this was why they had moved down to Pete's. They prophesied darkly that after Pete had moved his cattle away and only ours remained, we would be the ones to suffer. To keep up my prestige, I, of course, argued that this was all nonsense, that it was because the lions knew *me* and because I spoke to them that they left me alone. In my heart, and in private conversations with Isabella, I wondered just how long I could get away with that statement and what I would use for an explanation on the day when the lions did attack us.

During the construction period two baby duiker antelope were brought in by natives, and we bought them. Iz took over the job of raising them with a bottle until they could graze and feed themselves. A week or so later we bought a young oribi antelope from another native. Because of the odd little whistling noises he made, we named him Fwifwi.

It is very seldom that one sees an oribi, either tame or in a zoo. About the same size as a duiker, they are much redder, a bit taller, and not so common. Oribis are nervous, excitable little animals that inhabit open land by preference. Fwifwi became as tame as the duikers, and very dependent upon Iz. He was friendly with me but devoted to my wife, and would come galloping on his pipestem legs whenever she called him.

Here is an aspect of animal behavior which I have observed many, many times. Male animals seem to prefer and become more devoted to women than to men. With female animals it is the reverse. This appears to be true even with birds. But like people, no two animals of the same species react the same way or exhibit the same preferences, dislikes, or habits as another.

It was during the initial period of construction that Mwaming Thomas Sibyunni'byunni Mashonto was brought in by a native woman, who found him while she was out gathering wild fruit.

Thomas was a civet cat. He didn't, of course, acquire his full name until much later. Translated it means Mr. Thomas, Son of the Father of Birds.

Mr. Thomas was so tiny that Isabella, whose hands are small and delicate, could hold him neatly in one palm.

Civet cats are supposed, or reputed, to be untamable. When he was brought in, Tommy, although he could hardly see from his baby eyes, was full of fight and very dirty. By the time of his arrival we had moved our bed into the stone house. After sponging the little fellow off and forcing some warm milk down his throat from a medicine dropper, we put him in a small box lined with cotton batting and placed this on the floor beside the bed where we could reach him easily for night feedings.

For a time, the first night, Tommy was quiet. I flashed a light into his box, and he was sleeping, curled into a tight ball. Later he woke and began to whimper and cry. I got up, and warming the milk, fed him some. He wasn't quite so belligerent as before. Warm milk has a wonderfully soothing effect. But, after feeding, he didn't want to go to sleep. He rattled around in the box for a time and then began to cry again. Neither Iz nor I could stand this; the little fellow sounded so frightened and lonely crying by himself in the dark. So, raising the mosquito net, I reached into the box and got him. He bit me, of course, but it wasn't serious, and I stuffed him under the sheet. He curled up between Iz and myself and lay perfectly quiet, content that he had some form of companionship.

Half an hour later I awoke again. I felt as if I were on fire. I knew that Iz was awake also. Getting out of bed I lit the lamp and we turned back the sheet. The bed was literally black with fleas! Never have I seen so many. They were jumping and crawling to all corners.

I found a Flit gun and we soaked the sheets and the pillows with spray, killing hundreds of fleas. But the source of the trouble was harboring hundreds more. While Iz held him, I sprayed him gently, ruffling the coarse fur so that the spray got in among the hairs, and then I sprayed a towel liberally and we wrapped Tommy in it tightly and held him as if he were in a cocoon for five minutes or more.

When I undid the towel it was black with fleas, like the sheets. We sprayed his box and put him back while we ripped the bed apart, put on fresh sheets and pillowcases. We combed and brushed Tommy and then all three of us went back to bed.

It wasn't the pleasantest night we had ever spent, what with feedings and scratchings and twistings, but we did snooze a little.

The next morning, after breakfast, we washed Tommy in warm water with soap and creosote. Lots more fleas came off and died. We brushed him and combed him and he bit each of us several times. It was worth it. We got rid of all the fleas in the end.

We put Tommy back inside the bed, and from that day on it was his home and his castle. During the first few weeks he spent the entire day under the sheet and coverlet except when we uncovered him for feeding. At night, after we had retired and the light was out, he would crawl up onto the pillows and sleep curled around the top of Iz's head. She said he was hot, but he was so tiny and so appealing, she hadn't the heart to shoo him off.

So, Mwaming Thomas Sibyunni'byunni came into our lives. He met the duikers and Fwifwi, who also had the run of the bedroom and the front screened veranda. Any one of the animals could go outside whenever it wanted, but they seldom did so, as there was so much going on and so many natives about, they were afraid of venturing far from home. Iz fed them from a bottle, and fresh green grass was brought twice daily and put in a small heap on the veranda. The little antelope pushed it around and nuzzled it, but it was some time before they tried to eat the stuff.

The two duikers learned to drink tea before they ate grass. It was the custom for Lavison to bring tea very early. We had some before getting up, and I always drank cupful after cupful while shaving and getting ready to face the day.

In a spirit of play we offered a duiker the last bit of tea in a cup. It liked it. So we poured another cup, mainly milk and sugar. Cambric tea. It drank the lot, and its pal came over and wanted to try.

From then on Lavison always brought two small bowls on the tea tray, and every morning we four had tea together.

This early morning tea party attracted the attention of Tommy. He wouldn't be satisfied until he, too, had tasted tea. Another bowl was brought and Tommy given his portion with lots of sugar, as we had discovered he had a bit of a sweet tooth. Civet cats can't lap like cats or dogs because their lower jaw is underslung. Tommy lowered his lower jaw and part of his mouth into the bowl of weak tea and sucked. It was a most impolite sound, but it took him no time at all to drain the bowl. He loved it, and looking around for more, spotted a duiker drinking from its bowl. He scurried over, nuzzled the duiker from the bowl, and proceeded to empty it. He did the same with the second bowl while we laughed and the duikers stamped their little hooves and whistled in annoyance.

Every morning there was a battle over the bowls. Tommy always finished his ahead of the duikers, who were much more delicate drinkers. He did not like to be stamped on, so when he wanted to steal a bowl, he developed a trick of getting his head into a bowl and then pushing it over the cement and under a book case, where there was room for him but not for the taller duikers. Once he had a bowl there, he would finish the contents. He also found that he liked a certain type of broad, rather thick, leaved grass which was often brought for the duikers. He would eat quantities of this, disputing with the duikers and Fwifwi for more than his rightful share.

In these disputes with other animals Tommy never struck to cut. He hated the bedroom boy, Lubin, who made the mistake, in the beginning, of teasing Tommy. Occasionally Tommy would be late when the bed was being made up. He would then find a dark corner among the towels and curl up there. When Lubin found him in such a place, he would awaken him by making hissing noises and flicking a towel at him. This frightened Tommy, as he could not see well in daylight, and he never forgave Lubin. Whenever he had an opportunity, he would slash at Lubin's bare feet, and once he cut him open for a length of several inches and a depth of a quarter of an inch or more.

In his quarrels with the duikers Tommy would hiss and make cluck-cluck noises; he would raise the long hair on his back and bob and weave, threatening to strike. He never did. When he was a year old, Tommy weighed nearly thirty pounds and could easily have downed and killed one of the little antelope. The thought never seemed to occur to him.

Out in the bush civet cats are omnivorous. They eat quantities of berries and wild fruit, insects, lizards, mice, grass and, probably, caterpillars and small snakes, birds' eggs and baby birds. It is probable that they eat carrion, as civet cats will come to the high-smelling bait left for a trap.

Civets are lightning fast in their movements and their reactions. Tommy would stand on the floor in front of me and dare me to hit him. His head weaved back and forth and up and down like that of an extremely fast and clever boxer. I had to try mighty hard and have some luck on my side to be able to land a clip. It was all in fun, and once I clipped him, he would trundle off about his business of the moment.

Several times when my wife and I were about to retire and were sitting on the edge of the bed, talking over the day's affairs, Tommy, lying near us, would see a mouse run across the floor. His movements were so fast, they were difficult to follow. He was off the bed, onto the floor, and had the mouse before we were quite aware of what had happened. He would seize the mouse with a quick hard bite, then toss it in the air, let it fall to the cement, and watch to see if it moved. If it didn't, he'd hop back onto the bed and stretch out. Then we would all sleep peacefully.

chapter five

AS great masses of clouds began to pile up and the western skies in the evening changed from blue to violent orange, purples, reds, and pinks, we worked feverishly to complete the house, bring all necessary supplies out from the railway, and get everything under cover against the coming of the rains.

Charlie Portuguese, my *capitao,* had the men at work half an hour after sunrise, which came about four. After drinking several cups of tea in company with Iz, the duikers, and Mr. Thomas, I was out of the house as the men collected their tools and departed to the various working areas. At around eight or eight-thirty I returned for breakfast, for which, by that time, I really had an appetite. Then back to work at the forge, or on the tractor clearing land for plowing, or perhaps to study the walls of the new house and check with a mason's level to see that the men were laying the bricks and cement square and vertical.

We knocked off work at twelve when Charlie beat with an iron bar on a length of rail hanging from a tree limb. Two hours for lunch and rest and we resumed our tasks and kept at them until twilight fell. Ten- or eleven-hour days. Six days a week.

Even so, we could not complete all the work before the first rains. The old house had been 90 per cent rebuilt and a sloping roof put on. The walls of the new part of the house were finished, and we slapped on a sloping corrugated iron roof instead of the peaked roof we had planned. It would protect us during the rains, and under its cover we could finish laying the floors, plaster and whitewash the walls, and set the door frames, hang the doors, etc.

Cavadia delivered the grain we had bought to feed our staff, and we had this in storage. Field mice got into the storeroom and must have been very grateful to us for our thoughtfulness in laying up such generous supplies.

The brick kilns flared and smoked day and night until the last possible day. We used bricks at a tremendous rate. In addition to the thousands used constructing the addition to the house, many went into a building for our sows and the fine boar, in which I had laid a concrete floor and constructed farrowing pens. I had a workshop consisting of one brick wall and a large flat iron roof supported on stout poles, and there we carried on our smithy, carpentry, and mechanical work.

For the cattle, of which we had around a hundred to start, about half working oxen and half cows, we had built a large kraal in the native fashion. This is done by digging a trench two feet deep in a circle of sufficient diameter to house the cattle which will be put inside. Poles six to eight inches in diameter at the butt and sixteen to twenty feet long are set upright, butt end down, in the trench, which is then filled and packed with earth. Bundles of long green withes are collected, several withes are held together horizontally on the inside of the wall of poles and a similar number outside four feet above the ground. Wet green mopani bark or soft annealed iron wire is then laced back and forth between the poles and over and under the withes and drawn tight so that the upright poles are bound firmly and closely together. Another similar binding is placed three feet above the first.

A kraal made in this fashion is almost lion proof, and depending upon how fast the white ants eat away the poles, may last for several years. Lions will not jump into anything from which they cannot see an easy way out, and the poles were bound too tightly together for even a great male lion to force a passage between.

The compound of forty huts had been finished. Counting the wives of the forty natives in more or less permanent employ, and the children, over a hundred persons lived in our village under the rule of Charlie Portuguese. There were pens with grass-thatched roofs for the goats and sheep and the chickens. Dobson had built a one-room stone house some distance from the main building. What its purpose was, I never knew, but we rebuilt it, put on a roof of iron, and used it to store our flammable gasoline, kerosene, and oil and grease.

Trails and paths fanned out from the neighborhood of the house in all directions across the ranch. Along these I chugged in the tractor to tear and plow up land for the planting of corn and peanuts, and Charlie Matabele came and went with his oxen, dragging in logs for the sawboys and loads of firewood, poles for kraals and pens and roofs, and tremendous piles of thatching grass. Iz drove the truck, bringing loads of bricks for building and delivering needed materials. Clouds of dust rose from the sandy trails as the vehicles and cattle came and went and drifted high above the busy scene.

Sanitation and the control and disposal of waste was always a problem; it was impossible to induce the natives to use latrines. Fortunately, the baking sun, the torrential rains, the ants and scavengers destroyed the human waste, and it did not accumulate to become a nuisance. However, we could not allow our pigs to run loose on the veld to graze and dig for roots. This would have been the most economical way to raise hogs because there was ample wild feed, and it would have enabled us to reduce the supplemental feedings. But the hogs would also find and eat excreta. The danger of their becoming infected with tapeworms, trichinosis, or as the English call this disease, measles, would have increased a hundredfold.

When I had planned to have our hogs herded out on the flatlands, where their wallowing in the mud around the lagoons would help keep them free of ticks and where they could feed on the water-lily roots and green grass, I had failed to take the danger of trichinosis into consideration. This was an error, although not too grievous a one.

I had, however, given considerable attention to what may be called the "facilities" for the main house in which Iz and I were to live. From the beginning, in New York, I had determined that we would have an indoor bathroom. I was greatly pleased when the Crane Plumbing Company donated a tub, toilet, and washstand, and made many sketches of how I would arrange the pipes and plumbing. Above everything else I wanted Iz to have a fine comfortable kitchen and a decent approximation of a modern bathroom.

Constructing the bathroom and the outdoor cesspool both intrigued and puzzled the natives. It was hard to explain just what my purpose was, but they carried out my instructions as best they could.

The mulberry trees at the west side of the house stood some thirty feet from the wall. In part of this space, using the house wall as one side, we built a brick-walled room about fifteen feet square; the floor was raised four feet higher than the floor in the house. The side facing to the rear of the house was left completely open.

In this room we installed two one-hundred-gallon steel drums. They lay on their sides, and on the upper side each had a rectangular opening a foot long and eight inches wide to permit filling the drums with water. Each drum had brick and cement supports to hold it steady, but one was mounted much higher than the other so that a fire could be built beneath it. A one-inch pipe led from the lower edge of one end of each drum through the wall of the house into the bathroom, and one for hot and one for cold water was eventually connected to the bath, the toilet, and the washstand. This much the boys could understand and approve.

The vitrified clay pipe, through which waste from the toilet would be flushed, amazed and defeated them. They had never seen pipe like that before; they admired its luster and smoothness and thought it a great shame to bury it in the ground.

I had to blast to sink the hole which would be the septic tank. Blasting presented no problems because I was an old hand at handling dynamite, having been educated at Harvard to be a mining geologist and having worked as powder foreman, among other jobs, in mines before making my first trip to Africa.

When we had the hole cut out of the sandstone to my liking, we dug an inclined trench for the beautiful clay pipe and tunneled through the foundations of the house to a point below the spot where the toilet would be installed.

Do not be impatient with this somewhat lengthy description of what should have been a routine bit of construction. I am leading up to something. Unless there were similar facilities in Government House in Livingstone, our toilet was probably the first flushing one installed in Northern Rhodesia. It was certainly the first ever installed a hundred and more miles out in the bushveld. The natives began to understand its function as we neared completion, and their *ohs* and *ahs* sounded constantly as they discussed the whole matter in detail and speculated as to whether this new thing would work or not.

The boys had difficulty describing what I was doing because there are no words for such items as pipe, vitrified clay, water pressure, etc., in the native language. Any discussion, of necessity, had to be accompanied by long roundabout descriptions and much pantomime.

It was Mianje who brought matters to a head and solved all the questions which had been bothering our natives.

Mianje was a magnificently built woman who stood a little over six feet. She was the wife of our chief carpenter, and although she had been in my camps previously, I had never particularly remarked her until Iz and I settled on Ibamba.

She first came to our attention some weeks after our arrival, while we were still living in the grass huts beneath the fig tree. It was a few evenings after the one on which Lavison, not understanding the nature of pewter, had set a cocktail shaker he was polishing on some hot coals from the fire beside which he was crouched to have ashes handy for his cleaning purposes. The shaker had been a wedding gift from my brother and we had thought its shape, in the form of one of those large five-gallon cans farmers use to deliver milk to a dairy, attractive. The look of shocked surprise on Lavison's face when he picked up the shaker and discovered that the bottom half had melted away was so comical and so genuine an expression of sorrow at what had happened that we did not have the heart to berate him for carelessness. It was just one of the hazards of living as we were, and allied to the difficulty some houseboys have in learning that glassware will not bounce when dropped on a concrete floor or will shatter when shoved into a hot oven to dry.

Shaluma, who was Mianje's husband, approached Iz and me as we were nearing the end of our evening meal, and after apologizing for interrupting, requested permission for his wife to dance by the campfire after supper was done. Lavison, who was standing ready to remove our plates, joined in the conversation, explaining that Mianje had been bewitched when a little girl. The demon which had taken possession of Mianje masqueraded in the form of a zebra. Ever since her bewitching, whenever Mianje saw a zebra—we commonly called them convicts—or saw a part of one, the demon became active, and the only way by which she could rid herself of the spirit troubling her was to dance.

Although Lavison did not say so, he implied that the resurgence of Mianje's demon was rather my responsibility. I had shot a zebra the day before, as their meat is excellent eating provided every bit of the yellow fat is removed before cooking. When the bloody quarters of the zebra had been carried into camp, Mianje had glimpsed a portion, although the men carrying the zebra had shouted ahead as to what they were bringing.

We, of course, gave permission. I expected that the dance music would be provided by tom-toms, but instead a dozen or more men gathered near the fire, each holding an *m'pira*. Squatting together, each propped his *m'pira* on the ground before him, leaning the instrument against the dried half-shell of a calabash, which served as a sounding board.

They began softly playing in perfect unison a lovely tune which I recognized as "The Flight of the Dove." Full of rhythm and a haunting melody, the gentle music flowed from beneath the rapidly moving fingers of the musicians as they stroked the keys. It filled the air, rising with the sparks from the fire to die away among the limbs of the gigantic fig tree which formed a canopy above us.

Then Mianje came. Her only covering was a short skirt of tanned lechwe skin. Sinuous and beautifully proportioned in spite of her size, the tall Negress seemed in a daze. In her coal-black face, which was round and normally pleasant and happy, her eyes stared, dull and unseeing, from deep sockets. She had anointed herself with oil, and her skin shone like patent leather. Her feet were bare, and about her ankles had been bound anklets fashioned of tiny gourds filled with little pebbles which rattled as she stamped her feet.

For a moment Mianje stood with the firelight flickering and gleaming on her polished body. To Iz and me, watching, it seemed that she was far away in another world and conscious only of the music which was rising in volume and quickening in beat. Slowly she swayed, moving only the upper part of her body in rhythm with the music. Except for the notes from the *m'piras,* there was not a sound from the natives crowded about in a circle. She suddenly stamped her feet. The gourds rattled with a dry sound like that of the maracas used by Cuban musicians. The tune changed and became faster and more exciting. Mianje danced.

Powerful, yet lithe and graceful in spite of weighing nearly two hundred pounds, Mianje swirled and postured, swayed and leaped and writhed in as beautiful and expressive a dance as I had ever seen anywhere. Unlike much of the native solo dancing which is pantomime and tells a story or which is challengingly sexual, Mianje's dance was her own, a dance definitely to exorcise the demon within her, and as we watched, we could see and understand the struggle taking place before us. It was tremendously moving and absorbing, and we watched for more than two hours until, at last, the demon gone, Mianje sank, exhausted, to the ground.

I don't know just how it came about, but from that time on Mianje insinuated herself into our lives. It is most unusual for a native woman to, shall we say, take service with white people. Nevertheless, Mianje attached herself to Iz, and everywhere that Maseccasecca went, Mianje followed, unless she had work to do preparing her husband's food or repairing her hut or fetching water.

I saw Mianje often at the river, for she was very clean. She would bring her water jar to the bank, strip and bathe, and then fill the jar which, I guessed, held about eight gallons. Bending over from the waist, she held the jar between her hands, and then without perceptible effort, raised it aloft and balanced it, at a jaunty angle, on her woolly head. I thought that I was strong, but I knew I lacked the strength to pick up so heavy a weight just by the muscles in my arms.

In spite of her strength, her handsomeness, and her invariable good nature, Mianje could not be described as bright. She was like an enormous devoted puppy, and wriggled with pleasure just like a puppy when Iz would give her a cigarette or smile at her. Mianje doted on doing little things for Iz, such as errands or cleaning and brushing up the shelter, which she did enthusiastically but poorly. Iz tried to teach her to sew, but Mianje never really mastered the art. Her husband was far neater and more efficient at sewing.

Mianje came and went freely about the camp. She stole cigarettes at every opportunity and matches and, when the chance offered, sugar. But as Iz did not pay her for what little work she did, we made our reprimands gentle.

Mianje had, of course, heard all about the great mystery of the bathroom, the pretty pipes the *n'kos* had buried underground, and the hot- and cold-water tanks. A few days after the paint had dried—the concrete floor was black and the walls a light blue to a height of four feet and then white to the ceiling—Iz retired to the bathroom to attend to certain private business. Whether or not—because there were only the two of us—I had put a lock on the door by then, I have forgotten. Anyway, Iz closed but did not fasten the door.

Shaking with laughter, Iz told me later what had happened. Seconds after she had installed herself, the door opened quietly. Mianje stepped into the room, glanced about, and seeing Iz, crossed the floor a few steps and hunkered down in front of her. Iz ordered her out, but Mianje would not budge. There was nothing Iz could do except try to retain as much composure as she could muster.

When ready, Iz turned and pressed the lever which flushed the toilet. This was the moment Mianje had been awaiting. She bounded to her feet and rushed to peer into the bowl with its swirling water. Fascinated, she watched, and then turned to Iz, her eyes wide with admiration. By gestures and words she made Iz understand that nothing like that ever happened to Mianje. She hurried from the bathroom and raced to the compound to tell of what she had seen. Her description went all over the Mashakulumbwe country. Pete Cavadia and John and Florence Price heard it told by their natives, and even McKee, in far off Choma, told me the tale had reached the railway line.

So, in our lonely house far out in the blue of the veld, the simplicity of the native met the sophistication and practicality of civilization.

Several weeks before the rainy season the veld bursts into greenness. This is the very driest portion of the year. When we dug postholes or blasted stumps, or when the heavy gang disc plow I hauled behind the tractor turned up ground, there was not a trace of moisture in the excavated material. Yet at this time when one would have expected the vegetation to be most quiescent, the harsh dead-looking crowns of grass which had been left exposed to the searing heat of the rainless months of the dry season sent forth timid shoots of green; low, thorny little plants blossomed, and the trees began to bud new leaves.

A joyousness spreads through the veld. Springiness returns to the walk of the natives, and the women, working bent and industrious preparing fields for planting, sing as they swing their short-handled hoes. Heat and humidity are at their greatest, and sweat drenches every worker. But the naked children, sensing the change which is coming, gambol and dash about their games more furiously than before. A feeling of newness, of change and of rebirth, envelops the land, so that aches and pains are forgotten and a happy anticipation pervades everyone.

The game which, because of the drying up of the pans and waterholes scattered throughout the bushveld, have congregated in greater and greater numbers along the banks of the river and near the lagoons, become restless. In some fashion the animals know that the rains are coming and that feed and water will once again be plentiful.

I believe that even slight changes in barometric pressures are felt by and unconsciously reacted to by all creatures. Many times I have noticed that wild birds come more frequently to feeding trays and tend to stuff their crops when the barometer indicates the coming of a storm. Fish also react to pressure changes.

Just before and during this wondrous change from dying veld to living land is the time when calves are dropped by the buffalo, the wildebeest, the hartebeest and the roan, and eland antelope and the zebra foal. However scientifically and objectively one may view and study this phenomena, it is impossible not to feel and believe that there must be some great spiritual force guiding the destinies of all living things.

It is because they have observed these happenings during the centuries of their development that the natives endow the sun, the rain, and the wind with godlike attributes. Who is to say that they are wrong? The arrival or the nonarrival of the rain can mean life or death. Without the sun plants could not grow. It is the wind that carves the land, even resistant stone, and which distributes seeds.

In our white man's civilization and the conduct of our materialistic businesses, insurance policies and contracts for performance are written containing clauses of escape of payment or completion if such nonpayments or noncompletion are determined to have been caused by weather or other conditions which are "acts of God" and beyond man's control. So, in our superior way, do we acknowledge, however reluctantly, the existence of the natural forces to which the natives attribute personalities.

From the front veranda of the house Iz and I, enjoying a sundowner at the end of the day, sat and watched the game drift down the flat which stretched between us and the mission. Herds of striped zebra grazed slowly toward the river, the stallions neighing and suddenly, for no reason which we could see, engaging in short, furious battles, biting and kicking at each other. Wildebeest, mingling with the zebras, swung their heavy black and bearded heads and tossed their horns; abruptly they would drop to their knees to engage in determined butting matches, or two would race from the herd, single-footing with a grace and speed the finest horse could never equal.

Reedbuck whistled, and against the blackened veld where the fires had passed the orange puku antelope stood out sharp and clear. A flock of almost two hundred cackling guinea fowl scurried from the river each evening and hurried by on their way to find a tall tree in which to roost for the night. It was a mean thing to do, but periodically, so that we could have a change in diet, I would allow Jam or Charlie Portuguese to take a shotgun and follow the birds. Whoever it was would wait until the guinea had flown up into a tree and settled down, and then would creep beneath, and we, waiting and listening, would hear a shot.

Soon after the hunter would return, bringing any number from one to seven or eight fine, fat fowl. If I had permitted it, this would have been a nightly affair, for the boys loved to hunt, and they, too, found the guineas fine eating. The guineas, with their dotted plumage, bright blue heads, and yellow crowns, were decorative and they did no harm. We enjoyed their frantic antics and permitted shooting only at intervals.

For a month before the rains broke, the humidity increased, and for a short period became oppressive. Especially at night. The still hot wet air carried sound for long distances. The roaring of the lions as they emerged from the *saka* two miles from the house rolled over us as we sat on the veranda or at table for the evening meal. The magnificent sounds pulsed and flowed as the lions and lionesses swung their heads from side to side, exchanging information from troop to troop and lion to lion. Listening, we could differentiate between the males and females and trace their journeyings as they crossed the ranch.

Isabella, I am sure, never had the faintest feeling of apprehension because of the lions. They were with us always until Ibamba began to flood and the game moved to higher and bushier country. They never did us hurt or threatened the livestock, although it was a most unusual morning when I or the boys, going to work, did not find spoor in the trails and roads we followed.

Our natives came to accept the situation, and often in the still darkness Iz and I could hear them mimicking the lions as they sat about their fires in the compound and roaring back at them. Contrary to all the dismal prophesying to which we had listened before journeying to Ibamba during that first season, not a single lion bothered us in any way. Rather, they seemed to adopt us, to take a vital and deep interest in everything we did and to watch and inspect our work and our comings and goings. When the lions killed on Ibamba, they killed an antelope or a zebra, their natural prey. Never a cattlebeast. Our herds of cattle and flocks of goats and sheep came and went without molestation. Even the leopards, of which there were many in the papyrus along the river, where they hunted the fat cane rats, did not bother us, although our many dogs must have tempted them greatly. Dogs are a favorite food of leopards.

We continued adding to our family. One day a villager brought in a *mowan,* or crested crane. We immediately bought the young bird. It was just learning to feed itself, and for a time Iz fed it by hand, stuffing bits of dampened bread and crushed grain into its bill. We couldn't determine its sex so, just to cover all possibilities, named it Jane Emmeline John. Jane Emmeline John lived outside most of the time. Jane loved to walk beside us when we toured the estate, and kept pace with us stride for stride. She, he, it, played with the dogs, followed the work oxen, visited in the compound, and generally kept a bossy eye on all goings on. Although her, his, its, wild brothers and sisters could frequently be heard calling out on the flats or when flying over, Jane Emmeline John never left the immediate vicinity of humans. There was nothing to prevent it. She (as we decided to call her) just never did. Jane liked people.

Facts, or acts, such as Jane's devotion to people to the exclusion of her own kind, open up a wide field for speculation and study. Of all the hundreds of birds and animals which I have handled, I have yet to find one which, if acquired before its parents had an opportunity to teach it, did not readily adopt humans as foster parents and show a preference for them as against others of their own kind.

Which brings in the very argumentative question of inherited characteristics. Do or do not animals and birds inherit tendencies to become savage, to fear man, to be timid? These are mental or emotional traits as opposed to physical traits, or characteristics.

It is a generally held belief that a lion kitten, for instance, just because it is physically a lion, must grow up to be a dangerous and savage animal, or that a faun which you may have caught must grow into an animal which longs for the wild, free life of the woods.

Why should this be true unless mental characteristics are inherited? If mental characteristics are inherited, and thus are a basic emotional part of a mammal or a bird, how is it possible to tame an animal or a bird, as we tamed ours, or as hundreds of other people have tamed skunks, raccoons, foxes, deer, wolves, bears, tigers, elephants, warthogs, cheetahs, pigeons, macaws, myna birds, and so on and on?

I do not like the word "tamed," which the dictionary defines as "taken from the wild and made obedient." This strikes me as more applicable to the training to perform in an act by which certain men and women develop circus animal performances. Certainly we took or secured our animals from the wild. Never, however, did we in any way attempt to train or force or tame the creatures which came to live with us.

Free and wild on the veld, civet cats regularly deposit their droppings in certain well-defined spots of their own choosing. Tramping about Ibamba, we often found these deposits, which are marked particularly by an accumulation of hard dried seeds or pits from the fruits which the civets eat and cannot digest.

When Mr. Thomas was old enough to move about our house by himself, we placed a large enamel basin of water on the veranda so that he, and the duiker antelope, would always have water to drink. Why he did so, I do not know, but Mr. Thomas decided that the basin should serve as a dirting place, or toilet. Never in the years he lived with us did Tommy mess in the house. Invariably he found and used his basin.

Although Iz or I could tell someone who asked that Mr. Thomas was housebroken, the statement, in the accepted sense, was not really true. When a person says that an animal is housebroken, he or she usually means that the animal in question has had its little nose rubbed in a wet spot on the rug or been spanked and spoken to harshly and then hurried out of doors. Mr. Thomas was not subjected to such indignities. He solved his problem in his own way. Wild animals are very clean. When captured, unless housed under impossible conditions, no wild creature will foul its nest or its habitual quarters. Afforded the opportunities to do so, wild animals living with humans will leave a house to perform their toilet.

We did not teach or force our civet cat to sleep in our bed. He adopted the bed as his home of his own accord. We offered him his natural food of grass and berries and fruit and raw meat, but because of his curiosity he tried our forms of food and developed a great liking for baked custard, his sweet morning tea, chocolate pudding, and pumpkin pie. During the night Mr. Thomas patrolled the house and added beetles and other insects to his diet. He killed mice but seldom ate them, and he loved a bowl of milk.

When Mr. Thomas was brought to us, he was so young and so weak on his legs that he could not have moved from the place where he had been born except to nurse from his mother. His eyes were covered with a baby film through which he could, at most, see only dimly. He could only have known his mother by smell and by such gentle sounds as she may have uttered.

During the first days Tommy fought us because we did not smell like anything to which he had been accustomed. Our voices probably sounded harsh and loud and frightening. Just the act of picking him up must have scared him greatly.

At the time the native woman who brought him to us had found our baby civet it is impossible that his mother could have taught her youngster anything. He was too tiny, and neither wild nor domestic, neither tame nor savage. Most certainly Mr. Thomas possessed no consciousness of what he was or into what type, or species, of animal he was destined to develop.

Like all infant creatures, humans included, our child civet cat adjusted to the environment in which it found itself, became aware of the sights and sounds, the odors and the other creatures by which it was surrounded. Developing in this manner from infancy, our household environment, which would terrify an adult wild civet cat, became normal and natural for Mr. Thomas. Iz and I, Iz particularly, were the source of Tommy's food. We were the beings who played with him, talked to him, and gave him the warmth of our bodies. Whatever affection Tommy, in the wild, might have given to his mother, was given instead to Isabella, and inasmuch as he lived with us for far longer than he would have remained with his natural mother, he continued to give his affection to her for as long as he and Isabella were together.

We did *not,* consciously or otherwise, tame our civet cat. His association with us was, to him, wholly natural. He knew no other form of existence.

One of the questions most frequently asked of me whenever I have told stories of the many wild animals with which I have been privileged to live in intimate day-and-night association is, "But don't these animals revert, or become savage, when they grow up?"

Revert to what? Unless our civet cat had inherited mental or emotional characteristics which were so strong or powerful as to determine that it must develop into the savage and dangerous creature which is an adult wild civet cat, why should it become savage? Mr. Thomas's food was always ready to hand and prepared for him. He never faced the need to hunt and kill. True, he killed beetles and bugs, but that was because he liked to eat them, not because he needed food to fill his stomach; he killed mice mainly, I came to think, as a form of play or sport, for he seldom ate one.

We never saw Mr. Thomas make a serious threat to his companions, the duiker antelope, although he would quarrel with them. From infancy the duikers had been his associates and companions.

They never hurt him, so he was content to accept them. He accepted other animal associates on the same basis.

I have seen and been a party to this association and development of very young animals with humans so many, many times that I cannot believe that any so-called wild animal, if secured before its parents have been able to teach it, will or even is able to revert to what might be its normal timid or savage state of existence. The infant wart hogs, leopards, elephants, antelope, bush cats, cheetahs, rhinoceroses, buffaloes, zebras, owls, cranes, lions, hornbills, doves, hedgehogs, and turtles and tortoises which have passed through my hands have convinced me that it is the environment in which it finds itself and the teaching and demonstration of its parents which determine the development of a baby animal, and not inherited emotional or mental characteristics.

Mrs. Adamson depicts beautifully the development of a lioness in her lovely book *Born Free*. Here one can follow in moving detail the actions and reactions of a great wild creature living with human beings. You who have read this book will know how, instead of reverting, Elsa, the lioness, had to be coached and taught to fit her for what should have been her natural existence on the open veld. In *King Solomon's Ring* the famous animal student and psychologist Dr. Konrad Lorenz has written a most delightful account of a group of jackdaws which lived with him and insisted upon trying to feed him. The birds adopted the good doctor so completely, he could only be described as one of them. I could go on and on citing examples of the complete compatibility which can exist between animals and humans, but anyone who is truly interested can discover this for himself.

By these remarks I do not mean to suggest that the physiology of an animal does not play an important part in its development and in its habits. A lion equipped with powerful claws, tremendous speed and power, and mighty teeth and jaws has not been designed by evolution to graze on grass. Neither have its internal organs developed in such a manner as to make it possible for a lion to extract nourishment from herbage. A zebra or an antelope will refuse to eat meat, and should it forcibly be fed a meat diet, would die. Other animals such as civet cats, bears, hogs, and many birds are omnivorous in their diets and equipped by nature to digest most anything containing nutritious substances.

Neither do I intend to imply that a lion, raised in a home from kittenhood is not a potentially dangerous animal. It is, if for no other reason than its power and armament. Like human beings, lions sometimes get out of the wrong side of the bed, feel grouchy for some reason and want to be left alone, or suffer from an ailment or a small hurt. In such an event a lion may resent intrusion by a human and strike out, which is the only way it knows to fend another animal away if a warning growl is insufficient. When a lion strikes, it can tear a man's arm from his shoulder.

Such an action does not necessarily mean that the lion has reverted or that it has a mean temper. It is of no more consequence than a tart or rude rejoinder to a friend or a cry of "shut up" shouted at noisy children by their harassed and frazzled mother.

One of the greatest difficulties to be overcome when studying animal behaviorism is our tendency to measure reactions and intelligence and emotions in terms of human reactions, etc., rather than to try and project ourselves into a more objective plane.

As an example of what I mean, examine the studies made of chimpanzees. Scientists like to study chimpanzees because these animals are tractable, they are intelligent, and they very definitely have a place in, and a relationship to, the evolution of man. We sort of see our own image of thousands of years ago in the chimpanzees and the gorillas. Because we do see this image, we, or at least those scientists who study and report upon chimpanzees, are apt, inadvertently perhaps, to give an undeserved amount of credit to the chimpanzee and to put chimpanzees far up the scale of relative intelligence.

I do not for a second quarrel with the statement which is often made that chimpanzees can reason from cause to effect. But how is this reasoning by chimpanzees more wonderful than the acts performed by lions when they succeed in getting cattle out of strong pole kraals, or when driving game?

Confronted with such a kraal as the one which we built on Ibamba and which I have described, lions act as follows. The party—three, five, or more—approach within a hundred yards or so. There they will stand quietly for some time, surveying the scene and listening and testing the wind. One or more may even lie down.

Then they move. The lionesses and any youngsters which may be members of the group separate, and moving quietly, take up separate positions downwind from the kraal and some one hundred to two hundred yards away. The lion waits for a time, then he, too, moves and drifts slowly and as inconspicuously as possible up to the downwind side of the kraal. Once in this position he utters low moans and soft growls and paces back and forth until all the cattle in the kraal are awake and aware of his presence. Slowly and carefully the lion works until all the cattle are bunched together on the far, and upwind, side of the kraal, their backs against the poles and their horned heads facing toward the menacing beast outside and downwind on the side farthest from them.

When he has the cattle in this position, the lion suddenly and soundlessly rushes around the kraal and throws himself with a roar and growls against the poles right behind the cattle. He is so swift in his movements that the cattle are caught unaware; all they know is that suddenly the terrifying animal is right behind them and, from the nearness of the sound, in amongst them.

The group of cattle breaks and stampedes across the kraal in a mad rush to get away. As a nearly solid mass they hit the opposite side of the kraal, and down go the poles in a tangle of broken wood, torn bark, and trailing withes. The cattle rush downwind into the open, where the other lions are lying in wait. One or two are almost always killed.

Isn't this act by lions just as impressive an exhibition of reasoning as anything done by chimpanzees? The fact that lions vary this procedure so that game on the veld is driven through a defile in the hills onto lionesses waiting at the far end as much as a mile distant is to me, at least, as impressive as the chimp's using a pole to get a banana. It shows that lions are extremely versatile in their thinking and that they adapt a certain procedure to different circumstances.

Has anyone, however, seen the lion placed as high on scales of intelligence as the chimpanzee? The reason is that probably very few animal psychologists are able to spend the hours and hours out on the open veld which are necessary to study lions in their natural habitat. Another reason may be that the choice of position on the scale is somewhat governed by the fact that we, in our conceit, want to see the animals which have such an important place in our evolutionary tree high on the intelligence scale in compliment to ourselves.

chapter six

HUGE shadows cast by the rapidly moving masses of dark clouds crawled down the flats to seep deep among the trees on our high land and envelop the house. Sheet lightning flared and slithered among the clouds, touching their ragged edges with electric blue and purple light. Thunder rolled and muttered and a moaning wind blew cool and damp, causing the tall bottle palms to toss their heads wildly in the coming storm.

Around the house, in the workshop, and in the compound the boys hurried about, battening down and making everything as secure as possible. Tools were gathered and brought in and stacked, the truck driven under cover of a thatched roof, firewood carried into the kitchen, and the sheets of corrugated iron on the roofs were given a final check to see that they had been properly and securely fastened.

In the unfinished portion of the house where we had stacked and stored the bags of cement and lime and corn we laid out heavy green tarpaulins, to be pulled over the supplies in case the roof should leak. Unless there is a steep pitch to a roof of corrugated iron, it is difficult to lay the sheets so well that there are not nail holes or bent edges through which water might drip. Iz went from window to window, pulling the casements shut and fastening them.

A sudden bolt of lightning seared down and struck the ironstone ledge on which the house was built with a tremendous crash. Both Iz and I jumped as the noise hurtled through the house and a brilliant burst of light illuminated the interior. Thunder boomed overhead and reverberated from the metal roof, echoing and pounding through our home. One after another, so rapidly we could not count, terrific bolts of lightning struck the ledge and a curious metallic odor permeated the house.

Staring through the windows, we could see the thick limbs of the fig trees bending with the force of the wind. The palms were bent far over toward the ground and the fronds flew in the wind like umbrellas which had blown inside out. There was no rain as yet, but a darkness akin to twilight enveloped us.

The lightning passed and moved across the flats to burst and spray its light over the distant mountains. Thunder still muttered and grumbled in the sky, but the wind died down; for a brief interlude the veld was lighted by an odd violet-orange color and lay expectant and quiet. A dove cooed. The gentle sound came clear and lovely from one of the giant figs.

A few drops of rain fell, spattering and bouncing on the hard and waiting ground. The rain ran over the roof, the drops hitting on the iron with a sound of a myriad tiny hoofbeats. Then the skies opened; a deluge descended over us. The roar of the water pounding on the roof was so great, we had to shout to one another to make ourselves heard. Frightened, the little duikers crowded close to our legs, and Mr. Thomas, disturbed from his sleep in the bed, got out and prowled nervously about the room.

As the rain streamed down, Iz grew worried about Fwifwi and Jane Emmeline John. We failed to see where they were, but I assured her that they must have taken shelter. Animals are remarkably capable at caring for themselves.

Out on the flats I knew that the herds of wildebeest and zebra had turned their tails to the storm and were standing with the water running off their coats. The calves would be close beside their mothers and the members of the herd bunched together. On the tree-covered portion of Ibamba the kudu and the eland, the roan and sable, the bushbuck and the little duikers, grysbok, and steinbok would be huddled beneath bushes and trees, and the civet cats and mongooses, servals and bush cats, would be curled under piles of leaves or have taken shelter in clumps of tall grass. Grateful for the coolness and the water, the storm would not frighten them.

More suddenly than it had come, the rain passed and swept beyond Ibamba to bring freshening life across the land. With the cook and Lavison, Iz and I walked outside. Fwifwi came dancing and prancing across the grass, and from somewhere Jane Emmeline John appeared, placing her feet daintily in long strides as she hurried to greet us. Not a feather was ruffled, nor could I see that water had fallen on her back at all.

The stifling humidity which had pressed upon us for days had gone. The air was lively and cool and new. The ground steamed a thin mist which was slowly wafted away; a gentle breeze stirred the branches of the trees and the tops of the grass, showering the last droplets of moisture onto the thirsty soil. Here and there were puddles of muddy water, but these sank into the ground and were quickly absorbed. From the compound rose the shrill laughter and gaiety of the children, excited by the storm. One of the men beat a soft rhythm on a tom-tom to express his feelings, and a woman sang in a high falsetto voice. Our prideful Leghorn rooster arched his neck, stretched himself tall, and crowed. The hens clucked happily and came out of their house to peck at the moist ground. I could hear our cattle lowing as the herd boys moved them onto the flat which was the eastern end of Ibamba and lay in a wide curve of the river. It was good to be alive.

Only a few leaks had developed. While the storm lasted, Iz and I had gone about marking the spots where water dripped with a piece of chalk tied to a pole. When the sun returned, I called several boys and we brought tar and climbed to the roof. Iz tapped with her pole underneath to tell us where the leaks had been and we smeared hot tar over these and sealed the openings.

Contrary to the impression which the average American may have after watching Hollywood motion pictures of Africa, the rainy season is not one continuous downfall during which white people sit sweatily about, listening to the drumming of the water on the roof and trying to hasten cirrhosis of the liver by swilling bottles and bottles of square-face gin.

In Rhodesia, at least, the rainy season is a period of intense activity. The average fall of rain is about forty-five inches distributed over five to six months. This is the productive period for agriculture, and as soon as the ground has softened after the first few wettings, everyone gets busy preparing the land and planting.

With the help of the tractor, oxen, dynamite, and numerous natives I had managed to clear some hundred acres of stumps, small thorn trees, and palms and the crowns of grass and brush. Except on the flats, the soil on Ibamba was very light and sandy. Without the addition of chemical and green fertilizers and manure and humus it was too poor to grow much in the way of crops.

Nevertheless, we planted some eighty acres to corn—which is called mealies throughout the Rhodesias and South Africa—and some twenty acres to peanuts.

By the cattle kraal I had two large rectangular pits dug to a depth of about four feet. The natives cut huge quantities of grass, and this I had spread over the floor of the kraal to serve as bedding. The boys thought this was the height of nothing, and said so. Why on earth would Sibyunni'byunni put grass in a kraal so that the cattle could rest more comfortably? As the days passed, I had them fork up the soiled bedding, together with all manure, and pile this in the pits to rot. Only then did they begin to understand my motives. When I assembled our manure spreader wagon, loaded it, and then drove it behind oxen to the fields, the boys watched the kickers toss and spread the rotted bedding and manure over the prepared land, applauding vigorously every time a particularly heavy clump of material came sailing from behind the spreader. As in the case of the construction of the bathroom, there just were no words in the native language by which I could explain my motives before the boys could see the plan in actual operation.

Charlie Matabele and Charlie Portuguese took over supervision of the planting and cultivating. Mangineera and I, with a large gang, busied ourselves laying concrete floors in the new part of the house and then surfacing these with dry cement to form a smooth and polished surface. This was the first time I ever undertook to lay floors, and I learned a lot and earned myself a perfectly splendid backache.

In spite of the difficulties in building and the inevitable delays, the house neared completion and the fields outside were planted and other work continued. The walls of the living room and the dining room were plastered with mud and lime, smoothed, and then whitewashed. Iz painted the wood trim in the dining room Chinese red, and it was very gay and attractive. I made a tall corner cabinet with shelves and lockers at the base which I painted with black lacquer, and this held some of the glass and china. The dining-room table, large enough to seat ten comfortably, I made of thick heavy bloodwood planks, and the boys worked for hours rubbing and oiling the surface to a beautiful polish.

While we are discussing some aspects of our home-building, it may be of interest to answer some questions most frequently asked when we have returned to the States: What did we eat? How did we get our food?

Bread we baked whenever necessary, using homemade yeast to rise the dough. We had brought with us from Bulawayo several pound packets of compressed hops. Using a pinch of the hop leaves mixed in the water in which potatoes had been boiled, we added a bit of sugar and a touch of salt and flour and poured this warm mixture into bottles. The bottles were corked tightly, with the corks tied in firmly with string, and placed behind the stove to work.

Sometimes the mixture worked too well and the corks were blown from the bottles with resounding pops. Once or twice the corks held and the bottles exploded, scattering glass in all directions. When added to the dough, this powerful ferment made fine light bread, bread with far more taste and substance than the puttylike stuff currently offered so insultingly in modern chain stores as the staff of life.

When the rains came, we moved our vegetable garden from the riverbank, where the vegetables would have been drowned by the rising waters, to an area near the house and close to the dip tank. In Rhodesia, tomatoes grow almost wild and in great profusion. We grew both the yellow and the red varieties, and we had onions, lettuce, beets, carrots, white globe turnips, peas, snap bush beans, lima beans, and Country Gentleman corn.

The crucifer vegetables such as cabbage, broccoli, and cauliflower do not do well in the tropics, refusing to head up properly. Our cabbage plants grew to heights of two and three feet, branching out like bushes, but the young leaves were edible and tender. We tried artichokes and had some fine tall plants, but for some reason never succeeded in growing edible buds.

The natives grew quantities of various kinds of peas and beans, a cucumber with dull spines, pumpkins, peanuts, a melon with white meat and, of course, both Kaffir corn and mealies. Village natives constantly brought in produce for sale, as well as chickens, eggs, and occasionally a young goat or sheep. The eggs were small and had to be tested in water to determine how fresh they might be, because the native is not as fastidious as we, and the chickens were leggy and tough.

There were fish in the Kafue River, but most had a muddy taste and the flesh was soft and uninviting. Periodically our boys and their wives and children would stage a fishing party in the lagoon which gave Ibamba its name. First, they would close off the connection to the river with a fence made from the strong stalks of the papyrus which grew plentifully along the banks. Equipped either with cone-shaped baskets two or three feet long and eighteen inches in diameter at the open end, or with barbed fish spears, the men and women formed a line from one side of the lagoon, which was not more than three feet deep, to the other, and near the barricade of reeds. Then they moved, shouting and kicking up the water, down the length of the lagoon, constantly plunging their baskets and spears downward into the water and mud. It was surprising not only what quantities of fish but of what size these expeditions produced. I have seen them bring out catfish, or barbel, six feet long and weighing up to eighty pounds or more.

For meat we enjoyed quite a choice. There was game if we wished to shoot. Kudu, sable, eland, duiker and reedbuck antelope are excellent eating. Wildebeest and roan are apt to be tough and not quite so tasty. Puku and lechwe antelope feed on rank grass and water plants, and their flesh is sort of muddy- or even fishy-tasting.

Waterbuck is seldom good eating. Buffalo is fine, especially the tongue and liver and the rib and porterhouse steaks. Zebra meat is perhaps the most consistently tender and good of all wild meats, but one must remove every tiny bit of the yellow fat or the meat will have a strong horsy taste.

For wild birds we had our choice of the ubiquitous guinea fowl and *quales* or the knorhaan. The lesser knorhaan is a long-necked long-legged land bird which, when killed and roasted, has both white and dark meat on the breast. It is delicious eating, something akin to the dry meat of a pheasant.

Ducks of many species, teal, and spur-winged geese were plentiful on the lagoons. Spur-winged geese were not very good. The meat is exceptionally bloody and strong flavored and more than apt to be tough.

There were doves and sand grouse, both excellent, and now and then a greater bustard. The latter is as large as a turkey, and best shot with a small-bore rifle, as it is difficult to get within shotgun range: bustards prefer open ground, and run like the very devil when one tries to approach them.

For home-produced meat we had our hogs, which gave us chops and hams and loins varying a little in taste from wart hog and bush pig. We had good chickens and large eggs of our own, and sometimes killed a young goat, which is delicious eating and has a flavor like the finest lamb, a fat-tailed sheep, or a small ox.

Fruit was the one item of diet we could not grow or find on the veld. The wild figs were abundant, but each fruit was so full of ants, we could not eat it. There was a yellow hard-shelled fruit about the size of an orange, filled with a rather tart pulp which was good to eat, but these were scarce and ripened only at certain periods. We had mulberries, but most of our fruit came in cans and was expensive. Sugar, flour, tea and coffee, condiments, pickles, cheese, biscuits, pudding powders, chocolate and spices and dried fruits we had to buy in quantity and store on our shelves in tins and boxes and barrels and bags.

In front of and just below the wall of the long veranda we had a flower garden where Isabella grew tremendous zinnia plants covered with blossoms in every color. She also had petunias and verbena, and there were many wild lilies to be picked on the flats when the rains came.

Between the two mabunga trees on the front lawn I dug and cemented a rectangular pool about eight feet long and two feet deep. In this we planted water lilies gathered on the flats, and the blossoms made a lovely splotch of color beneath the canopy of bougainvillaea stretching from tree to tree above.

Jane Emmeline John adopted the pool as her own and spent much time standing in the water. The motionless bird, with its golden topknot and soft grayish-blue feathering, surrounded by water lilies and framed by the purplish red flowers of the bougainvillaea, formed a picture which would have delighted a Japanese painter.

Immediately about the house and for a distance of some two hundred feet the boys kept the grass cut short. The expanse could hardly be called a lawn, but the mowing did help to discourage some of the mosquitoes which swarmed during the rains, and the green grass formed a striking background for the orange coat belonging to Fwifwi, the mousiness of the grazing duikers, and the black, white, and reddish coat of the young lechwe antelope we had accumulated.

The Kafue River began gradually to rise, and the water flowed into the lagoons and into gullies cut into the flats by previous rains. Up these huge black barbels pushed their whiskered faces, searching for food and places in which to spawn. The natives speared these great fish by the hundreds of pounds, split them, and smoked them over fires. The air around the compound stank with the smell of smoking, partly rotten fish.

On the bushveld beyond the edge of the flats, where the land rolled endlessly westward until it met the Atlantic Ocean and eastward toward the Indian Ocean, the pans and waterholes which had lain as beds of dry mud filled with water as the rain pelted down. Fish and frogs which had lain dormant in the dry mud revived, and the frogs added their song to the sounds of the awakening veld. The large game animals began to move off Ibamba, fearful of being trapped by the slowly rising waters. As the sable and roan, the wildebeest and zebra and the eland moved, so moved the lions, and during the rains it was only exceptionally that a lion visited on the ranch.

This necessary movement of game, or migration, dictated as it is by the need for water and for grazing, presents one of the greatest problems to the conservationist who wants to establish refuges for the wild animals. Because of climatic changes which cause the disappearance of their food and drink, antelope and zebras, giraffes and elephants must travel long distances if they are to find new feeding grounds and live. This compelling need to migrate means that any refuge, to be successful, must be of gigantic area; this, in turn, means conflict with natives, native grazing needs, and the farming and ranching of white settlers. The greatest foe of wild creatures today is neither the hunters nor disease. It is the need of constantly expanding populations for land.

Leopards, which we trapped now and then, had been living among the papyrus along the river. With the rains they came onto the high ground of Ibamba and occasionally tried to catch a dog. We had a great number of dogs of every conceivable breed or mixture of breeds, among them a pair of nearly true brindle great Danes. A reasonably good example of the fine ridgeback breed, a bitch named Spotty, grew to be the nearest thing to a house dog which we could allow.

By the beginning of the rains our household of animals consisted of the two duikers, Mr. Thomas, a young reedbuck named Flags, and a dove named Tweetie, not to mention Fwifwi and the lechwe, which entered occasionally to look around the living room and sniff in the kitchen. It may seem strange that with such a houseful, we had not adopted a dog. The reason was the prevalence of rabies, both the active type and that called "dumb rabies." On the veld and during the nights the dogs, roaming free, often fought with jackals and small cats, and sometimes chased hyenas. Any of these could be carriers of rabies, and the disease was so prevalent and is so horrible and the cure so terribly painful that no one took chances by making too much of a pet of a dog—no matter how fine an animal.

Snakes, too, moved from the flooding lowlands, and for a time we had trouble with them and had to be on the lookout constantly. Isabella lowered herself into one of the large wicker chairs in the living room one afternoon and a long thin *m'swemma* snake slithered from under the cushion and writhed across the floor. *M'swemmas* are fearfully poisonous and vicious. Lavison quickly ran and fetched a shotgun, and Iz blew the snake to bits on the concrete floor.

Portions of the face of Ibamba changed as land which had once been thornbush, or dotted with mahogany and bloodwood trees, sprouted green with waving mealies or the short bushes of peanut plants. Logging and wood roads were cut into the bush. Mosquitoes, breeding in the water spread by the river, came in such swarms as to make it nearly impossible to leave the carefully screened house at night. If we did, we walked into such dense clouds of insects that they could actually be felt beating against the face and any other exposed parts of the body. Some nights the hum outside the windows rose to an angry whine. When the wind blew from the northeast, the scent from the millions of water lilies was almost nauseating, it was so strong and permeating. The hippos left the deeper part of the river and walked along the edge of the bush and lay, during the day, hidden in the grass only a few yards from one of our roads. Huge flocks of red- and black-billed little cranes with white vests and black backs marched in serried ranks across the veld and around the house, picking up the insects forced onto the shorter grass by the flooding. Our cattle waxed fat, and the sows threw fine litters of squealing little pigs.

One day when the mealies were just beginning to sprout above the ground, word came to me from my blood brother, Chief Sheasongo, that some of his people had captured a lion cub and that he wished to give it to me as a present. Jam was dispatched to fetch it. It was a trip of sixty miles to Sheasongo's village, and we waited anxiously as the days passed and Jam continued absent.

It was several years since I had had a lion. They are, beyond all others, my favorite animals, and I waited in a fever of expectancy and worry. Jam should have been able to go and come to Sheasongo's in five days, and when he did not show at the end of that time, I began to fear that the little lion had died or that some accident might have happened. Young lions are delicate animals, and not easy to raise. Even in the wild it is seldom that more than one or two of a litter survive.

Then one day Jam came walking down the road from the compound to the house. Over his shoulder, hanging from a pole, swung a small cage made of bark such as the natives use to bring in chickens. He drew up before me and slowly lowered the crate to the ground. Inside I could see a small animal, but I nearly wept when he reached in and brought forth the most miserable example of a baby lion I have ever seen. It was skin and bones, its eyes, tremendous in the bony head, were kittenish blue but watery and dull. It could not stand. Its coat was matted and filthy and it cried pitifully.

Although natives know how to fashion crude nipples from reeds and bark, the villagers had tried to force the little lioness—it was a girl—to eat meat and fowl. Feathers still lined the cage, and feathers can raise the very devil with a youngster's tender insides. Adult lions pluck birds, using their rasplike tongues to pull out feathers, but the baby lioness was too young to have learned this. It was only too obvious that the little girl was suffering from severe gastric and intestinal troubles.

We gathered it up and carried it into the house, where we sponged it off with lukewarm water and dried it with a warm towel. The little lioness tried to be savage and growl and bite, but it was far too weak. We warmed milk and, with a teaspoon, fed it tiny helpings, pouring the fluid into a cup made by pulling the under lip away from the gums and letting the milk run into its mouth between the baby teeth. It swallowed painfully, but gradually, after an hour or so, it stopped trembling and lay exhausted and quiet.

We named our little lioness Paddy because of her huge flapping front paws, which looked even larger than normal because of her emaciated condition. She weighed between five and six pounds, and it was obvious that she had been captured before she had been fully weaned. Her little stomach just had not been ready for the rough diet offered her, on which she had chewed in a desperate attempt to alleviate her hunger.

Iz and I, with help from Lavison and Jam and Mangineera, went to work. After cleaning Paddy up outside, we felt we had to do what we could to clean her insides.

Lavison brought hot water from the kitchen and Isabella a hot water bottle and enema tube from the bathroom. Jam fetched a grain bag, and we wrapped Paddy in this to prevent her scratching us with her sharp claws and to hold her without squeezing her too tightly. Then we gave her a soapsuds and olive oil enema. It wasn't easy, and Paddy certainly neither liked the process nor co-operated. But we had to get as much of the poison in her system out as possible, and get it out quickly. I knew it was dangerous to give so young and weak an animal such forceful treatment. Her heartbeat was very slow and feeble, and the enema and the straining might prove fatal. Unless the accumulated fecal matter, the feathers, and the poison in her intestines could be drawn out, Paddy would die. It was a kill or cure treatment.

Under any other circumstances the sight of a large white man crawling about the floor with a purple enema tube and bag in his hands, following a tiny snarling lion kitten while three anxious natives tried to help and a beautiful girl crooned and hovered over the frightened, angry animal, might have been amusing and comical. To us it was deadly serious. When the enema brought results, we almost cheered. The poisons were being evacuated and the mess was of no account. The floor was cement and could be washed and mopped and disinfected.

The experience was terribly exhausting for little Paddy. When it was over, she lay quivering and completely drained of strength. We warmed a sack in the oven in the kitchen and wrapped her warmly. We tried to give her a little lukewarm milk to which we had added a few drops of cod-liver oil. Paddy swallowed less than half a teaspoon and let the rest dribble from her mouth as she lay on her side.

If we were to pull the baby through, even more drastic measures were called for. There are no books on the care and feeding of young lions, so I had to guess and to use past experience as a guide. Something to tone up Paddy's system, give her an appetite and stimulate her heart, was indicated. I chose strychnine, which is, of course, a deadly poison in the wrong dose. Guessing at the quantity, I measured a bit of nux vomica, which contains strychnine, onto the end of my knife, and mixing this with a little scraped raw meat and blood, forced the pill down her throat. She bit me twice in the process.

Strychnine is pretty quick in its action. Twenty minutes went by as we watched anxiously. There were no signs of spasms or of twitching. I felt the heart action. Maybe it was just wishful thinking, but it seemed less irregular and the kitten's labored breathing had eased.

We waited for an hour and then repeated the strychnine, only this time I floated the powder on milk. Hour after hour we kept this up, far into the night. By the time we stopped, the lioness had taken nearly a quarter of a teaspoon of nux vomica. We called it enough, and tucking her into a box filled with warm rags and cotton batting, placed it beside the bed and fell asleep, exhausted and praying for a miracle.

Either the strychnine worked or our prayers were answered. Paddy was alive the next morning and seemed stronger and more interested in food. For the second day we followed the same procedure, increasing the amount of milk slowly and adding cod-liver oil every other time. We were just guessing wildly at how much strychnine a lion that size and weight could take without becoming poisoned, but as it seemed to be working, we continued the doses.

We were counting on the milk and the oil to help counteract any strychnine which might be in excess of the kitten's power of absorption.

We continued the treatment for a little over a week, reducing the nux vomica toward the end and finally cutting it out entirely. By this time Paddy's appetite was coming back. She began to drink lots of milk, mixed either with blood or cod-liver oil. We ground fresh liver and fresh kidneys and scraped meat for her and fed these in small quantities.

Mr. Thomas watched all these nursing activities with the greatest interest, and so that his nose would not be too far out of joint, he was given some of the ground meat and milk with the little lioness. At first Tommy hissed at Paddy and put up his back hair, but he soon accepted her as another member of the family and came and went, paying little attention.

When we took Paddy outside to get some sun, she met the dogs and, of course, shared the rooms and the verandas with the duikers and Fwifwi when he came into the house. The little antelope showed no fear whatever of the tawny big-pawed little creature, and watched it rather disinterestedly. Paddy made friends with them and smelled them carefully all over to be sure she would know them again, and then more or less left them to their own devices.

Within a month Paddy was eating well and was strong enough to climb onto the bed by herself. There she would stretch out on top of the spread, pushing it down tight so that it would seem that Mr. Thomas, sleeping beneath, must suffocate. But he wouldn't come out and the lioness never actually lay on him.

So another youngster which was too young to have been taught by its parents joined the household. No one had told Paddy that she was a lioness, or that lions did not customarily associate with dogs and civet cats and crested cranes and certainly did not live on amicable terms with young antelope. Not knowing what she was supposed to be, Paddy just made friends with everybody and every animal and bird, galloped about the house, took baths in a washtub in the kitchen, gamboled outside, and generally had fun and grew.

Christmas was approaching. Both Isabella and I came from families which always had a Christmas tree and made much of holidays and birthdays. As I went about the veld, I kept my eye open for a tree of some sort which might have a shape approximating that of a spruce or fir. Isabella had been saving the silver paper from packets of Flag cigarettes and had quite a pile on hand. In the evenings, while Paddy dozed in one of our laps or on the floor beside us and Mr. Thomas padded about the house on his nightly search for beetles and mice, we cut the silver paper into long thin strips. We would use this to decorate the Christmas tree.

We had a few boughten ornaments. To add to these, Iz saved the shells from hen eggs and the brown, stronger, and faintly spotted shells of guinea-fowl eggs. The natives, walking about Ibamba, were constantly finding guinea nests and bringing in the eggs. Most of these we set under hens to be hatched so that we would have a fine flock of young guinea fowl for broiling.

Isabella formed the eggshells into little baskets, cutting the shells with nail scissors so that the edges were scalloped or cut into series of points. These she painted or decorated with designs in different-colored sealing waxes. Others, which she blew instead of cracking open, were made into balls and colored. Hanging from a thread, they were very pretty. She cut out stars from cardboard and painted these gold and silver, and I fashioned some icicles by twisting bits of bright tin from cans.

There is an enormous satisfaction to be gained by making things. It is akin to the pleasure derived from planting seeds and bringing a garden to a fruition of blossoms or edible vegetables. This was a very happy and contented period for Iz and me. Outside the lands were beginning to be covered with the new shoots of corn and the green leaves of peanut plants. The vegetable garden was doing well and flowers bloomed before the house. As we walked about, the lechwe antelope walked with us and capered and pranced and trod on the growing vegetables and Jane Emmeline John stalked beside us, uttering throaty soft sounds by way of conversation. Paddy and Tommy and the duikers and Fwifwi were well on their way to becoming healthy, splendid creatures, and Tweetie, our pigeon, flew into the living room, coming like a winged bullet through the kitchen and the dining room each evening to roost atop Iz's sewing basket, which rested on a high book case. From the safety of her perch Tweetie would survey the room, watch Paddy and Mr. Thomas with one beady eye, coo a few times, and then settle down to sleep. Flags, the young reedbuck, stumbled and skidded on the cement until he found what he thought was the softest spot, and then lowered himself clumsily to the floor and dozed.

Mr. Thomas had matured sufficiently by this time to begin producing the civet for which his species is named. This is a gummy brown substance of a waxy consistency, and is produced in a large gland just beneath the root of the tail. Civet has a very pleasant scent, and is, of course, highly prized as the basis for many very expensive perfumes.

Each evening as Isabella and I sat waiting to be called for supper, we would hear the springs of our double bed creak slightly. Then there would be a soft thump as Mr. Thomas jumped from beneath the bedclothes to the floor. Within a minute or two his sharply pointed black-and-white nose would appear around the corner of the parapet separating the living room from the conservatory. His nose quivered with anxiety as he sniffed the air, trying to discover who and what was in the room. Becoming bolder, Tommy would thrust his head into view, and his black shoe-button eyes would scan the room. He would sound his cluck-cluck-clucking noise—which was almost exactly like the sound a hen makes to call attention to the fact she has laid an egg—and Iz would cluck-cluck back at him.

Satisfied that everything was in order, Mr. Thomas would descend the two steps to the floor of the living room, and after another cluck-cluck, find Iz and greet her by sniffing at her bare legs and giving a swift lick with his tongue. Then he would come to me and give me a sniff but not a kiss, and then go off to find Paddy and annoy her with a hiss or two and to badger Flags.

Having greeted everyone and announced his presence, Tommy sought the leg of a chair or the round coffee table or the corner of a door or corner of a wall. He would then lift his tail high and back toward whatever he had selected for his attention and position himself carefully so that his civet gland was aimed correctly. A backward step as he opened his gland and he deposited a thin smear of civet on the table leg or the corner of his choice.

After a time every leg, every corner, every door had a brown mark on it at a height of five inches from the floor. The scent of civet filled the rooms. It was not strong and was rather pleasant, and although the brown deposits were not perhaps sightly, we never tried to remove them.

chapter seven

PADDY grew to be a husky little lioness full of fun and games. She and I would roll on the floor and wrestle, growling and yelling and messing up the room. With her teeth and claws she tore my shirt to ribbons, and soon I had to put on a special old one in order to save anything fit to wear. But in all our rough play it was only by accident that she ever scratched me. When she did and I showed it to her, she would sniff the trickle of blood and then moan and cry and push against me and lick the hurt, doing everything in her power to tell me that she didn't mean it and that she was sorry. Gradually, as she grew bigger and bigger, she learned to keep her claws sheathed, and it was only in the excitement of the wildest kind of boxing and playing that she forgot herself and let those great hooks slide from their sheaths.

Living as Isabella and I did with our animals day after day, night after night for weeks, for months, for years, is an experience which, most unfortunately, is enjoyed by relatively few persons. When a person obtains an animal so weak and young that it has to be taught to eat, and subsequently raises that animal to adulthood, the animal develops into something far more alive, vibrant, and interesting than some creature which has been purchased in a pet shop and whose previous training and development is unknown. Which is why I dislike to have the word "pet" applied to Paddy, Mr. Thomas, the duikers, Fwifwi, or Jane Emmeline John.

These animals were not pets in the accepted sense of the word, any more than they were tame as that word is commonly used. Tiny, untrained, and inexperienced when brought to us, these recently born babies just adapted themselves to life as they found it and grew into adults, much the same way as Topsy is reported to have grown.

Isabella and I devised formulas to meet each animal's special needs. We doctored them as best we could when necessary, and hovered and watched over them as devotedly as any human mother ever watched her first-born child. To us they were children, our foster children. Each in his or her own way looked to us for nourishment, for play, for comfort and understanding. As time passed and we all developed together, we came to know what each little look or glance could mean; what the small and gentle sounds they uttered were meant to convey to one another or to us; we could tell almost instantly when one of our foster children was under the weather, disgruntled, or experiencing the changes and emotional upsets which come with puberty. Day after day, night after night, we watched their little jealousies, their loves, their rages, and their fears as they were exhibited, either to last or fade.

A keeper in a zoo can never grow to know his animals as we knew ours because we did not inspect the animals' cages at five in the evening, turn out the lights and lock the doors, and then go home to sleep. When we retired for the night, more often than not our foster children retired with us, often in the same bed or at least the same room. When we ate, they ate with us; when they played, we played with them. Our animals became as much a part of our household and were just as dictatorial and demanding of our time and affection as human children in, shall we say, a more normal family. There was no wire, there were no bars or railings between us and our animals. We did not view them across dry or water-filled moats or have the need for high-pressure water hoses to separate them when, and if, they quarreled.

It is because I have lived in such close association with wild animals, and domestic animals too, for some forty-five years that I bristle violently when persons who do not have an iota of my experience accuse me of anthropomorphism.

I use the word "anthropomorphism" in its generally accepted sense of "attributing human traits or emotions to animals." Scientifically, of course, this definition is absurd because human beings are only a species of animal. Through the development of our brains, the use of our hands, and the invention of speech, words, and writing, we have reached a higher stage of development than other animals. Or at least we believe that we have and so tell ourselves constantly. No one, of course, can be certain that this is really so. One's opinion must rest upon the values one expects from life. If a happy and contented life can be defined as one free from worry, free from a daily threat of disease, free from lying, rape, mugging, and restrictive controls and the necessity of conformity, it seems to me somewhat speculative whether human animals are much, if any, better off than a little brown screech owl flitting in the twilight or a proud lion stalking across the veld, accompanied by his wives and family.

Of one thing I am fairly certain: animals, wild animals particularly, enjoy a far greater degree of self-confidence than human animals. Domestic animals tend to lose their self-reliance and to lean more and more upon others, generally their human masters, for support. This is especially evident in the breeds of dogs which have been developed during recent decades. Especially have the fine old cocker spaniel and the proud collie and the great Dane been debauched.

I do not intend to argue here whether the words "love," "hate," "jealousy," "fear," and others used to define emotions should or should not be used to describe the emotions of animals other than human. So far as I am concerned, there is no argument, and I am hopeful that, as this story of Isabella's and my life on Ibamba with our foster children unfolds, you will come to think as I do. Which is that all animals, some to a lesser and some to a greater degree, experience emotions, and that they react basically in much the same manner as do humans.

It is only natural law that this should be true. All living matter, both vegetable and animal, evolved from an identical original source. The two great kingdoms followed different lines of evolution and each kingdom, within itself, developed various and different species which came to be unlike any other. These species, ever changing, ever trying new varieties of leaves, or horns, or skeletal structure or tooth development, tails, smooth or rough bark or wind-blown seeds and color variations, evolved into the myriad forms which we know today.

All mammals, all birds, all reptiles possess a nervous system. The rudiments of such systems are found in micro-organisms. These nervous systems react to heat and cold, to noise, to light. The fact that the nervous systems of some creatures react more violently to certain stimuli than others only serves to prove the universality of the nervous system. It is largely through the messages received and transmitted by nerves to the brain that emotional reactions are developed. This being true, it is then manifestly impossible to deny emotions, rudimentary or otherwise, to nonhuman animals.

Emotions are not palpable, concrete things which can be coldly classified and catalogued. Emotions are the very ferment of life, and we do not know, we may never know, what is life. Man cannot yet make an acorn, an egg, or a spermatozoon.

There is so much that we humans could learn from study of the emotional and psychological behavior of other, less complicated animals if only we would disabuse our minds of the thought that we are different in any basic manner. To devote the enormous amounts of time, energy, and money which we do to attempting to understand ourselves, without first having learned to understand simpler forms of life is, for me at least, comparable to attempting to learn mathematics by starting with integral calculus instead of first mastering arithmetic and geometry. This may explain the instability and unsureness which pervades the professions of psychology and psychiatry.

Believing as I do in the basic oneness of all mammalian life, I shall continue in my anthropomorphic way, using the words "love," "jealousy," "hate," and "fear" to describe, as best I may, the actions and reactions of our family of foster children.

With so big and powerful an animal as a full-grown lion one must always be careful. I definitely do not mean afraid. Just careful. Never, if you can avoid it, put your animal companion into such a position as to make it fear and feel that it must fight. And don't whip or beat animals. If you have brought an animal up properly to respect your authority, there should be no need of a lash. You may force an animal to obey in this way, but you can never win its trust and love. Using a whip is like crashing a bottle on a horse's head between the ears to break it of rearing. You can certainly train a horse this way, but you will never be able to get near its head to put on a bridle without a struggle.

Tommy was between five and six months old and weighed about fifteen pounds. One day I was standing in the living room with a bunch of lemon leaves in my hand, which I was crushing to smell the perfume. Probably I was toying with the idea of concocting an anti-mosquito lotion or something. The mosquitoes which came up out of the flooded flats at night were simply incredible. As Iz and I sat playing a game of hearts after supper, we could hear the steady zizz and buzz outside. Malaria mosquitoes. The Mashakulumbwe district was highly infected.

While I was fooling with the lemon leaves, I dropped a couple. Mr. Thomas was around, poking curiously here and there, searching for a stray beetle. He saw the leaves fall and came to investigate. He sniffed at them, and then suddenly he flopped to his front knees, twisted his head sideways, and rubbed his cheek back and forth across the leaves. We watched, chuckling with amusement, as Tommy literally went into rhapsodies over the lovely smell.

Iz got some perfume and put a large drop on the floor. Tommy came over, sniffed, and did the same thing. In the course of the next few weeks we tried all sorts of smells on Tommy. He reacted violently to most, but his favorite, it developed, was pure household ammonia on a bit of cotton. The fumes made his beady little eyes water, but he adored the stuff, and would rub one cheek and then the other on the cotton until it was plastered flat to the floor and the ammonia all squeezed out.

Keepers in charge of the big cats in zoos throughout the world will probably be aghast and dismayed at the revelation that anyone can reduce the largest, proudest, and most disdainful lion to a groveling, mooning creature by offering it a whiff of perfume.

After hours, when the visitors had left the park, my present wife,

Sandy, and I were privileged, at a zoo which shall be nameless, to go behind the rail which separated the cages of the lions, tigers, leopards, and pumas from the viewing area and play with the inmates through the bars. We offered one old and particularly disgruntled lion a whiff of catnip oil. The lion found this mighty interesting, but the smell which sent him into a complete tailspin was that of the cheapest and strongest perfume we could buy in the five-and-ten-cent store. When a dab of cotton soaked with perfume was tossed into this lion's cage, he fell apart completely. Moaning and gurgling, he would flop onto the floor and rub and rub his cheeks on the bit of cotton. At such moments of ecstasy the lion was utterly oblivious to the presence of humans and paid no attention when we reached between the bars to rub his body or pull an ear. Other lions on which we have tried our perfume experiment reacted exactly the same way. Lionesses do not appear to be quite so susceptible, nor do leopards and tigers, at least the ones we met, react as enthusiastically as lions.

Tommy always came to the supper table and went from Iz to me and back again to see which of us had the most interesting food. He enjoyed cooked meat, but there was no use offering him a piece which was on the tough side. He would accept it, chew on it tentatively, then spit it out and look up inquiringly, as much as to say, "Heh, are you eating that stuff? What's the idea? Can't you do better?" Then he would shuffle down to Iz and beg something from her.

Tommy's favorite foods were chocolate pudding and baked custard. He enjoyed these so much that Iz used to bake him a special little custard all his own every once in a while. He would guzzle the entire dish and beg for more.

Paddy would eat almost anything except raw vegetables and fruit. At breakfast time she had a bowl of oatmeal porridge with milk and sugar. She liked stews and roast meats and would eat roasted potatoes and vegetables if mixed with the meat. She got all the kitchen scraps and bones, and whenever she could, would sneak a dressed chicken from the kitchen table and gallop off with it in her mouth. It was a wonderful sight to see Paddy gallop from the kitchen with a chicken in her mouth, pass under the dining-room table, rush through the living room, up the conservatory steps, and under the bed in our room—with the cook after her, waving a dish-clout and cursing fluently in native.

Paddy had a well-developed sense of humor. Indeed, most lions do. She loved to hide behind a door and leap out when Iz or I passed. As she got big, she was strong enough to knock poor Iz down, whereupon Paddy would sit on her and wash her face with her tongue. This was amusing to me, but hard on Iz. Paddy's tongue was like a rasp, and too much licking would take the skin off.

Two weeks before Christmas, Charlie Portuguese and Mangineera took me aside one morning when I was working at the forge. I could tell from the smirk on Mangineera's face and the slight grin which twisted Charlie's upper lip that they had some sort of a request to make. This one turned out not to be as outrageous as some they occasionally dreamed up.

Christmas, they informed me solemnly, was coming. As a holy day Christmas, of course, meant nothing to either one. But from previous years with me and from the talk of the natives from the Kasenga Mission they knew Christmas as a day for jollification, presents, and general celebration and no work.

They could not, they informed me solemnly, properly celebrate Christmas day without beer. I nodded agreement. Beer, I agreed, was a necessity, although I could already see in what direction the two were planning to lead me. To make beer, Mangineera continued while smiles spread across both his and Charlie's face at their success so far, grain was needed. I agreed again. You cannot make bricks without straw nor beer without grain.

It would, they told me, take two weeks for the women to prepare the grain and ferment it properly. That I knew was true. So, they ended their dissertation, would I, Sibyunni'byunni, who was their generous employer, their friend and counselor, a great hunter and a *matakatsi* of lions, give them two bags of corn to be prepared for beer? Two bags was four hundred pounds.

I pretended to ponder the question because I wanted to learn just what other ingenious arguments they might produce. But they knew and I knew that they knew I would give the grain. Which made them very happy, and they promptly dropped the work they were doing, shouted to the compound for the women to hurry to the storeroom, and Charlie marched off to issue the corn. I was just a trifle astonished to see the speed with which the women appeared, each one carrying a basket. It was obvious that they had been lurking behind their huts, waiting for Charlie Portuguese to call them. The entire compound, I am sure, must have taken part in discussions the evening before as to just who should approach Sibyunni'byunni and when and how.

South of the Equator, Christmas arrives in the middle of summer. Neither Iz nor I were individuals with warm thick blood—the type of person who just adores to get frostbitten skiing on some frozen slope rather than to sit sensibly by a warm crackling fire—so the absence of snow was of no moment.

The same anticipations, apprehensions, and excitements which fill the air in America in the days before Christmas also pervaded Ibamba. The children and the women rolled their great eyes and smiled coyly at Iz and me at every opportunity. Some did little jigs and dances to bring themselves to our attention so they might not be forgotten when the great day arrived. Each night the tom-toms pulsed and throbbed from the compound as the natives danced and sang about the beer which was brewing and about how wonderful Sibyunni'byunni and Maseccasecca were. Their words, drifting on the still night air, would, the singers knew, reach us as we sat in the house or on the veranda. They sang about Paddy and Mr. Thomas and the duikers and about our past deeds of hunting and catching and of great feasts and funeral dances. The nights were gay indeed, so gay that no vast amount of work was possible during the days, for everyone was too tired from singing and dancing to work.

Christmas is, of course, a two-day holiday throughout British territory because Boxing Day follows immediately on the twenty-sixth. A few days before the great event Iz and I began sorting out the various presents we had purchased: particularly fine skinning-hunting knives for Jam and Mangineera; a fine pocketknife with several blades and gadgets for Charlie Portuguese and Charlie Matabele; a white shirt and white shorts for Lavison; lengths of gay brightly colored cotton print cloth for Mianje and certain other wives of our more important natives; khaki shorts or a shirt or a trade blanket for others. The general laborers, those without special skills and with whom we did not have the personal contact which we had with our houseboys and the gunbearers and hunters—carpenters, sawboys, drivers, and garden boys—received extra rations of grain and salt; a half-pound packet of sugar; some cigarettes or tobacco. For the children we had strings of bright seed beads and small bundles of cheap sweets.

It took a bit of doing to be sure that we had something for everyone. There were nearly a hundred souls, young and old, living in our compound.

Along the eastern boundary of Ibamba the Kafue was rising steadily. The river had not yet overflowed its banks, but the flats stretching for miles and miles along each side were very wet, and the ground, soft and spongy. The lagoons were filling, and the stream beds which reached like fingers from the flats into the higher tree-covered bushveld were either full of water or filling rapidly. Travel, except on foot through mud and water, was impossible. For the next four or five months, depending upon the quantity of rain, Ibamba would be isolated from the outside world. We would send notes back and forth by messenger to the mission, and Shamakembie came and went to the *boma* at Namwala with the weekly mail. Otherwise, Isabella and I were alone with our natives and our animals.

We were very happy and contented. If Isabella felt any qualms because of our lonely situation, she concealed it perfectly. Coming from a large family in which Christmas had always been a day for the gathering of friends and relatives, and from the gaiety and excitement of New York during the weeks of Christmas and New Year's, it was remarkable how naturally she adapted to her new life.

Only one flaw rose to mar the holidays. For some reason—I can only figure this was pure nastiness—Gordon Reade, the Magistrate, chose this time to send us a stern note, stating that he would no longer countenance our placing a note to Pete Cavadia in our mail bag.

The day before Christmas I found and brought in a small evergreen thorny tree which I trimmed into the general shape of a Christmas tree. Iz made up a kerosene case, the light type of box in which two five-gallon tins are packed for shipment, filled it with fresh vegetables from the garden, and sent it to the Prices at the mission along with another to Pete. Curiously, we were the only people who had an assortment of vegetables.

Charlie Matabele and Charlie Portuguese selected a small, young, and they hoped tender ox from our herds of cattle which, by Christmas, numbered about three hundred head. I shot the beast, and the men cut it up to be ready for distribution. Iz and I, of course, as was our privilege, had first choice, and took a standing rib roast, a piece of liver, and the tongue and the fillets. Meat, particularly meat with fat on it, is a great need of the natives. In usual circumstances they do not get much fresh meat to eat, which is one reason that a hunter never has difficulty in securing men to work for him. Meat is almost as intoxicating as beer, and natives will sit down and gorge, when they have the opportunity, until their bellies are painfully distended and about all they can do is stagger off to some spot where they can lie down and sleep it off.

Christmas Eve I mounted the tree on a stand and brought it into the living room. The duikers and Fwifwi, who had come in out of the rain, had, of course, to nuzzle and examine this new thing from every angle. Paddy, too, had to participate, and Mr. Thomas, when he came, sniffed the tree and promptly backed up to it and deposited his sign of civet on the stand. Which made things official.

With Lavison and Sixpence, the cook, and the kitchen pickaninny who scrubbed the pots and pans oh-ing and ah-ing and getting in the way, we began to decorate the tree. Paddy insisted upon batting with a huge forepaw at the dangling ornaments, and several delicate eggshells, which Iz had worked so hard to create, were broken. The little antelope were fascinated with the proceedings, and smelled each new ball or star or length of silver paper until their curiosity was satisfied. Tweetie watched with a round black eye from atop the workbasket, and Tommy continually got underfoot. When all the ornaments were hung, the tree looked very pretty, and when we added the gay candles, it was scrumptious.

We dared not put the presents beneath the tree because our foster children might become too curious during the night. For safety's sake I put the tree on a table; the boys went to the compound, and Iz and I and Paddy turned in. The duikers and Fwifwi and Flags retired to the veranda, and Mr. Thomas was left to patrol the dark and silent house.

As we lay in bed courting sleep, the throbbing rhythm of the tom-toms being beaten in the compound rolled through the windows and echoed from the walls of our bedroom. We could hear the singing and chanting of the natives and guessed that they had decided to sample the beer. From far away other tom-toms pounded and throbbed from the mission, where another dance was in progress. The sounds of the small falsetto drums, the thin tightly drawn skins of which were being beaten in a fast, tricky rhythm, blended with the deep, booming, pulsing beat of the long-throated drums to produce an exciting, enveloping syncopation which is the basic appeal of all true jazz—a far cry from "Silent Night."

Christmas morning we were awakened early by the chattering of the natives assembled by the kitchen door. Lavison brought our tea and the bowls for the duikers and Mr. Thomas and then helped to carry the presents into the living room and into the kitchen. The sweet music of *m'piras* filled the air, smothering somewhat the murmur of the people waiting for us to appear.

When we did throw open the door, we were greeted with cries of delight and a chorus of shouted "Christmas bockes, Christmas bockes," which could only be interpreted as requests for the Christmas boxes of goodies and presents.

Charlie Portuguese and Lavison distributed the bundles we had prepared. Then the heavy quarters of meat were carried to the chopping block and Mangineera and Jam cut and whacked the red flesh and the white hard bones and the slabs of heart and kidney fat into portions so that every family received its share. Singing and shouting, the natives trooped off to the compound, the women carrying their rations of dripping meat on their heads and balancing their portions of sugar and grain and salt in baskets on top of the gory loads.

The houseboys and the gunbearers and hunters were then given their more special gifts, and they, too, left for the compound and the hilarious beer drink which would begin as the meat roasted on the fires. At last Iz and I were able to exchange the gifts which we had for each other.

The foster children were not forgotten. When we had our rib roast, there was the specially baked small custard for Mr. Thomas. The antelope received lettuce and carrots as a treat, and Paddy, an especially fine thigh bone from which she greedily sucked the marrow.

It was quite a day. When in the evening we lay back in our chairs to admire the candles on the tree, the songs and the tom-toms of the natives celebrating in the compound flowed into the house. Paddy, having been chased from the rug by Mr. Thomas, lay on the hassock with her enormous forepaws draped down one side and her hind legs dangling on the other. I took a picture of the scene with the Christmas tree in the background, and we had it for years until we lost the greater part of our negatives and prints while we were in the West Indies during the last great war. I wish I had it to include in this book.

As the flood waters rising in the Kafue reached their peak in late February and the beginning of March, the entire flats—which cover an area nearly two hundred miles long from north and west of the Namwala *boma* to the railway line at Kafue station and are some fifty to seventy-five miles wide—became covered with water ranging in depth from a few inches to six feet or more. Our cattle could no longer be herded on the lush green grass growing on the flatlands of the ranch, but grazed among the trees on the higher ground and along the bordering land between the island—which was the bush-veld and on which our house was built—and the encroaching waters.

Here and there across the flats the dark tops of conical anthills could be seen protruding above the surface of the flood. The grass kept pace in growth with the rising water and the tips of the long stalks waved in the breezes blowing across the vast and empty area. When the floods receded, the grass would stand six to twelve feet high to dry out gradually and then be burned off by the natives, who would start tremendous raging fires to get rid of the harsh growth which their cattle could not eat.

Water lilies grew in prodigious numbers; the red, blue, white, and yellow blossoms and the broad green lily pads dotted the surface of the water wherever the grass did not choke their growth. In the evenings, as gentle moisture-laden breezes drifted over the flats and through our house, the heavy, strong scent of the water lilies filled the rooms with perfume.

During these months of rain Isabella was busy with the vegetable garden, her flowers, painting inside the house, and putting final touches here and there to make things more homey and comfortable and, of course, feeding and taking care of the foster children. For a time we had a young bushbuck antelope which Iz raised, but when it was strong enough, we allowed it to return to the bush, as it seemed unhappy and did not fit into the household.

When out hunting one day on the far western edge of Ibamba, three miles from the house, where the mopani forest began, I unintentionally creased a zebra stallion about eighteen months old with a bullet. We put ropes on the animal while it lay unconscious. I doctored the cut on its head and found the skull undamaged, so we coaxed and forced the zebra to walk to the house after it had recovered its senses. It fought and tried to bite us and kicked with fury, but finally we put a halter on it and staked it out on the lawn at the end of a long strong rope.

We kept the stallion for only a few days. When we were sure that it had suffered no permanent injury, we freed it, and the last we saw of our "convict," he was galloping happily away along the edge of the bush on his way to rejoin the herd. As we watched him go, I could not help thinking that some of his disgust with us might well have been engendered by our having tagged him with the absurd name of Horace.

There was always work to be done. The fields of corn and peanuts needed constant cultivating, and there was new land to be cleared of trees and brush. The cattle had to be inoculated against anthrax and blackleg and East Coast fever and to be branded. Bull calves and young boars needed castration and the teeth of the piglets had to be cut to prevent them from chewing their mothers' nipples to ribbons. Twice a month all our domestic four-legged stock were passed through the dipping tank.

The first few times cattle are run through the dip nothing ever goes right. Most of our cattle were of the long-horned rangy native breed. They could leap and run like antelope.

Our dipping tank was a long narrow concrete structure sunk into the ground. At the entrance end the tank wall rose vertically and the tank was about six feet deep. The depth of the tank lessened gradually down its twenty-five feet of length, so that the bottom rose at the exit end to form a ramp up which the cattle, which had to swim the first fifteen feet, could walk to leave the tank.

Serving the entrance to the tank was a kraal built in the form of a triangle with the small end opening onto the tank. The cattle, in small herds, were driven into this kraal and then pushed, shoved, and herded toward the small end and made to jump into the tank. Unless their horns were too wide-spreading, the animals went completely under the solution with which the tank was filled. In this way every part of their bodies was soaked with the tick-killing fluid, and it had a chance to penetrate through the hair on their hides as they swam and reach every one of the horrid insects which had burrowed their biting beaks into their hides. Bont, blue, and brown ticks infested Ibamba, indeed all Rhodesia, and as they were the main carriers of stock-killing diseases, it was imperative to rid the cattle of them as completely as possible.

Dipping was an event of great excitement, for the boys especially. It required the efforts of nearly a dozen men to force the cattle through the crush kraal and into the tank. Approaching the jumping-off place for the first time, an ox would brace its feet and refuse to move. It could not turn and go back because the poles of the narrow neck of the kraal pressed in on each side. A native, stripped for action, placed his shoulder under the tail of the animal and tried to heave it forward and make it jump into the tank. Sometimes the boy was successful and sometimes not. Regardless, the boy usually became covered from shoulders to feet with excrement, to the unbounded joy of his hilarious shouting companions. Once in a while a native would seize an animal's tail and bite it to make it jump, or give the tail a twist.

On occasions an ox or a cow would bunch its four feet close together right at the lip of the tank and give a tremendous leap, hoping to clear the water, only to land upside down. When this happened, we all rushed to the edges of the tank, grabbed the horns, the tail, and the hind legs, and literally flipped the animal over, righting it and then turning it around so it could swim to the exit. Some of the oxen had spreads of horn so wide that when they jumped, the horns caught on the sides of the tank and held them suspended. Then we had either to twist the animal's head sideways so that it could pass along the tank, or lift the ends of its horns and walk along the tank sort of half carrying the animal while it swam with its legs.

While dipping was in progress, the air rang with shouts and yells, the shrieks of laughter and the curses of the natives. The cattle lowed and bellowed and the dogs barked and yipped until they, too, were caught and thrown into the tank to rid them of their ticks. Sometimes Fwifwi or the duikers or the lechwe would approach the tank to watch the dipping, but the uproar quickly became too much for them and they scuttled for safety and peace.

The tick-killing fluid which was added in measured quantities to the five thousand gallons of water in the tank was an extremely poisonous preparation. Had any of the cattle drunk any of the solution in the tank, it was more than likely that they would have died; every precaution was taken, and each animal passing through was watched intently to see that it did not swallow any of the bath. Before being herded into the dip kraal, all animals were watered so that they would not be thirsty.

Snakes became a problem. It has been my experience that generally one sees very few snakes in Africa. They are there, but they hide or get out of the way of approaching people. As the waters, rising around Ibamba, covered their holes and hunting grounds, the snakes were forced onto the high land to which the mice and insects and others of their food had retreated. Walking the paths about the ranch, we had to watch for the slow-moving and belligerent puff adder and, at night, for the grayish night adder. Once or twice we saw mambas whipping across the lawn, the forward third of their long slender bodies carried high off the ground. The natives killed several spitting cobras around the chicken pen and in the compound, and *m'swemmas* got into the house once or twice.

In the evenings we almost always had a fire, either against the dampness, for cheerfulness, or because it was just plain cold. Before the fire there was an old bit of a rug and a hassock. Paddy loved to lie on the rug and toast herself. So did Mr. Thomas. Finding Paddy there first, he would sniff to be sure which animal was lying there, then his back hair would rise and his tail would fluff out and he would lower his head toward the floor in striking position and hiss and growl. Paddy would ignore him. Furious, Tommy would make darting motions as if to slash or bite. Still no reaction from Paddy. The little cat would then study the situation, and deciding upon the proper attack, would dart his head forward and nip Paddy smartly on a leg or her tail. That would bring a reaction. The little lioness would roll over or raise her head and wave a great paw in Tommy's general direction. Sometimes she would give a plaintive growl. But she wouldn't give up her place until Tommy nipped her again, whereupon she would slowly get up and, protesting, climb onto the hassock. Mr. Thomas, having won his point, would toast for a while, just to show who was really the boss around the house, and then go off on further explorations.

On my second trip in to the railway after the road had dried out Iz accompanied me, and we went to Choma instead of Pemba. There were a lot of little things which she needed to buy. We left Paddy behind in the care of Lavison, but Tommy traveled with us in a special box.

Because of the condition of the road we camped one night going in. We let Tommy out of his box, and he had a great time wandering about the camp, sniffing at all sorts of new and delicious scents. When it came time to retire, Iz took him onto her cot with her and, so far as we know, he spent the entire night there sleeping.

At McKee's hotel we established ourselves in a double room. Tommy's box was placed beside Iz's bed, and he was allowed out to familiarize himself with his new quarters. We filled his dirting bowl with water and placed him on the bed, but he wanted to run around after being cooped up on the long trip.

After a wash-up we walked over to the store to look around. We left Tommy shut in. For maybe an hour we talked with 'Kee, and then went to the tiny bar for sundowners. It was nearly seven before we returned to our room to freshen up for dinner.

Tommy was missing! I hadn't noticed as we entered, but I remembered that the door had been unlocked. The bedroom boy making his rounds to let down the mosquito nets had left the door open, and Tommy had gotten out.

At once we got out the flashlight and began to search and call about the front and to look under the flowering shrubs and bushes. No answer came to Iz's cluck-clucking. We searched around the back and in every possible place. Other people, ready for dinner, came and helped. But we couldn't find our little foster child, and finally went in to the dining room to eat dinner hurriedly and return to carry on the search. Although we hunted and called for a long time, we had no luck, and eventually returned to our room, heavy-hearted and trying to tell ourselves that we would find Tommy in the morning. Just in case Tommy might wander back during the night, we left our door open onto the veranda.

It was only about a half an hour after we had retired that we were startled by wild screams from the room next door. A woman was yelling mightily for help. Iz was first out of bed. I think she guessed what the trouble was. I followed her onto the veranda and into the next room, where Iz was standing in her nightie, holding Tommy tightly in her arms while an old biddy in the bed, under the net, was still screaming. 'Kee came on the run, carrying a gun. In the excitement of quieting the woman down we figured out that Tommy must have slipped out while the bedroom boy was making up our room, and gone into the next. He probably hid under the bed until the woman came in, went to bed, and put out the light. Then he tried to lift the net with his nose, as he did at home, and climb into bed. I can't say I blame the woman for being startled. How could she have known that the "savage beast" was only Mr. Thomas, and that all he wanted was comfort and safety?

chapter eight

YOUNG animals are like children. Which, of course, they should be, as children are only the young of the human animal. Paddy and Tommy, the duikers and Fwifwi, each had lively curiosity. Just like your child or mine, each had to investigate a candle, the kerosene lantern, the fireplace, and to learn about fire the hard way. The animals played, just as children play, running and jumping and rolling and twisting and chasing each other so that their muscles and firm little bodies developed and grew.

As weeks passed, the antelope tried higher and higher jumps and would run in larger and larger circles. As they became surer of themselves, they ventured farther from the security of the house and into the vegetable garden. They learned what to eat and what not to eat by tasting, spitting out cabbage but nibbling on the tomato fruits, although they avoided the vines. They would stand on the grass, stiff-legged and alert, their petal-shaped ears cocked forward and their eyes wide and round, and watch the, to them, huge cattle being herded into the crush pen preparatory to entering the dip tank. At the first resounding smack and splash as an animal hit the dip, away they would go, dashing for the safety of the house.

Our foster children exhibited very little fear. Like most people, I was brought up with the belief that various animals were instinctively afraid of certain other animals. I doubt very much now that this is true. I believe that knowledge of what to be afraid of is learned, either by experience or through the teaching, by example, of other animals.

I have seen a young wart hog, raised with the family, walk right upwind to a leopard, one of its most notorious enemies, and try to make friends. Our antelope showed no semblance of fear when they first encountered Paddy and Tommy. They played with the dogs and felt safest when in the company of humans. I once had a leopard, named Binkie, which grew up from kittenhood with a police-dog puppy and a young black goat. The three animals played and roamed together, and all three slept huddled together on an ancient couch on the veranda.

It is not only among animals living with humans that I have seen this lack of fear demonstrated. More than once I, with my trackers and hunters, have walked right up to a baby wildebeest, or zebra, lying on the veld while its mother was away to water, and laid our hands on it without the slightest difficulty. Indeed, the first reactions of such young animals is to accept a finger to suck, or to push and butt at a button on a jacket in the hope of finding milk. The smell of man, supposed to cause such paroxysms of fear in the hearts of animals, means nothing to a baby antelope or other baby animal.

The close and utter dependence of pets upon their masters and mistresses brings up another question. That there is such a thing as parental love, or affection, among animals is beyond question, I think. Ranchers and farmers know how fiercely a cow will defend her calf. Lions are most dangerous when accompanying their kittens, and will fight furiously to protect them. Birds will dart at, and otherwise try to frighten, an intruder who comes too near their nest.

But do the kittens, the fledglings, the calves, and foals feel affection for their parents? If they do feel such affection, does this develop gradually through association, or is it instinctive?

When wild lions roared outside the house on Ibamba, Paddy paid little heed. The first few times this happened, she would listen, but she made no attempt to answer or to move to the door to go out. Later she paid no attention at all. Paddy was contented and happy. She was well fed, protected against the elements, and she had companionship all day and night. Indeed, she was far better off with us than she could ever have been free on the veld. Sounds uttered by her own species apparently made no appeal to any latent instincts.

There was little to have prevented either Tommy or Paddy from running away had they so desired. The doors of the house were usually open. Everybody, the antelope, ourselves, the houseboys, came and went freely. Tommy did get lost once when he went out alone, but when we found him, he was obviously trying to find his way back home from the tall grass where he had been exploring.

Does this complete acceptance of Iz and me as satisfactory parents indicate that baby animals must *learn* to love their parents? I am inclined to think it does. If this is true for baby animals, isn't it also true for baby humans? Can you honestly state that you believe that a human baby a few weeks or a year old feels love for its parents, and that it would pine if taken away and some other equally loving and tender persons substituted? I am afraid I could not say that for my own children at that age.

The word "instinctive" is one which has been grossly overworked. Too often the word is glibly offered as an explanation for acts the motivating cause of which we do not understand. Instincts do play a part in the lives of all animals, but their influence, particularly in animals high on the scale of intelligence, is largely limited to actions revolving around birth, breeding, and death. Generally knowledge, the patterns of behavior, are acquired through experience. They are not inherited.

Outside, the big wild lions were returning to Ibamba and the great *saka*. Shamakembie, bringing the mail from Namwala, met a lioness and four cubs walking along a track on the ranch one morning, and we spent a night and two days trying futilely to find her—with larceny in our hearts, of course. At night lions roared more and more frequently, and their spoor crossed and recrossed the ranch.

The three lions of the previous dry season returned. Or at least a party of three lions came and visited us quite regularly. As before, during the night they walked all about and examined everything. The dogs would bark furiously and raise cain, but the lions never bothered them, nor did they bother the animals which also slept outside.

Once or twice a week it was not at all unusual, when Isabella and I would be sitting in the long living room, for her to raise her head and listen. Outside, on the dry grass, only a few yards from the lighted windows, we could hear lions walking around the house. In an endeavor to find out how much meat a wild lion could eat at one sitting, we weighed haunches of zebra and chained them down not far from the house, then sat on the back veranda and waited for the lions to come and eat. In the moonlight, as we watched, one or possibly two lions got away with one hundred and seventeen pounds of meat! And they ate it all right in our back yard!

Lions killed all about us. They took cattle from the Kasenga Mission and from the village to the north of us. On the back reaches of the ranch, not far from a large shallow waterhole, the lions frequently killed zebra, "lion pudding," and an occasional wildebeest. In the *saka* they got bush pigs and, once, an eland bull which had come to feed on the wild oranges which were quite plentiful there.

As was inevitable, on several occasions the herd boys, tagging along behind the cattle as they grazed or moved from lagoon to lagoon, saw lions. The lions either stood and watched for a while or slowly stalked away. They never threatened the cattle or the herd boys who, believing in my power to control wild lions, no longer bothered to carry guns.

A native brought in a baby wildebeest which we immediately adopted and named Popeye. Wildebeests and hartebeests are reputed to be born crazy because they are always up to such antics on the veld. Hunters say that they cannot help being a little on the nutty side because of the mass of maggots which live inside the scent glands on each side of the head and which must drive the animals batty with their wigglings and squirmings. It is not unusual to find short pieces of heavy grass or a bit of twig imbedded in the exterior opening to these scent glands. They probably were forced into the openings when the animals rubbed their cheeks hard against the ground to ease the itching.

It was difficult for Popeye to switch from mother's milk to even diluted cow's milk. Formulas for young animals are not easy to evolve. Experienced animal handlers guard their formulas with the greatest secrecy. For some days and nights Popeye suffered from stomach troubles and wind and gas. She was too big to pick up and burp like a baby, so I would have to get out of bed, light a lamp, pull on some shoes, and get her outside where I could push and cajole her into a fast walk or trot up and down a path to work out wind, hoping and praying there were no puff or night adders lying about.

Popeye fitted right into the family. She learned to be pretty well housebroken, and like the other foster children, came and went as she pleased. It was a beautiful sight to see Popeye single-footing across the lawn in a last gallop before coming in for the evening to add confusion to the situation before the fire. Because Popeye, like Paddy and Thomas, developed a liking for the rug and for toasting. She was as large as a Shetland pony, long-legged and gangly. And she knew what she wanted.

Popeye didn't care which of the others was occupying the favored rug. Finding Paddy there, she would lower her head, snuffle through her broad black nose, roll her eyes, utter a whinnying sound, and stamp her front feet. Her eyes bugged out and she would lower her head as though to butt with her baby horns.

Whoever was occupying the rug usually ignored all these preliminaries. A few more snorts and puffs and Popeye would get down to business. Approaching carefully, she would raise her front feet with their sharp hooves and deliberately stamp on whoever was on the rug. This accomplished her purpose. Whoever was there moved, and Popeye would triumphantly stand on the rug, go around once, fold her front feet, then her back legs, and sink down in a compact bundle and toast contentedly. Once she was established, neither Paddy nor Tommy could shift her, short of biting her really hard. Which seldom happened.

Each of our foster children had his or her little peculiarities or habits. Popeye watched Paddy and Mr. Thomas climb into Iz's or my lap and cuddle down to sleep. She apparently decided this was something she should try, and selected Iz for her first attempt.

Carefully backing up to Iz, who was sitting in a deep wicker chair, Popeye placed her hind legs against Iz's knees. We both watched, astonished and curious as to what Popeye had in mind. Suddenly she humped her hind quarters upward and thrust herself backward to land sitting in Isabella's lap. Her hind legs stuck out straight from the chair and parallel to the floor. Her big eyes rolled wildly and she puffed and blew through her muzzle as her front hooves slipped on the cement with her efforts to retain her sitting position.

I laughed so hard that tears ran down my cheeks. Which was mean, because poor little Iz was flattened into the chair, holding the broad behind of a wildebeest calf weighing almost as much as she. I have seldom seen anything quite so ludicrous as a wildebeest sitting in a chair, and it was some moments before I could get up and help Iz to extricate herself.

Popeye was either pleased with the sensation she had caused or really enjoyed sitting, because she tried this several times later on, and we had to keep an eye on her. She would never do this unless there was someone in the chair, and it was well, when Popeye backed up and had that certain gleam in her eye, to be sure the chair in which either of us was sitting was strong and solid. Popeye tried her sitting act with me once when I was on a light wooden chair, and we ended up on the floor amid a tangle of broken chair legs and rounds. To save the furniture, we finally had to break Popeye of this habit by slapping her vigorously on that portion of her anatomy which she wished to deposit in our laps.

With the ending of the rains, as the ground dried and became firm, I laid out the foundations for the long building which would house the laboratory and all the equipment we had brought from the States. The walls were to be of burned brick, and Mangineera again dug himself a hole near the clay pits and with a large gang of natives worked day after day, forming the gooey mass of clay and sand into bricks. Charlie Matabele busied himself with his spans of oxen, hauling in huge loads of firewood to be burned in the kilns, and the sawboys worked hour after hour with their long ten-foot lance-toothed saws, slicing mabunga and mahogany logs into boards and beams to be dried and cured in the shade against need.

About this time we began to feel the first effects of the financial and business depression which was creeping over America and was later to spread throughout much of the world. We maintained a rather voluminous correspondence with our friends, one of the most informative and active of whom was Franklin D. Roosevelt, an old friend of my family's. We exchanged frequent letters in which I told him of our progress in setting up the research station, our difficulties and little experiences. He would write back tales of his fishing excursions and send us advice and information about conditions in the States. Roosevelt, "Uncle Frank," was a director of the American Museum of Natural History, and he had helped me as best he could during the time when I had spent so many months trying to raise the money to found the station. It had been through the good offices of "Uncle Frank" that I had secured the support and backing of Madison Grant and Henry Fairfield Osborn and numerous other men of prestige and importance.

It was during this period that I began reporting my personal observances regarding political trends, observations concerning the beliefs and functions of important officials and residents, and information bearing upon economic developments in Central Africa to Roosevelt, a personal task which I continued to perform for him for many years, regardless of where I might happen to be.

The fact that it required a month for mail to reach us from the States made very little difference once the initial gap had passed. Personal news, anecdotes, and opinions from our friends were just as welcome and just as valid and interesting when we did receive them as they would have been three weeks earlier. The time lapse, however, did make a great difference in our reaction to the news of the world. On Ibamba we did not read the news of any event until at least a week or ten days after it had happened. By the time the overseas papers reached us, the story or the event had been forgotten by the African papers, which were by then chasing some newer item of gossip or speculation. We came to learn that the events which were so boldly headlined and reported as if they were the very stuff of history were, in all actuality, only passing events of small moment, except to those most intimately concerned, and that their consequences extended but little beyond the day of their occurrence. The conference, the decisions, the travels of important officials, by the time we read about them, were largely done with and forgotten.

More important than our personal mail was notification that settlement of my parents' estates was being delayed and that the sums expected to result from the sale of buildings which my father had owned in Kansas City and elsewhere, and his interests in ranching and farming lands, could not measure up to original expectations. I received certain sums more or less regularly as the assets of the estates were liquidated, but these were less than I had been led to believe they would be.

Consequently, we immediately began to cut expenses. It had never been our thought that we would be able to bring Ibamba into profitable development in less than five years. Cattle mature slowly, particularly the type of range-grass-fed cattle we owned. It required several seasons to bring newly cleared land into full production. When we had sailed from New York, it had been our expectation that we would have sufficient money to permit the slow development of the ranch and to supply funds with which to build the station. As the situation in America worsened, it became more and more evident that we could not rely so heavily as we had done upon receipt of money from the States.

As a result we decided against incurring the expense of corrugated iron for the roof of the laboratory building. Instead I designed a steeply pitched roof which would be covered with thatch. Properly put on, thatch makes an excellent roof. It is much cooler than iron and not noisy when the rains pelt down. The grass and the poles on which the thatch would be laid could be secured for only the cost of labor. The drawbacks were that thatch is very inflammable, and despite our efforts to clean the grass before laying it on the roof, some dust and dirt continually drops to the rooms below. Also, thatch is a haven for mice and insects.

We were determined to get the laboratory started. After all, it was the main reason for our having come to Africa. As beggars cannot be choosers, we fell back upon the use of grass rather than postpone the building until the business situation might clear up and we would again begin to receive ample funds.

Thatching is something of an art. Although every male native knew something about how to thatch a roof because every village hut was roofed with grass, competent and careful thatchers were not common.

To begin with, the grass, standing from five to eight and nine feet tall, must be cut when fully ripe and as dry as possible. Out on the flats our boys wielded their sickles and cut enormous quantities, which were tied with bark into bundles eighteen inches to two feet in diameter. These were carted to the building site on the truck and dumped in huge piles.

Other boys then cut the large bundles open and reassembled the grass into bundles, each of which was some four to five inches in diameter at the thick end. These bundles were bound as tightly as possible with strands of mopani bark stripped from trees on the western edge of the ranch and kept wet and pliable in tubs of water.

Beside each mounting pile of small bundles we built a rake, or cleaning rack. This consisted of a length of two-by-four through which had been driven a number of ten-inch spikes, so that the pointed ends rose from the wood like the tines of a rake. This spiked piece of timber was mounted on two stout stakes driven deep into the ground. A native seized one of the small bundles of grass, swished it down with a thump onto the spikes, and then drew the bundle lengthwise through the spikes, combing out any broken lengths, the leaves and seeds. When done properly, each bundle was tossed aside as a clean bundle of long, polished stalks of grass bound tightly together and of a more or less uniform length and diameter.

While the grass-cleaning process was going on, a roof foundation consisting of hard mopani rafters fastened together at a steep pitch was put into place. The laboratory building was twenty-five feet wide and eighty feet in length. Each half, or side, of the roof was nearly thirty feet wide to allow for necessary overhang; a tremendous expanse of thatch. It was even more difficult to build the supporting rafter construction because we could secure no trees long enough to supply single beams. Each beam had to be built up from two or more lengths of the hard difficult-to-work mopani.

Once we had the rafters up, literally hundreds of yards of round poles were nailed into place, running parallel to the length of the building and about fifteen inches apart horizontally. It was to these poles that the grass thatch would be sewed. These thin straight poles were cut in the mopani forest around the pan at the western corner of Ibamba. You may perhaps conceive of the great amount of work we had to complete when you visualize the enormous quantities of grass, of poles, and of timber for the rafters which had to be hauled long distances by truck, and the tons of bricks, the endless quantities of firewood, etc., which had to be moved.

Dividing the chores, Iz and I worked like beavers. When I drove the tractor, she handled the truck. It was quite a feat for my little mite of a wife to manipulate that overloaded truck through sand and wet ground, back and load and deliver her cargo where wanted, and then return for more. But day after day, sweating in the hot cab, covered with the dust and debris from the grass which was thrown onto the truck or with the dirt from the loads of bricks, she drove the truck and we got things done. Small as she was physically, and feminine in every way, Iz developed muscles in her forearms and biceps which would put many a football playing teen-ager to shame. In spite of the sun, the hot dry winds, the work, and the fact that she developed a pair of shoulders which would have been the envy of many a lightweight wrestler, Iz remained a radiant, lovely girl.

About this time a messenger came from my blood brother, Chief Sheasongo, bringing news that my brother intended to visit me in ten days' time. I was delighted, not only because I was genuinely fond of and had great respect for Sheasongo, but also because I had not seen him since Isabella and I had reached Ibamba and I had long wanted her to make his acquaintance.

There was almost as much protocol surrounding the travel of a great African chief and his meeting with another chief as today surrounds a summit meeting of heads of states. Informed of the coming visit, Charlie Portuguese immediately asked for, and got, a group of workers to start construction of a new and fairly large hut in which Sheasongo would be able to stay during his visit to Ibamba. This was begun at the edge of the compound.

Large quantities of grain were distributed to the women known to be the best and most careful brewers, to be fermented and made ready against the dancing and celebrations which would surround Sheasongo's visit to his blood brother, *N'Kos* Sibyunni'byunni, and his *N'Kosikase,* Maseccasecca. Charlie Matabele, Jam, and Mangineera looked over the herds of cattle with speculative eyes and discussed which of the young oxen should be chosen to furnish meat for the feastings.

Here is perhaps as good a place as any to explain the difference between the words *n'kos* and *bwana* which one sees used in books about Africa. In Rhodesia *n'kos,* which is a Zulu word brought north by the Matabele, was used as a title of respect. It means chief, and was not conferred lightly upon any white man. *Bwana* literally means only a man of some substance, and is not in any way a title. Because most white men were persons of substance, the word *bwana* came to mean "white man," and the natives used the word in a descriptive way. Bwana Makuba, which came to be the name of a copper mine, originally referred to a prospector of considerable physical size who was called *Bwana Makuba,* or the large white man, by the natives in his employ. *N'kosikase* was the feminine of *n'kos.* Isabella's name, *N'Kosikase* Maseccasecca, translated, meant, "the Chieftaness Who Is Always Smiling." *N'Kos Sibyunni'byunni* meant "Chief, Father of Birds."

We were, of course, kept apprised of the approach of Sheasongo. On the afternoon of his arrival the compound was in a complete dither of excitement and anticipation. Many of our boys and their wives had come from Sheasongo's village, and they were eager to hear the latest news and gossip and, naturally, looked forward to the celebrations. Natives just love a party.

Jam came to the front veranda to tell me that Sheasongo had reached the northern boundary of Ibamba and was even then coming down the road which we had cut through the bushveld. A wide grin spread across his handsome dark face as he spoke because Jam, although a Barotse, had hunted from and lived for many years in Sheasongo's village. Others of our top echelon of natives congregated by the veranda. Each decked out in his finest freshly washed and pressed shirt and shorts. Tall and short, some broad of shoulder, and some skinny like Shamakembie, from many different tribes, they were a heterogeneous but impressive group of men.

Lavison, resplendent in his white shorts and shirt, appeared and carefully opened the screen door at the end of the veranda and fastened it back against the parapet. He brought two chairs and placed them like thrones facing outward through the doorway. These were for Isabella and myself.

Softly at first we heard the music of the *olimbas,* the xylophones, sounding from the direction of the road through the trees beyond the compound. As the music swelled in volume, the keening cries of welcome uttered by the women in the compound cut piercingly through the melodious music and we knew that the chief was passing by the huts of our people.

Isabella and I took our seats. Jam, Mangineera, Charlie Portuguese, Charlie Matabele, Shaluma, Shafumu, Lavison, Longone, Tickie, Shamakembie, and Sixpence ranged themselves on the veranda behind us. Ordinarily, of course, they would never have dreamed of entering our house in such fashion, but this was a most special occasion. It would not have been fitting for me, *N'Kos* Sibyunni'byunni, to meet with *N'Kos* Sheasongo without the presence of my men to support and back me up. That *N'Kosikase* Maseccasecca was present was a concession to my race. Ordinarily women are not present except as spectators in the background at such meetings.

As the procession which was coming neared the house, the musicians increased the tempo of their music and beat frantically upon the long *olimbas* which they carried before them, supported by leather thongs passing around their necks. The song echoed in the rooms behind us; I heard Paddy growl, and the duikers left the veranda and hid in the bedroom.

The first to appear around the corner of the house were several young men, naked except for breechclouts, their bodies shining with the oil which had been rubbed over their skins. Slowly, while the music flowed about them, they approached the area before the veranda door. One laid down a fine mat made from split palm fronds and carefully smoothed this out. A second man unrolled the skin of a maned lion and laid this on the mat so that the head skin pointed in my direction.

Although slavery was illegal and everyone would deny its existence, I knew that these young men were slaves of the chief. As the first two stepped back, another came, and in the center of the lion skin he placed a wide, beautifully carved and highly polished stool.

There was a flourish on the *olimbas.* The group of men standing behind the slaves parted and Sheasongo strode forward. He was magnificent. A cape of leopard skin, the deep orange and the black spots shining in the late sunlight, hung about his wide shoulders. Amulets and charms and a beaten snuff spoon hung from his neck. On his head was a straw hat of native make, decorated with brilliantly colored feathers. Around his waist he wore a fresh brightly colored length of patterned cloth, and his forearms were covered from wrist to elbow with wide bracelets of elephant ivory.

The music ceased abruptly. Solemnly, with great dignity but without a word, Sheasongo seated himself facing me on the stool. A slave handed him his scepter, which had been carved in the shape of a ball on the end of a slender handle from the horn of a rhinoceros. Taking the scepter in his right hand, Sheasongo placed the ball end on his right knee. There wasn't a sound from the entourage behind him or from the women and children who had followed from the compound.

Steadily, his dark eyes piercing and bright, my brother stared into my face. My gaze took in again the high cheekbones and the great hooked nose, the thin lips which betrayed his partial Arab ancestry.

A feeling of power and decision radiated from Sheasongo. No one could sit opposite him without knowing the vitality, the cruelness, the charm, the life-and-death authority of the man. He was one of the last of his kind, a final example of the terrible warrior chiefs who once had ruled throughout the land.

In silence we stared into each other's faces, each reliving in his mind past associations and past discussions and deeds. Breathless, the assembled people waited for me to break the silence, which must last for just so long as to indicate to all that neither of us was impulsive, but not so long as to be rude.

Charlie Portuguese coughed softly behind me. It was my cue.

"*Dabonwa,* Sheasongo," (I see you, Sheasongo).

"*Dabonwasi,* Sibyunni'byunni" (I see you also, Sibyunni'byunni).

We proceeded through the ritual questions as to the state of his health, then of my health, of the condition of his village, of my village, of his crops, of my crops, and whether the rains had been sufficient or insufficient, the hunting, profitable or unprofitable.

With these relatively unimportant questions out of the way—I say unimportant because each of us knew the answers before asking the questions, and we only posed them because of the protocol which bound us—we got down to a real fireside chat. It was between three and four years since we had seen each other, and there was much to be told and to be discussed. The counselors and elders ranged behind Sheasongo joined in the conversations, as did Mangineera, Jam, and Charlie Portuguese and others. Jokes and reminiscences flowed between us. It was a most enjoyable visit, and I, for one, felt closer to my blood brother than I had in a long, long time.

The sun sank close to the far horizon, and Sheasongo was sitting in the shadow cast by the house. He had walked a considerable distance that day, and I knew he must be weary. I mentioned this, and at the slow nod of his head, I told him:

"A house has been prepared for your comfort. We have slaughtered an ox in honor of your visit to me and beer has been prepared for all. The day has been long and your journey wearisome. Tomorrow the sun will rise again and we can talk at length. Go now, my brother, and feast and rest. May the night and a fire bring you peace and comfort."

Assisted by two slaves who darted forward on each side to raise his arms, although Sheasongo was in the prime of life and strong, the chief rose from his stool. He was an impressive figure as he stood looking at me. His countenance was dark and imperious and arrogant, his attire, splendorously barbaric. Standing stiffly erect with his broad shoulders thrown back, he was every inch the image of a great and powerful ruler.

"I go, Sibyunni'byunni," he said. "I go with joy in my heart because I have seen you and found you well. Tomorrow will be another day. When the sun has warmed the land, I shall come and we will talk. Rest in peace."

"Go in peace," I answered as he turned away and his retainers gathered up the stool, the lion skin, and the mat to follow behind him.

You may wonder at my mention that at such a date in the history of Rhodesia, Sheasongo possessed slaves. Slavery had, of course, been abolished—legally, at least—many years before. The young men known as slaves, of whom there were six or eight, were actually youths whose parents had given the boys to Sheasongo when very young. The chief provided for their every need, just as he did for his own sons. In his way he was fond of them, and although they had to obey his every whim and serve him, they lacked for very little. The youths received no pay for their services, they could not marry without his permission, and their lives were at the disposal or whim of Sheasongo.

It was told, although I never had proof, that when Sheasongo's son by his first and therefore chief wife died, Sheasongo went off into the bushveld which surrounded his village, accompanied by two of the slave youths. One carried the rifle of which Sheasongo was so proud and which, because of his chieftainship, the government allowed him ownership.

Sheasongo, so the story went, returned alone from this excursion. The slaves never were seen again, and all in the village assumed that Sheasongo had shot the young men and buried them so that his son would have servants in the world to which his spirit had gone. If true, the act was only that of a man trained in and still wedded to the traditions of his tribe, one who refused to admit the existence of the new order brought to his land through conquest by the whites, of whom, in the majority, he did not approve. In the lexicon of we whites Sheasongo's act would be classed as murder. In his world, the world in which he had been raised from infancy and in all the customs in which he devotedly believed, his killing of the youths—if he did kill them, and I believe he did—was not murder but a necessary ritual. It is significant that no one would ever talk and that no proof of Sheasongo's reputed acts could be found. He was never prosecuted.

Among the retainers who accompanied Sheasongo was a slave, a Mankoya native, so old and wizened that he tottered a little as he walked, and the skin on his belly and his upper arms lay in crinkled folds. His name was Shamoanna, and he was chief *olimba* player to Sheasongo.

Shamoanna spoke a form of the Mankoya language so archaic, few could understand him. But when he hung his *olimba* from his skinny neck or squatted on the ground with the cumbersome instrument before him and played, everyone understood. For there was no one who could match him in his remembrance of songs and tunes or who could wield the light, tiny hammers with which he struck the notes so skillfully or so quickly.

Only chiefs have the prerogative of having their own *olimba,* or xylophone, player or players. It was royal music in more senses than one, and the important chiefs, when on the march, were always accompanied by one or more *olimba* musicians.

It was fine, indeed, to see Shamoanna again and, of a morning, to be awakened by his music as he played beneath the window of our bedroom. That Shamoanna played for me was strictly within the limits of the protocol which regulated his life, for I was a chief, and not only a chief, but the blood brother of Sheasongo, who, he believed, owned him body and soul.

Sheasongo stayed with us for three days, and we had a most happy time together. Isabella admired and liked my brother greatly, and he, on his part, was gracious and respectful to her, although, as a general rule, Sheasongo took little notice of women and favored them with no respect at all. In his pattern of life women were to bear children, to work in the fields, and to prepare the food, not to sit as equals with men. Women, in Sheasongo's world, were chattels to be bartered or sold, and at all times they were to be subservient to men.

Iz and I were expecting an addition to our family all our own. We made preparations to go to the hospital in Livingstone, nearly three hundred miles away. We planned to drive down in our very old and open Dodge touring car.

Although we were filled with anticipation and worry and hope—the coming baby would be our first child—the comfort and safety of our foster children was much on our minds. How could we best arrange things so that they would not be too lonely—would be sure to have enough to eat and drink, and have room to play? After we had left, we could not be certain what would happen. It was even possible that one might wander away, looking for us.

In the end we divided the house. Tommy was to have our bedroom and the front veranda, which he could share with the duikers and Fwifwi. This would give him both space in which to roam and look for bugs and his beloved bed in which to sleep during the day.

Paddy was to have the second room and the back veranda. Popeye and Flags could use the living room and go and come as they pleased. Lavison was put in charge, and dire were the threats I spoke to him of what would occur if anything happened to the foster children. Lavison was a good boy, and as he had been with me for years, was accustomed to having to take care of the master's assortment of animals. But we drove away with heavy hearts. As we rolled toward the railway line and along the dirt and graveled road to Livingstone, we realized what a hold our little family had on our hearts and thoughts. We missed them dreadfully.

Livingstone was hot as always. Down in the Zambezi Valley it is usually steamy and humid even in the winter months. After our isolated life on Ibamba the dirt streets seemed crowded. It was difficult for us to adjust to having so many people around, even though many were friends of long standing. But finally Iz's time came, and she was delivered of a baby girl. It was a difficult delivery, which meant that we had to be absent from Ibamba longer than planned. There was a great deal of work going on and nobody except Charlie Portuguese and Mangineera to supervise. After ten days we decided that I should make a quick run up to the ranch, stay a day and a night, and then return, by which time we hoped and expected that our daughter would be strong enough to travel the long, hard, jouncing road.

I took off long before dawn and drove by headlights up the road to Pemba, where I had breakfast with Hard Jones in his little pub. Then on out into the blue and toward Ibamba.

I was worried about Iz and the baby, and as I drew nearer and nearer to Ibamba, worried about the progress of the work and the condition of the animals. Nevertheless, I forced myself to drive slowly and carefully, watching for stumps, for thorn branches in the road which could prick through a tire easily and leave me with a puncture to fix. Several times I had to stop while the boy with me filled the radiator from the water can in the back.

It was late in the afternoon when I drove over the slope on which Kasenga Mission was built and headed across the intervening flat for the ranch. As I drove off the flat and climbed the rise toward the house, I could see natives hurrying about and saw Lavison come out of the veranda and stand ready to greet me.

His face was long and solemn when I drew up behind the house. I took one look and asked, "What's the trouble? Are Paddy and Mr. Thomas all right?"

"They are alive," he replied. From the tone of his voice I knew that he was withholding something.

"What is the matter with them?"

"Come and you will see," he answered solemnly, and turning, led the way toward the veranda.

I climbed out quickly and followed. Lavison led the way into the bedroom. I glanced quickly at the bed. There was no bump under the sheets.

"Where is Mr. Thomas?" I demanded quickly and harshly.

Silently Lavison pointed to a built-in closet. Approaching, I called and cluck-clucked. There was a faint noise and what might have been a cluck-clucking answer. I called again and, very slowly, walking stiffly and painfully, Mr. Thomas came out of the closet.

I stared at him, aghast. He was skin and bones. His eyes were gummy and wet. His fur had lost all its fine sheen and was sticking raggedly in tufts and bunches. His tail dragged. Worst of all, Tommy seemed scarcely able to put his feet on the floor. I stooped and gathered him up and held him close while my eyes filled with tears. A thick lump rose in my throat.

I whirled on Lavison. He backed away from me.

"It was not I, *N'Kos*." The words rushed from his lips as he saw the anger in my face. "After you and Maseccasecca left, Mwaming Thomas would not eat. He would not go in the bed. Come." And he walked onto the veranda, motioning me to follow. "Day and night, day and night, Mwaming Thomas ran on this." Lavison laid his hand on the top of the stone parapet which enclosed the veranda to a height of three feet. I stared at the top. When we had left, it had been gleaming white from a fresh coat of whitewash. Now it was a dirty rusty color.

Gently I turned over one of Tommy's feet. The pads were raw and bleeding. With tears running unashamedly down my cheeks, I picked at the crusted top of the parapet. The rust was blood.

I held Tommy close and whispered to him. He whimpered and laid his little head against the bowl between my neck and shoulder and cried like a baby.

Stolid though he was, Lavison's face worked with emotion as he watched. Other natives, carrying in parcels and baggage, watched with their mouths drooping open. It was a tribute to Mr. Thomas that they tiptoed about and were careful to make no sounds laying the suitcases down on the cement.

When I could speak without betraying too much of the constriction in my throat, I issued orders. The cook was to prepare supper for me and a custard for Mwaming Thomas. The bed was to be made up at once. I would eat in bed. The *capitaos* were to carry on as usual. I would see them in the morning.

Lavison opened the door between the bedrooms, and Paddy came rushing in and tried to climb all over me. I fondled her and fended her off at one and the same time as I held Mr. Thomas close against me.

Walking about while the bed was being made, followed everywhere by Paddy, I greeted the duikers and Fwifwi, who came running in from the lawn, and patted Popeye on the head. As I entered the bedroom, I kicked off my shoes and loosened my shorts so that they tumbled to the floor and I could step out of them. Lubin had the bed ready. After he had pulled off my socks, and although there was still light in the sky, I climbed in, taking Tommy with me. He curled up as close to my neck as possible. I pulled the sheet over him and he lay trembling against me, his little nose quivering and his body racked with whimpering sobs.

Paddy climbed onto the bed and lay across my feet, her wide paws outstretched on the covers, and watched with big solemn eyes. Popeye wandered in and stood rolling her eyes at me as I lay in bed, and cocked her floppy ears forward to listen to Mr. Thomas.

When supper was brought in, I sat up and took the tray, and taking some custard in a teaspoon, offered it to Tommy. He sniffed and reluctantly tried a little. Then he snuggled down again. It wasn't food he wanted. He wanted affection. Never have I seen such a demand and need for love and care from an animal, whether wild or domesticated. No dog or cat which I have ever had wanted so much loving.

Gradually Tommy's crying subsided and he stopped trembling. Lavison brought hot water and we mixed a weak solution of permanganate and gently sponged off his feet, softly working off the caked grains of lime and the dirt and hardened blood. Tommy seemed to understand what we were trying to do, and although he whined several times and pulled back on his feet, he made no cries, nor did he attempt to jerk away. He just lay quietly in the crook of my arm. I sponged his eyes with boracic water and dried them, and brushed his fur to throw off some of the dirt.

Then we settled down for the night. I was dog tired from the long trip, but I woke during the night several times to give Tommy small helpings of custard and to offer sweetened milk. It seemed that I lay for hours staring into the dark with Tommy pressed tight against me, whimpering, whimpering. Paddy pressed against me from the opposite side, but she slept.

By morning Tommy had stopped crying and had fallen into what could only have been a sleep of exhaustion. I eased myself out of bed, pushing a pillow against Tommy to make him think I was still there, covered him, and stole out to wash, shave, and straighten up and have breakfast. I left Lavison in the bedroom with orders to come and find me, wherever I might be, when Mr. Thomas woke up.

He slept all morning. At noon I wakened him to examine his feet and to put salve on them and wrap them lightly in bandages. His eyes had cleared, and he watched me work and sniffed eagerly at my hands and arms. When I cluck-clucked to him, he answered softly. He ate more custard and toyed with a little scraped meat and drank some milk. Then I tucked him back on the pillow and covered him and he seemed content.

For the rest of the day I was able to get about the ranch, with Paddy following me wherever I went and Popeye galloping and playing around us. Fwifwi, too, was very glad to see me, but the duikers more or less accepted my return and continued in their placid way. Jane walked with us on our tours and once chased Popeye, but lost the race because Popeye could really run when she had a mind to.

I knew that I would have to leave the next morning. I prayed that if I made a fast trip and that if the baby and Iz were in shape to travel, we could return before Tommy had injured himself further.

I thought of trying to take him with me, but decided against that. He was in no shape to travel. Seeing him in his condition would upset Iz terribly. With the baby on the return trip, it would be impossible to give Tommy the care he would need.

I would have to be absent at least three days, probably four. One to go, one in Livingstone, and two to return. I gave Lavison instructions as to how to care for Tommy's feet, and we agreed that he was to be kept shut in the bedroom and not allowed on the veranda. He was to be offered all the dishes for which he usually had a preference.

I did not dare to tell Iz in what condition I had found Tommy. She was well and the baby was much stronger. We decided to make the trip the following day, and to stop at Hard Jones's for the night rather than to try and push through in one long day.

Bassinets were not to be had in Livingstone. So we purchased a large, rectangular heavy wicker mail basket about thirty inches long by twenty inches wide and fifteen or sixteen deep. We had a mattress made to fit, and Iz fashioned a net of mosquito netting to cover the top.

On the return we had the top up to keep the sun off and we took it as easy as possible. At Pemba we were welcomed royally; Mrs. Jones did everything to help, and Pete Cavadia insisted upon standing a round of drinks in celebration. This was the first white baby for the Namwala-Mashakulumbwe district in many, many a year.

The following day we drove slowly. We stopped at M'Beza so that bearded Tommy Dugan could admire the baby, which he did, and then drove on past Kabulamwanda and Marla to the mission, where we had tea and John and Florence also admired our daughter. We were mighty proud of her.

As we crossed the final flat and the house loomed ahead, I tried to prepare Iz for Tommy's condition. I was afraid of what might have happened after I had left. In spite of her natural preoccupation with the baby, Iz was very upset and almost cried.

She did cry when she saw him. But although Lavison said he hadn't eaten after he discovered that I had gone, he was in much better shape than when I had first returned. And he would have little to do with me. Once he found Iz, I was second choice. Tommy wanted his mummy, and old, however kindly, father just wouldn't do at all.

It was quite a homecoming. All our natives had to see and admire the baby and express their satisfaction. Paddy was continually underfoot and being stepped on or over. Iz alternated between carrying the baby and carrying and crying with Tommy. Popeye got a tear-wet kiss on her funny quivering muzzle, and Fwifwi danced around Iz like mad. Like Tommy, he, too, had missed and wanted his mother.

Eventually things quieted down. The mail basket was set up on a bridge table by the bed, with a lamp close by on another table for night feeding. The bags were unpacked and some presents distributed. After an early supper we five went to bed: the baby in her basket, Iz and I in the big bed, with Tommy pressed tight against Iz, and Paddy across my feet. Popeye insisted upon sleeping in the bedroom also, but sometime during the night went out onto the veranda, where it was cooler, and slept with the duikers and Fwifwi.

Our little family was together again, with one very important increase. The arrival of the baby created complications. The morning after our return Iz took the baby in her arms and walked out onto the lawn to look things over. Fwifwi dashed up and danced around and stood on his hind legs to see what she was carrying. When he determined that the bundle was alive, jealousy got the upper hand. He stood in front of Iz and reared on his hind legs and tried to stab the bundle with his short but very sharp horns. He even jumped in his efforts, and made such a fuss that Iz had to retire into the house and shut Fwifwi outside.

The duikers did not seem to be bothered. They were placid little chaps and just went their contented way. Popeye was interested and would peer for minutes at the baby, rolling her eyes round and round and snuffling. Paddy liked the baby and smelled her gently and seemed to understand that the baby girl belonged and that she must be nice to her.

Mr. Thomas was another matter. He would lie on the foot of the bed and never take his beady eyes off the child as she lay gurgling and turning while Iz bathed or changed her. At first Tommy made threatening noises deep in his throat, and it was only too obvious that if we left the baby alone with him for a second, he would spring at her. Tommy loved Iz so fiercely that he found it terribly difficult to reconcile himself to the fact that there was another who took precedence. Gradually his active animosity wore off, but we could never trust him around our daughter.

Paddy, on the other hand, virtually adopted the little girl, and would lie quietly on the bed with her great paws stretched out before her and watch Iz's every move as she tended the child. When the baby cried, Paddy cocked an interested ear and turned her head sideways and looked very anxious and inquiring.

Working hard, using boards from packing cases, I fashioned a very passable imitation of a kiddie coop. Not only was it strong, with a hinged top, but it could be folded flat like one made by a professional. I used a picture in a Montgomery Ward catalogue as an example. In this, Buncher, as the baby was nicknamed, was safe from insects and from Tommy.

Did I say safe from bugs? Well, she was until the evening we forgot to put the legs of the coop in tins, and ran into the bedroom in response to agonized wails to find our darling literally being smothered with hordes of black ants. After that we were doubly careful.

When a great lion sounded off from the edge of the back grain field, everybody listened. We had no choice. When that tremendous booming voice rolled into the house, it echoed and bounced from the walls and the tin roof. I won't say you couldn't hear yourself talk, but one did have to shout. The voice of a full-grown wild lion, letting it go all out and brazenly, is something to hear from close by. It makes the roarings which resound in a zoo sound puny and as if made by kittens.

The first time this happened after our return from the hospital, both Iz and I rushed to the bedroom. We were scared that the tremendous sound, booming into the dark room, would not only waken the baby but frighten her. It awakened her all right, but there she lay with her feet in the air, cooing and gurgling and sort of trying to point in the direction from which the sound was coming. Later, when she could form something approaching words, she would lie and listen and say, "Henoo, Henoo." Which became the lion's name. The great voice carried no fear to the child. She thought it was fine entertainment, just as she considered Paddy the most natural playmate a baby could have.

Other youngsters were brought in by the natives. We acquired a very ugly black baby ground hornbill. When full grown, these birds are as large as an American turkey and have a great curved bill. On the veld they live on snakes, mice, insects, and seeds and fruit. A ground hornbill will eat anything. So we named ours Garbage.

At first we fed Garbage on balls of soft cooked meal. It wasn't necessary to put these on a plate. We just tossed them to him and he caught them neatly and swallowed them whole and croaked for more.

As Garbage grew, a great friendship developed between him and Jane Emmeline John. This was beauty and the beast with a vengeance. Everywhere the tall, beautiful bird with the gold topknot went, Garbage waddled along behind. They were inseparable. Jane mothered him and would stand over the ugly bird and pick around his head gently and sort of groom him and get bugs off him.

Garbage developed a bad habit of roosting on our seed plats, which we had supported on pole frames in the shelter of a grass hut. He was so heavy that he tramped down or broke off the tiny growing plants. So I had to shoo him away constantly. I used to keep a light switch in the shed house, and whenever I caught Garbage roosting there, I would beat him lightly. He would squawk and grunt and flap his way out. Immediately Jane would come dashing up, wings outspread and uttering raucous cries. She would beat my bare legs with her elbows and talk to Garbage and lead him away; then, when the black bird squatted down, she would hover over him and pick him and comfort him.

Jane could, but seldom did, come into the house. Garbage was forbidden. He was too dirty. So he would often stand outside the veranda door and beg to be allowed in. Mr. Thomas used to take great delight in standing inside and calling Garbage all sorts of names and refusing him admittance.

As our second dry season began to draw to a close, the game came in closer to the house, seeking the water in the river. The lions became more numerous, and seldom a week passed that we were not visited by from three to a dozen or more wild lions. The great *saka* at the back end of Ibamba was the lions' favorite retreat. Although I didn't get out there very often—it was a mile and a half to two miles from the house—we heard lions roaring nightly as they came out of the dense growth, where they had been sleeping in the shade, and looked and sniffed the situation over preparatory to their nightly hunt.

One night two males met outside the house around the back, not far from the kitchen, under one of the wide-spreading wild fig trees. They fought about something, probably a female. The sound was terrifying and terrific. Worse, it woke up the baby. Paddy listened with intense interest from in front of the living-room fire. But she didn't even bother to get up; just raised her head and pricked her ears. I went to the kitchen and into the storeroom at the end of the long building. The roars and growls and fighting had subsided. There was a bit of a moon, and I decided to step outside and see what I could of the happenings. Very gently and slowly I eased the knob and opened the door. There was quite a step down. To my right, as I stepped out and down, there was a good-sized thick bush. Just as I swung out and touched the ground, a huge lion rose up from under it. He stared at me for a second, and I at him. Then we both departed: I into the house in a hurry and he off across the grass. I am sure he was just as startled and scared as I was.

chapter nine

SO another dry season passed, and the masses of clouds again began to pile up to the west and lightning flickered from cloud to cloud and the gorgeous colors faded one into another, bringing the tall bottle palms into swaying black relief. The months during which Iz and I would be cut off from the rest of the district were fast approaching. We faced our isolation confidently, although the continuing business depression was very disquieting and we realized keenly the responsibility which had become ours with the arrival of Buncher, our daughter.

Because we had torn up and plowed lands the season before, we began our plowing this second year before the rains actually fell. It was hot, dusty work. The sandy soil got into the tracks of our small tractor and ruined the drive sprockets and bearings and rollers. Even had this not happened, we had discovered that a tractor, during those early years in Northern Rhodesia at least, could not compete with oxen. Gasoline and kerosene cost the equivalent of a dollar and a half a gallon, not counting the sums we had to lay out in deposits on steel drums and on transportation from the railway line. The costs of mechanical farming proved far too high to be continued, just as we slowly discovered, also, that it did not pay to grade upward the quality of our ranch cattle.

The major, almost the only, market for beef was represented by the thousands of natives employed at the copper mines to the north of us at N'dola, Luansha, Bwana Makuba, and Elizabethville. To supply the demand, cattle buyers traveled up and down the railway, buying at auction or by private arrangement. These men wanted quantity, not quality, for their money.

Although supplemental feeding and the introduction and use of quality bulls resulted in somewhat heavier cattle and animals with finer meat, the buyers did not, indeed could not, weigh the cattle bought. They estimated the weights and made their offers, keeping always in mind the inevitable shrinkage which would occur during and as a result of shipment. The buyers knew that a native would rather receive two pounds of fairly tough meat in his ration or for his money than one pound of beef which was tender and sweet. As a result, we ranchers who had begun or were contemplating improving our cattle abandoned the practice. Only a few, like Mopani Clarke, who could afford the long pull necessary to develop herds of quality cattle, continued the procedures.

It was during this second rainy season that the locusts first appeared. For months we had been reading warnings in the Livingstone *Mail* about locusts, and government agriculturists had been publishing directions of what countermeasures to take if and when the insects arrived. But until that year the locusts had confined their activities to other parts of Africa, Kenya, Ethiopia, Tanganyika, etc. Since white men had been in Northern Rhodesia there had not been a serious invasion. So although we read the stories about the locusts and clucked sympathetically over the reports of damage which the hordes of insects inflicted, we were not prepared for what happened.

Like most everyone, I had read stories in the Bible concerning plagues of locusts. At various times I had seen reports in the newspapers of locusts which devastated grain-producing countries. These countries had always seemed far away and were inhabited by people whom I knew little or nothing about. In my mind I pictured a swarm of locusts as merely a large crowd of grasshoppers.

I knew from my reading that the swarms were voracious in the extreme, but the actual damage which they could do, the actual size of the swarms, was something no one who has not experienced locusts can picture beforehand.

It was Charlie Portuguese who first saw the locusts. He was on the lawn, and I went out to see what it was at which he was pointing. At the horizon I could see a great dark mass of what looked like smoke lying far down over the flats. The rains had soaked everything, and I knew that the dark mass, moving and boiling miles away, could not be smoke from a grass fire. Gradually it increased in size, rolling up and up above the line of demarcation between the vast stretch of grass and the cloudy sky. From where we stood watching in awful silence, the mass looked like a gigantic thunderhead.

Other natives had joined us, and I heard worried murmurs of "*chiquiqui,*" locusts. I just couldn't believe that that enormous mass was composed of flying insects. Then, slowly at first, it began to move and to sweep toward the range of low mountains to the east of the flats. The mass flattened somewhat to form a long wavering cloud which steadily pushed toward us, following the mountains and the edge of the flats.

Within an hour, as we watched, the mass began to pass between us and the mountains across the river. It blotted the hills from sight and seemed to be miles in length. How deep and how high it was could only be guessed. I estimated that the mass was some half-mile high. It must have been miles in thickness, or width, horizontally, to give such an impression of denseness.

That first swarm did not come onto Ibamba. But it was not many weeks before a swarm did come.

Can you imagine a swarm of grasshoppers so dense, so large, that if they flew over Manhattan Island, the entire city would be cast into shadow and darkness?

Can you picture in your mind a cloud of flying insects sixty miles long by fifteen miles in breadth and five hundred feet in depth? No one can. The number of locusts required to make up such a swarm is beyond human counting or imagination.

We saw just such swarms. Their shadows darkened Ibamba. They appeared over the far horizon like great palls of smoke, coming swiftly up the wide flats which stretched before the house. Huge reddish clouds, moving, rising, falling, coming into and passing swiftly from view. Incredible, terrifying clouds comprised of ravenous flying insects.

Chiquiqui! Chiquiqui!

Sight of that first swarm of locusts sent chills of fear racing up the backbones of Isabella and myself. It appeared so enormous, although, as we came to know later, it was actually a small swarm of a sort of exploratory nature. Fast moving, swelling in size and then constricting, it was palpable and yet impalpable. At one moment, staring in horrified fascination, we thought that we could see through the myriads upon myriads of fluttering insects, only to have the seeming transparency darken and close as millions of the flying locusts pressed forward upon the leaders.

Deeply worried and frightened by what we had seen, Iz and I conferred at length with Charlie Portuguese, who had seen locusts before in other parts of Africa, and with Mangineera and Jam and Charlie Matabele. I fetched the copy of the paper in which were printed the instructions from the Department of Agriculture. We read these through carefully two and three times.

Noise and smoke and movement were recommended to try and keep the locusts out of the fields and to frighten them away if they had landed. Farmers were advised to have piles of wood ready in the fields to light so that fires could burn all through the grain lands and be smothered with green material to throw off clouds of smoke. The government advised that anything which would burn and make smoke, old tires, tar, wet hay, old rags soaked in kerosene, used crankcase oil, anything and everything, be collected and be piled in and around cultivated lands and that bottles of kerosene and bundles of kindling be kept handy so that the piles could be fired quickly.

There was more, but this involved the use of poison baits and we had no poison, and now that the road to the railway was soggy with rain, no way by which to bring out hundreds of pounds of arsenic.

As there were still two hours of daylight left and I was gravely worried, I got the truck, and collecting a gang of natives, drove out into the bush and had them load up with all the dead dry wood they could find. Leaving the men to collect further quantities, I drove back to the cornfield nearest the house, where Charlie Portuguese had another crew waiting and had them unload the wood and begin to pile it in heaps throughout the field. It was a sixty-acre field, but by dark we had managed to set up a series of woodpiles all around the edges. Through the field, from corner to corner, we ran lines of other piles to help protect the center. With the first light on the morrow I ordered Charlie Matabele to take oxen and haul in all the wood he could and for another gang to pile up wood in the bush where I could collect it with the truck. Jam, Mangineera, and others were put in charge of arranging the piles, filling bottles with kerosene, daubing the piles, after they were built, with some of the tar which we had for our roofing jobs, and making sure that everyone in the compound, old and young, men and women and children, knew they would be expected to dash into a field immediately a swarm attacked. They were to run up and down the rows of grain, shouting, yelling, beating on tom-toms or tin cans and waving their arms to prevent the locusts from settling.

Neither Iz nor I comprehended what an attack by locusts could mean. Despite the anxious looks and the gravely spoken warnings of our devoted boys, we felt that, having followed the government's recommendations as fully as we could, we would be reasonably safe.

How little we knew! How inexperienced we were!

For the next two days we did not see any locusts. Travelers, natives passing through, told us of damage to the north and to the east and the west, but they were grinning and shrugging their shoulders, and we failed to heed the warnings or to take into account the fatalism of the people.

At the constant urging of Charlie Portuguese we continued, however, to haul in wood to protect the several fields, to cut wet green grass and make other preparations. At night the compound, in contrast to the usual pervading gaiety and chatter, huddled dark and silent under cover of the darkness. The immense land, stretching for hundreds of miles all about, brooded as a miasma of fear and anxiety swept through the villages. The days were clouded and sunless; the air was hot and humid, and no breezes blew. It was as if the entire Mashakulumbwe district lay waiting for the thrust of some deadly blow.

All tried to continue with the tasks assigned, but every eye was turned toward the sky. We had put a lot of effort into preparing our fields. The depression, which had begun in America and was deepening there, had spread to Africa and crept into Rhodesia. Faced with a seriously diminishing income, Iz and I had decided to try and hurry things along agriculturally, and try to raise enough grain over and above the needs of our natives to sell sufficient to carry us through the coming year.

As I walked through the fields in which the grain plants were standing six to eight inches high and beginning to tint the formerly bare soil a lovely shade of verdant green, I thought of how disastrous it could be if the locusts really came in hordes and literally ate us up. Staring about me, it seemed incredible that insects, even so large as locusts, could completely devastate the broad wide lands. My ignorance comforted me, and in the evening I tried to pass my confidence along to Isabella.

Chiquiqui! Chiquiqui!

The shrill, nasal cry was raised by a native woman. At the words Iz and I hastily pushed our chairs from the luncheon table, for the alarm had come during the time of the midday rest period. Sixpence dashed from the kitchen, and grasping an iron bar, hammered on the length of rail dangling from a mulberry tree. *Chiquiqui, Chiquiqui.* No one but I could hear the cook shouting, for the ringing booming noise rolled over the fields, drowning the sound of voices.

Dashing from the house, Iz and I gazed about. There they were, pouring over the trees. Clouds upon clouds, rank upon rank, insects innumerable. Natives rushed from the compound—men, women, children, even women with babies on their backs. Out they came on the run, and disappeared into the cornfields. This was war.

Charlie Portuguese, Mangineera, Jam, and others came running for the bottles of kerosene and the boxes of matches and bundles of dry grass we had made ready. Grasping their bottles, they ran swiftly from one pile of wood to another, thrusting dry grass beneath, soaking it with kerosene and coal tar, and touching the whole off with a match.

We had placed the piles of wood every thirty yards around the grainfields. Smoke billowed from them in heavy white-brown clouds and rolled over the grain. Tom-toms throbbed. The shrieks and yells of women and children sounded from amid the serried ranks of growing corn. Tin cans were beaten.

We battled with frenzied noise and smoke and heat. Yells and the deep, throbbing boom of the drums swelled to a fearful din. I added the roar of the motor to the sounds as I started the truck to bring wood and grass to keep up the smoking fires. Running, dancing, leaping figures, fantastic in the palls of smoke, dashed up and down the fields. A droning, rustling sound filled the air as the millions of locusts fluttered over and about us. Battle. War. Our food supply was threatened. More wood, more grass, more smoke. Hours and hours of carrying, stoking; hours of shouting and yelling. Lungs and throats grew raw with the clamor and the acrid smoke of tar and wet grass. The tom-toms throbbed and leaped. The locusts were upon us.

Teatime came and passed unnoticed. The shouters were lagging. Half of them had not eaten. The hastily abandoned pots in the compound smelled of burned food as I drove past to fetch loads of grass. I ran into the fields to give encouragement. The fearful racket rose again in volume. Isabella, her face black with grime, had the women join hands and run in lines up and down the rows. Swarms of locusts flew from the ground. The grain rustled and snapped as the insects leaped from the leaves. I lost sight of the women in the cloud of insects. And still locusts were pouring in upon us from the veld. A seemingly unending river of flying insects was descending upon us over a width of three miles. The sky was darkened. The rustle of wings and the faint droning filled the air with a continuous hum. Over this rolled the steady booming of the drums and the roar of the motor fighting through the damp plowed soil from fire to fire.

The house had vanished. A brownish-red swirling cloud of insects indicated where it stood. But of the iron roof, white window frames, or solid stone walls, not a sign could I see.

A white figure dashed from the cloud enveloping and clinging to the house. It was Isabella. I saw her waving her arms and running about, and then she vanished.

Wood, wood. Grass. Kerosene. More tar. Up and down the lines of fire we went, coughing and yelling. Smoke choked us. Our eyes streamed with tears. And still that ominous droning filled our ears. Was there never to be an end to this river of insects? They filled the air. The ground was smothered with them. Every fence post, palm tree, every blade of grass, the truck, even the huts of the natives were covered with quivering, feeding insects. Locusts. Locusts everywhere. Fighting them was like fighting the flakes of a snowstorm. They were there and not there. We chased them from one patch only to see them settle in another. Behind, still more arrived to take their places. As they fed, they dropped behind them little balls of chewed-up grass. The ground was dotted with these. They dropped them as they flew, and my hat was covered. I even found some in my pockets and the cuffs of my shorts.

Then, with the setting of the sun, sullen and myopic, behind heavy clouds, the river of oncoming locusts thinned. But although the newcomers ceased to pour in upon us in such numbers, the almost incredible number of locusts hovering over the grain appeared to increase. I exhorted the weary workers to further efforts. For I thought the locusts were leaving.

Did I say leaving? That was what we thought that evening as they rose in swarm upon swarm and flew to the bushveld surrounding the fields. As twilight stole over the smoking fields, the last fluttering insect left.

With Iz and the *capitao* I walked over the scene of battle. The fields were trampled and torn with footprints. Much growing grain lay flat, mashed by rushing feet or the whirling wheels of the truck. A heavy, sodden smell of rank smoke, newly turned earth, snapped green grain and gasoline fumes hung in the evening air. In the sixty-acre field adjoining the house there still remained much grain, despite the naked chewed stalks which rose forlornly in the rows.

Encouraged, for we had thought to find the damage even greater, we took the path leading to another field, which we had wrested and cleared only that year from the virgin veld. It was a forty-acre patch, half of which I had planted to corn. The remaining half I was reserving for potatoes and onions.

We had progressed only a few yards along the road which had been cut through the bushveld when we stopped with gasps of astonishment and horror. Before our startled gaze opened a scene worthy of prehistoric times. Insects by the hundreds of thousands had settled everywhere to pass the night. Every tall blade of grass bent under the weight of clinging locusts. The road was a crunching carpet. Each step stirred up myriad fluttering insects. In the fast-vanishing sunset glow, the wings, quivering as the locusts vibrated them, imparted a shimmering sheen to the veld. The trunks of the trees were so thickly covered with clinging locusts that they became pillars of shivering insects. The branches, the stones, fallen logs, stumps, and bushes were covered so no vestige of their original shape or color could be detected. From the uncounted beating wings rose a rustling which flowed over the usually silent bush with an ominous persistence.

As we walked along, batting the swarming locusts from our faces and clothes, our hearts sank lower and lower. What chance had we against such incalculable numbers? It was no surprise to come out on the inner field and find it bare and barren, as if newly plowed. Not the tiniest stalk of corn remained. Nothing green could be seen except a few rank-smelling weeds which had escaped the cultivator. Along many of the rows we found round holes. Here the locusts in their voracity had dug under the ground to secure the last possible bit of stalk.

There were also many, many other round holes, the significance of which we did not then understand. Later we found that these were egg deposits, but this first evening we were spared that knowledge.

It was a weary, discouraged couple who sat down to dinner that evening. Our hopes for meeting the farm machinery and fertilizer bills we had incurred were bound up in our securing good yields of grain. Because of the depression our income was vanishing and our holdings depreciating. Grave worry had been weighing down our spirits for many months. And now locusts.

We had lost twenty acres out of the hundred and thirty we had planted to mealies and peanuts. But there was still time to replant, and if we kept up the fires and smoke, we should be able to save at least a hundred acres of grain. At six bags to the acre, this would mean money enough, plus the dribble from the States, to carry on in a small way. We went to bed more hopeful and more determined.

I turned out at daylight. There was not a locust to be seen. The dew lay heavy on the grass. Swishing about, I got the truck started and went off to fetch wood and grass, so that the smoke piles should be ready. Fortunately, the tops of the trees which we had cut for wood for the brick kilns lay about the veld and it was easy to collect them.

It was well I turned out early. The locusts were still with us. I had failed, when I first left the house, to distinguish the motionless forms from the bark and the stones to which they clung. As the sun rose and warmed and dried the veld, the wings of the locusts dried, also, and fluttering up from the grass, the trees, the stones and logs and paths and bushes, they descended upon the grain.

Again the shrieking women and children ran along the grain. Smoke billowed forth. The drums throbbed and the motor roared. Hour after hour, all morning, all afternoon. Not a moment's rest. Wood, wood, more wood, and still more wood. Water to relieve parched throats. Grass to smolder and tar to stink. On and on we fought.

On the far edges of the ranch, three and four miles away, locusts which had not reached the fields the day before rose in their millions and flew upon us. The fields became an indescribable scene of battle and confusion, exhaustion, and exhortation. We were fighting for our food, our very means of living. On and on and on, dashing amidst clouds of insects as thick as drops of rain in a storm.

The house was invaded. Grass which we had placed on the iron roof to alleviate the heat was eaten. The flowers vanished as before a giant mower. Zinnias, petunias, gaillardias, nasturtiums, asters went down before the onslaught. The ragged lawn was a creeping, crawling carpet of feeding locusts.

The vegetable garden was threatened. Isabella carried great bundles of grass, toiled and worked and encouraged women and the garden boy to heroic efforts. But she could not be with them every moment. The baby had to be fed and bathed and cared for. As soon as she left, tired bodies relaxed and the locusts got amongst the peas and beans.

Food was forgotten. Everyone on the ranch was pressed into service: Sixpence, the cook, Lavison and Lubin, drivers, herders, hunters, carvers, visitors, women, and children. We worked and yelled and ran until so weak from hunger that we just had to eat. I divided our people into groups. While some ate, the others worked. But the locusts gained on us. We were losing the battle.

Counting the tiny tots beating tin cans, there were some hundred souls on our side. Against us were arrayed uncountable millions. To run over, to smoke, to protect more than a hundred acres was impossible. Human bodies just could not be forced beyond certain limits.

We were bone weary that evening as we straggled from the fields and left the locusts departing to sleep in the bush. But it was nothing to the utter exhaustion we experienced in ensuing days.

Our first battle with the locusts lasted for twelve consecutive days. Morning after morning we dragged our weary bodies forth, hoping against hope that this would be the last day of battle. Hour after hour we fought a losing fight. At night our sleep was troubled and restless. Visions of flying insects would not leave our minds. Our aching bones cried out for rest, but we could not sleep. Our grain, our food, all our work to build a home was being eaten away before our eyes. Where would we find money to pay for seed, for wages, for fertilizer and machinery? Where would we find food if this kept up?

Firewood became more and more difficult to find. Supplies of dry grass became exhausted. We dug up old piles of bedding, tore down unused huts and a half-completed pole cattle kraal. The poles had been cut at great labor and not a little expense, and brought a considerable distance. No matter. The grain must be saved. Into the smoking fires they went. I pulled down a shed built to cover delicate seedlings of sandalwood, rosewood, and bamboo. The grass roof kept us going about an hour. The poles somewhat longer. The dip shed went next, and then the dip kraals. Nothing was safe from our frantic search for wood and grass.

At the end of our twelve-day battle we viewed the wreckage. In no other words could one describe Ibamba. Gone were the trim straight lines of fencing. The neatly thatched seed houses, the shed over the long dipping tank, were things of memory only. Jagged holes where posts once had stood, litters of broken grass and bits of bark and tangled lengths of barbed wire were all that remained. Ringed about and scattered through the once green and serried fields of grain lay evil-smelling smoking heaps of ashes. Deep ruts crossed and recrossed the lands. Here and there lay a neglected pole, a wisp of grass. A few stalks of corn, miraculously surviving the onslaught of the locusts and the destruction of many running feet, stood up brave and alone. But our hundred and thirty acres of corn and peanuts were gone. Chewed stubble, ragged bits of leaves, and a carpet of little chewed pellets was all there was to remind us of what had once seemed such promising lands of growing crops.

Wearied and discouraged as we were, Charlie Matabele and his drivers yoked the oxen and commenced clearing up the fields and replanting. But nearly every day swarms of locust passed to remind us of how futile our efforts could be in the face of such tremendous numbers of insects.

For nearly a month no big swarms descended upon us. Our new grain germinated and grew. Some of the old plants revived and sent up new growth. Yet always over the enormous flats of the Kafue River gigantic swarms of locusts wheeled and settled or, rising in the morning, passed in a swiftly moving reddish cloud beyond the horizon.

During these feverish despair-filled days Christmas came and passed almost unnoticed. We had very little spare money with which to buy presents and lacked the enthusiasm to pore through catalogues in a search for gifts which we could afford. Iz did manage to order two or three small simple toys for Buncher, but that was it. We had a tree and we trimmed it with homemade decorations as before, and with such of the boughten ornaments as we had saved. Bravely Iz concocted a deep-dish pumpkin pie—pumpkins were one of the few vegetables the locusts did not eat—and she had a custard for Mr. Thomas.

Jam hunted long hours day after day. I had removed the restrictions I had imposed upon shooting on Ibamba because we had to have meat, no matter what the costs. Our storeroom was still piled with bags and bags of grain, but it was so painfully obvious that no one could look forward to a crop with the ending of the rains that we cut the daily ration from two and a half pounds of whole grain to two pounds and tried to make up the difference with meat or fish.

Two days before Christmas Jam shot a kudu bull in the great *saka,* and the next day we slaughtered an ox. But there was no beer, and the only Christmas "bockes" we could give out were handfuls of salt. In contrast with the wonderful Christmas of the year before, there was little dancing and singing. The older men and women, those who had passed through the periods of drought and adversity which are all too common in the life of natives, walked with solemn, anxious faces and downcast eyes. Only the children, who could not comprehend the magnitude of the disaster which loomed over all our heads, and who derived excitement and fun from the noise and running, the smoke and the tension, which pervaded and blanketed the cultivated lands, were happy and cheerful.

Mr. Thomas caught and ate the locusts which got into the house. This was not because he was trying to be helpful. He just liked to eat locusts, and out on the veld the omnivorous mammals and the insect-eating birds waxed fat. But their efforts were as nothing compared with the incredible swarms which descended upon the land.

The little antelope, Fwifwi and the duikers and the lechwe and

Popeye, were disconcerted and upset by the numbers of locusts which flew up into their faces as they tried to browse on the badly eaten grass. To Paddy, of course, the locusts meant little. When outside the house she tried to play with them, rushing about and flapping her great forepaws in the air in efforts to bat down the zooming insects as they rose from the ground before her rushes. She killed a few, but her endeavors were as futile as our own. Her efforts, of course, were play in contrast to ours, which were such a deadly serious business. Paddy had a kudu thigh bone for Christmas.

Still swarms darkened the sky and cast enormous shadows over the land. From the railway a hundred miles away reports dribbled in, carried by wandering natives. Choma was infested. So-and-so at Pemba had given up, and pulling his plows, had discharged all his employees. The government sent out notices on how to combat the locusts and warnings of the coming hoppers. The poison offered us for use was too expensive for most. The value of our hoped-for grain would not support the purchase of spray pumps and chemical smudges.

With grim smiles we read advice to plant sweet potatoes, manioc, cowpeas, and peanuts. Locusts, we were informed, would not eat these crops. They ate *our* peanut bushes. And where were we to find cuttings and seed at such a late date? And what would we use as a substitute for money?

The plows were kept going. Long, even furrows rolled over, to be harrowed and planted. Tiny green shoots poked their heads above ground. Carefully and faithfully we cultivated and hoed.

For a time affairs took on a brighter hue. The trees put forth new leaf. We still had vegetables, for we guarded and fought for these with determination, and my indomitable wife had planted more flowers.

Then one day one of the plowboys, working up the lands we had reserved for potatoes, came to me carrying in his hand a curious little sausage-shaped thing. It was a cluster of tiny sacklike envelopes, the whole an inch-and-a-half long. With a sickening sensation I realized that this dried-up brownish thing was a cluster of locust's eggs. The potato field was a mass of them, my native told me. The newly turned furrows were dotted with hundreds and hundreds of the small brown sausages.

I hurried over to see for myself. Not only were the unused potato and onion lands packed with eggs, but the twenty acres of newly sprouting corn as well.

Calling Jam and Mangineera, Shamakembie and Charlie Portuguese, I sent them off to go over the thirteen square miles which comprised Ibamba and bring me reports of what they found.

Large parts of Ibamba had flooded or had become marshy during the rains. Locusts will not lay their eggs in wet ground. From the reports brought to me that evening, there was no doubt, however, that the entire dry, sandy part of the ranch, which was an island in the water-logged land, had been used as a laying ground. We were face to face with the fact that within a short period we should have to defend ourselves against millions of hoppers, or young locusts which cannot fly.

Reorganization became a necessity. The tales we heard of the voracity of hoppers caused our experience with the adult locusts to pale into insignificance. When the eggs hatched, so we were told, the young locusts were very tiny. But in a week they were the size of small big-headed grasshoppers. In two weeks they were an inch and a half long. In three they were fat and heavy. This growth came at the expense of all the green food obtainable. Once they reached a certain size, the hoppers started moving in veritable rivers across the country, eating everything and moving continuously in the search for food and still more food.

We read tales in the paper of trains which were delayed because the rails were covered with hoppers. The wheels of the locomotives could not grip the rails because of the mashed bodies of the immature locusts. Natives came from other districts with fearful stories of whole areas absolutely denuded of growing things by the passage of swarms of hoppers.

There was only one thing to do. The oxen were taken from the fields and started plowing furrows around the borders. Behind came all the available workmen with shovels and picks. It was back-breaking work and frightfully discouraging, for as we worked, heavy torrential rains descended on us and filled up our trenches and washed away the carefully cut banks. Persevering, sweating, cursing, we eventually dug two lines of trenches ten yards apart around all the lands. These trenches were two and a half feet deep, with perpendicular sides. The excavated earth was thrown up in a loose pile on the sides nearest the fields.

This was the only defense possible. The hoppers, as they came across country, would reach the trenches. Into these they would fall, and we could trample them, burn them, drown them, and smother them with earth.

Poison, to be mixed with water and sprayed over the hoppers and the growth upon which they were feeding, was being distributed by the government. One had to pay cash, of which we had none. We had already spent far more money than the value of what grain we might reap could ever total. Also we had many cattle, goats, and pigs. They would eat the poisoned herbage and die as well as the hoppers.

Trenches, fire, and work were our only weapons. The eggs did not hatch as quickly as we had been told that they would. So we plowed the potato lands to a depth of four inches and turned up thousands of egg clusters, which dried and died under the fierce sun. We quartered the fields and dug trenches to separate one patch from another. All told we dug more than four miles of hopper trenches.

While doing this, we managed somehow to find the time to cut, disinfect, and plant sufficient seed potatoes for twenty acres. We pulled, trimmed, and transplanted from seed beds enough young onions to plant seven acres, and cultivated the corn and peanuts.

Where, as in the case of heavy disc plows and harrows, we required much power, we ganged the spans of oxen, using as many as twenty-six to pull a single implement.

The first hoppers appeared following a ten-day dry spell. At once we fired the grass. Veld grass grows six feet tall and is rank and coarse. With the wind behind, it made a roaring fire. Huge columns of smoke rose in the air and covered Ibamba with a heavy pall. Trees were badly scorched and grazing destroyed. Hot as was the fire, and widespread—we burned the entire island part of the ranch—it apparently had no effect whatever on the hoppers. The fires forced us to graze our cattle along and on the wet marshy lands. Many developed scours from the excessive moisture in the grass, and their hoofs and hocks became affected.

At first the hoppers appeared as tiny insects grouped in circular patches. These spread and joined others. The hoppers grew, as well as multiplied, until the entire ranch was a squirming mass. Winged and flying locusts appeared at the same time, coming from goodness knows where.

We fought as best we could. The battle was not so spectacular as the ones we waged earlier in the year. There was drum beating only when flying swarms descended, for the hoppers were not frightened by noise. We waged war silently and grimly, squashing every hopper that escaped our fires. Around and around the fields we went with oxen dragging a soil pulverizer and harrow and heavy logs. We beat with sticks, branches, shovels, and sacks. When the oncoming hungry hordes reached our trenches, we manned the ramparts and killed millions. But they filled the trenches and swarmed over. Worse still, they hatched out within the fields themselves.

We were too few, too tired, too poor and discouraged to fight successfully. We did the best we could. But it was hopeless. The hoppers ate our potatoes, cutting off the tops so that the tubers beneath failed to develop. Growing grain they ate to the ground. Peanuts dried because the top growth was gone.

We saved some vegetables, a flower or two, and the onions. These last, in fear of locusts, we had planted away from other crops on the rich banks of the river. The water was receding, but there would be sufficient moisture for many months.

To complete our downfall, late rains fell along the Congo-Rhodesia border and ran into the many affluents of the Kafue. Instead of continuing to recede, as it always had since records had been kept, the Kafue rose again and our onions were inundated and washed away.

Onions were scarce and growing scarcer. A grim situation was worsening as far as fresh foods were concerned throughout the entire territory. At the time when we should have harvested ours, onions sold for from eighteen to thirty cents a pound. Had it not been for the unusual floods, we would have had forty thousand pounds.

The crop damage by locusts was complete. Coming as it did when we were just starting in to develop Ibamba, we lost, as well as our crops, all the fertilizer, all the labor, all the planning, work, and hopes which had gone into those locust-ravaged lands. Compounded by our financial losses caused by the business depression which was now world-wide, it was a grievous blow below the belt.

From 100 acres of well-fertilized cultivated cornland we reaped 60 bushels of shelled corn. We should have reaped 2,300. Our 20 acres of potatoes gave 11 bags. We should have been busy sacking nearly 300. Our peanuts failed utterly. We pulled only enough nuts to fill 6 bags.

We read an account in the Bulawayo *Chronicle* of the locust threat to Southern Rhodesia and the damage occurring in other areas. It sounds incredible, but on one of the great sugar estates at Sena on the Zambezi, in Portuguese East Africa, the manager found that locusts had laid eggs throughout the cane fields. He gathered all the workers together, men, women, and children, and sent them into the lands to pick up all the egg clusters which they could find. It is, of course, impossible that all the eggs could have been found. Yet, from one estate, natives, picking by hand, uncovered and piled up *thirty tons* of locust eggs.

chapter ten

DESPITE all our problems, we had not lost sight of our original intention to start a research station for the study of wild animals on Ibamba. We had a vast quantity of scientific equipment still packed in the cases in which it had been shipped. To set this equipment up properly, however, I needed a great many accessories such as copper tubing and brass connections to pipe the gas for burners and the sterilizer, a sink in which to wash glassware; solid, rigid tables and benches on which to work; shelves for storage and many other things. The floor of the laboratory should, of course, have been made of concrete with a smooth surface which could be washed down regularly. There should have been windows which could be closed against rain or wind and these should have been screened to keep out bugs and dust and vagrant blowing leaves.

The sawboys had cut a number of fine thick mahogany and blood-wood planks to be fashioned into tabletops, and we had strong three-inch-square timbers to form legs. But unless these could be set in cement, the tables would not be rigid enough for proper scientific work.

Because of the depression we lacked the money with which to buy the extras needed. Indeed, instead of having money, we owed a considerable sum to the bank, which had allowed me a generous overdraft. The bills mainly were for farm equipment. I tried to negotiate with G. North and Company, the agricultural firm from which I had bought the plows, the soil pulverizer, the harrows, the cultivators, and the planter, offering to clean up the machinery carefully and repaint it and then return it to them. The implements had only been used for one season and were in fine condition.

Already, however, the locusts had created such havoc throughout the entire territory that North, although very friendly, could not consider my proposition. They wrote to me stating that they understood my position and realized that under the circumstances they could not expect payment for some time, but that they could not take back the machinery. Practically every farmer and rancher in both Northern and Southern Rhodesia was trying to negotiate the same sort of plan. North had already taken back as much as they could afford, and as conditions worsened, their stocks of used implements piled up without the faintest chance that they could be sold.

In a period of eight to ten months Northern Rhodesia had gone broke. Many settlers, discouraged and nearly penniless, pulled up stakes and returned to England or another country. Production at the copper mines dwindled as prices for the metal dropped and the demand lessened everywhere. As a result the native work force was cut drastically and we who were dependent upon the mines as a place to which to sell our grain and cattle watched our markets vanish.

Over the land from the South Atlantic washing the shores of Angola to the Indian Ocean on the east, from the Congo southward into Southern Rhodesia and the northern Transvaal, the locusts swept in their unbelievable swarms back and forth across the sky. They died by the millions, but before dying they laid, and the hoppers followed by the tens of millions. Starvation stalked the territories. The gardens of the natives, usually verdant with pumpkin, mealies, Kaffir corn, beans, and spiny cucumbers, lay pitiful and desolate and unproductive. Over wide areas the grass had been badly damaged and eaten off, so that flocks and herds found it difficult to graze enough to fill their bellies. Cattle wandered bellowing and moaning softly with the hunger inside them. The sheep and goats rose on their hind legs and even learned to climb a little in their efforts to reach the few green leaves on the bushes and the smaller trees. The herds of game migrated and shifted constantly in the search for food. Animals of many species sought refuge on the flats, where there was moisture and water and where grass grew; but the grass was harsh and tough and contained little nourishment.

Starvation stalked through the villages and grain prices rose to fearful heights. Some of the traders who had fat bank accounts considered buying up grain and storing what they could buy as a speculation, but the government was strongly against such practices. We negotiated a deal with Pete Cavadia and succeeded in purchasing enough grain to see us through for the next ten or twelve months if we were careful, and in this we were very lucky. As the dry season progressed and the swarms of locusts remained to darken the skies, we knew that the next planting season would be another time of battle and struggle, of noise and smoke and exhaustion. The more rugged and determined, or those who had no choice, spit on their hands, tightened their belts, and prepared to fight. Those who were wiser or financially able left the territory.

On Ibamba we dug in for the siege. As Pete delivered the grain, I poured tons of it into our 500-gallon water tank and sealed this for safe keeping. The remainder, in 204-pound bags, we piled carefully in the storeroom, where we kept a constant number of mouse and rat traps baited and set. Every morning each trap held an animal, but even so we could not keep pace with the rodents. Weevils, too, got into the grain and did a lot of damage.

Paddy was developing into a splendid young lioness. As she neared her first birthday, she weighed a little more than a hundred pounds; her head was heavy and broad, and her canine teeth, long and strong. She and I engaged in terrific wrestling matches each evening on the floor of the living room. From the uproar one might have thought that I was being torn to pieces, but it was seldom that I was even so much as scratched.

Buncher and Paddy were inseparable friends. The lioness had adopted our daughter. To such an extent that we had to be just a wee bit careful as to how we chastised our little darling. When Buncher cried, Paddy reacted instantly. If the lioness thought that Buncher's crying was because of something we had done, her ears were drawn back flat against her wide skull, her eyes glared, the black lips curled away from the shining teeth, and Paddy snarled a warning to us to be gentle. Whether Paddy might have attacked either one of us if she thought Buncher was being injured, we could only guess. Her fierce motherly devotion to the child indicated that she would not hesitate.

Tommy, too, was growing. Older than Paddy, Tommy weighed close to thirty pounds and was as large as a spaniel dog. His low-slung body was nearly three feet in length, and with his long bushy tail he was six feet over all. When he and Paddy climbed into and onto the bed, there was not much room for Isabella and me. When we had Buncher with us, the situation was really crowded.

Buncher was beginning to try to toddle. Not yet a year, her legs were not strong enough to hold her up for long, but she found that by clutching Paddy's ear, she could hold herself upright. Paddy positively radiated pleasure and contentment whenever Buncher crawled over her, pulled back her lips to see her teeth, and hauled on her ears or her huge, furry paws. Neither Iz nor I ever felt a qualm that Paddy would hurt our baby. She was more devoted, more intelligent, and more careful of her adopted child than the finest dog could have been.

It was fascinating to watch the parallel development of the lioness and the child. Paddy, of course, developed both physically and mentally at a much faster degree. Nevertheless, Paddy learned to adapt herself to her environment in exactly the same manner as did the human child. She, as did Buncher, learned by experience, by trying and testing, tasting and touching and listening and watching. So far as we could tell, Paddy also developed emotionally much as did Buncher. Both experienced jealousy. Both were frightened at times and felt scared. The young lioness, left alone, became lonely, just as our daughter, and cried for or sought companionship. Paddy knew anger, and she could be stubborn as a mule when certain moods were on her. At other times she was gay and full of tricks, wanting to play hide-and-seek, to wrestle, or to go for a walk. That Paddy fully experienced that emotion which we call love both Isabella and I were fully convinced. She showed this in her need to be with us, in her care for us, and in the manner she approached and looked at us. So far as our lioness was concerned, her entire world revolved around and centered upon Isabella, Buncher, and myself. Just as Mr. Thomas's world centered on Isabella and, in part, on me.

Love, affection, devotion—whatever term you prefer to describe the emotion which governed the relationship which existed between Paddy and Mr. Thomas and Isabella and me—had very little, if any, basis in sexuality. Although, as I have stated elsewhere, male animals appear to attach themselves more devotedly to female humans than to males and female animals attach themselves most often to male humans, I have never noticed the faintest indication that this attachment is in any way dependent upon or influenced by sex. In the wild, although zebras and wildebeest constantly graze and herd together, I have never seen a zebra stallion attempt to mount a wildebeest cow nor a wildebeest bull show interest in a zebra mare —even during the breeding season, when the females were in heat. Although, of course, if a zebra stallion did succeed in covering a wildebeest cow, the mating would not be fruitful of a calf or foal.

Between the duiker antelope and ourselves there was no such feeling as existed between us and Fwifwi, Paddy and Thomas. The duikers were just placid unafraid little creatures who did not mind being handled by us. Such handling had become natural to them, and our home was their normal, natural habitat because they had never consciously known another. Popeye was more demonstratively affectionate than the duikers—she nuzzled us enthusiastically at every opportunity—but she was not devoted or loving in the way or the sense that Paddy and Tommy loved and were devoted. When we had to leave either Paddy or Mr. Thomas alone, each pined and was miserable and lonely. Popeye did not even miss us.

Garbage stayed with us because there was always food; he was not disturbed and he felt safe. He came when called, but that was mainly if not exclusively because he had learned that when we called him, it meant that we had food. Garbage's motivating organ was his stomach not his heart.

I could never make up my mind as to just why Jane Emmeline John stayed with us. True, we fed her. But she secured most of her food, which consisted of insects, small frogs, lizards, and grubs, for herself. She apparently enjoyed walking beside us when we strolled about the lawn or walked to the vegetable garden, and while doing so, chattered to us. Or so it seemed. Jane always came eagerly to greet us in the morning, but we provided nothing special for her in the way of shelter or protection. Although wild crested cranes often flew calling over Ibamba and Jane both heard and watched them, she showed no inclination to join them. Having been raised from a fledgling with and by humans, Jane just preferred human company to that of her own kind. This, I am sure, was caused more by environmental factors than by any feeling of affection for the humans by whom she was surrounded.

We had stored the scientific equipment in the north end of the long thatched-roofed laboratory building. It seemed a shame, after all the work we had put into the brickmaking, construction, and thatching, not to make more use of the structure.

Iz wanted to have her precious Leghorns closer to the house, where she could keep an eye on them and on the dozens and dozens of young guineas we had raised. We decided to make a part of the northern half of the long building into an inside henhouse with a large wired run outside. With brick left over from construction I built a wall inside about thirty-five feet from the storage end, which I ran up twelve feet, leaving space in which to set a door. Adjoining the wall, so that the door opened into it, we constructed a wire enclosure with chicken wire across the top so that the hens could not fly up and over the wall. In this enclosure I built nesting boxes and roosts and we covered the floor with chaff for bedding. We knocked a hole through the outer wall and inserted a door about four feet high. This led out into the outdoor run, which was also covered across the top with wire to discourage the hawks and eagles which continually swooped and hovered over Ibamba. Some of the handsome black, red, and white Bateleur eagles were powerful enough to pick up a full-grown hen and carry it away.

In the center of the laboratory building I began to set up a sort of office and workroom. I needed a quiet place in which to study and do my writing and work up my notes, and if I had a place to put them, I wanted to use certain of the simpler pieces of apparatus.

At the opposite end from the wall separating this space from the chicken house I built another wall, also only twelve feet high, with a door. The fact that neither of the inside walls ran up to the peak of the roof permitted the air to circulate, and the building always remained cool and comfortable.

In the thirty-foot-long office room we set up a long, heavy bench against the wall facing the house, which was some sixty yards distant. We put two windows in the wall about fifteen feet apart and above the bench, which gave me a fine light. I found enough screening to cover these windows and two casements which I had intended to use for some other purpose but had not gotten around to doing.

We set a square table toward the center of this room, and the carpenters constructed a crude sort of couch against the wall opposite the one separating me from the chickens. The floor we made of damp hard-packed clay, and we set several shelves up where they would be handy. With a single straight kitchen chair for me to sit on, the room was a nice place in which to work without interruptions.

Iz and I knew that at some future date we would have to move Paddy from the house to an enclosure. It was not that we were in the least bit fearful of her, because no animal could possibly have been more gentle, more obedient, and more devoted. But Paddy was growing—like the proverbial weed. Despite her very inauspicious start in life, Paddy gave every evidence of developing into an extremely large lioness. The bones in her wrists and legs were thick and strong and heavy. Her skull was broad and her eyes set wide apart, which, incidentally, I believe is one of the signs of a trustworthy lion.

It has been my experience, after raising and handling many lions, that one should beware the lion or lioness with a narrow skull in which the eyes are set relatively close together. Narrow-skulled lions occur more frequently among zoo-bred lions than in the wild, but there are a few, and they are generally mean and vicious. As if they always carried a chip on their shoulders and bore only contempt for the world in their hearts. In zoos, under even partially decent conditions, lions breed frequently and easily. All too frequently, actually, so that lion kittens are almost a drug on the market. Many of these zoo lions are inbred and are pretty poor specimens in comparison with the splendidly muscled, big-boned lions of the veld.

Paddy would have to be moved from the house because she would just be too big. By another dry season Paddy would weigh between 250 and 300 pounds. This would be too much for our furniture, not to mention the space which she took up on the bed. Already she was too large to bathe in the washtub which stood in the kitchen, although she persisted in trying to squeeze herself in, with the result that the kitchen floor was flooded with water.

We could have trained Paddy not to sit in chairs, lie on the bed, or bathe in the tub. She was extremely intelligent, anxious to do what we wanted, and amenable to instruction. There was another and more compelling reason why we would have to move her.

Quite evidently, Paddy was developing into what the natives called a black lion. She was not, of course, black. Had she been, we would indeed have had something extraordinary. I have never heard of a melanistic lion, nor, for that matter, of a melanistic tiger, although there have been, and are, white tigers. Mangineera and Charlie Portuguese frequently pointed out to Isabella and me that the long guard hairs growing through Paddy's fur were black. Lions with black guard hairs, the boys stated emphatically, were the most dangerous kind. They were the lions which turned man-eater, and whenever a chief or a witch doctor died and was reincarnated as a lion, that lion, or lioness, always had black guard hairs.

Jam, the Charlies, Lavison, and Mangineera were not at all afraid of Paddy. Sixpence, however, was beginning to get just a bit chary of our growing foster child, and when she stalked into the kitchen, raised her great head, and calmly took a dressed chicken off the table, he no longer walloped her with a dishclout or chased her out of his domain. Paddy knew Sixpence was afraid of her, and it just made her that much more arrogant.

When the compound boys met Paddy as she paced along a path or meandered to the garden, they gave her a wide berth. The lioness never chased a native, although I saw that several times she was tempted to do so because she loved to tease people. There was no harm in her yet, but fear of her tremendous strength and speed, her terrible claws and great teeth, was developing among our natives. I could not always be with Paddy—she came and went much as she pleased—so for her own protection it became evident we would have to put her in an enclosure. A panicky native, a visitor, perhaps, might throw a spear at her. Then anything might happen. A wounded lion can do fearsome damage.

So we planned to build an outdoor paddock for Paddy and to give her a room in the laboratory building next to my office space. This would give her a quiet place to which to retire when she felt so inclined, protection from the elements, and while I was working, we would be able to talk to each other over the wall. We were so reluctant to move Paddy that I put off construction of the paddock until near the end of the dry season.

When the plowed lands had dried out sufficiently, we cleaned up the debris from the many fires built to try and smoke away the locusts and set the plows so that the shares cut to a depth of only four inches. Four inches was the depth at which most of the locust eggs were laid, and by dragging the plows up and down the fields, we turned up thousands of egg sacks to wither and die in the fierce heat of the sun. We missed other thousands, and these hatched and developed into hoppers which crossed and recrossed Ibamba in uncountable hordes, devouring everything remotely edible.

It was obvious to both Isabella and me, as indeed it was to every other settler throughout the territory, that when the rains returned and the time for planting arrived, we would be faced again with the dreadful menace of the locusts. Discussing our situation, we decided that we would not quit. The temptation to do so was tremendous. There were still many unrealized assets remaining in my parents' estates—as those who lived through the depression years in the early and middle thirties will remember, it was virtually impossible to dispose of real estate or such things as an office building—and if we returned to the States, there was the possibility we might salvage some funds with which to make another start. On the other hand, we had invested so much money, time, and effort in Ibamba, it seemed cowardly and unwise to cut and run. Cowardly because, although at least theoretically we had sufficient assets to cover our indebtedness, our assets were in America, where they could not be touched by our creditors even if we went into bankruptcy. If we pulled out, they would be left hanging. Besides, I felt a strong moral obligation to those firms which had contributed so generously to help start a research station. It would not be right, just because the squeeze was on us, to pull up stakes and abandon the equipment. These, at least, were our oral arguments. Neither of us admitted that the honest fact was we had lost our hearts to Ibamba, and to the free, wild, untrammeled life; we hated the thought of returning to the strictures and compulsions of what our friends liked to call "the civilized life."

We reduced the number of our natives as far as we could and still have enough to work the ranch. After the devastation we had wrought in our battles with the locusts, there were many repair jobs to be done. The barbed-wire fences had to be restrung and new posts put in. The dip kraals and the shed over the tank had to be replaced, as did the covering over the seed beds. Above all, the vegetable garden had to be revitalized, and we started a gang clearing a large piece of ground on the riverbank where the soil was rich and black and to which water could easily be carried from the river.

Cavadia, along with the Prices at the mission and the Greek trader at Marla, had expressed interest in buying fresh vegetables from us each week if we had a surplus to sell. So we planted rather extensively and in considerable variety, and watched over the developing, sprouting garden with fierce determination. Periodically, sometimes two and three times a week, sometimes not for ten days, smoke billowed up from the riverbank in dense clouds and the pandemonium of tins being beaten, shouts, and yells rose in the air as the garden boys and all others strove to fight off hungry swarms of locusts which had spotted the luscious green of the growing vegetables.

In many areas of the world, when disaster strikes among the farmers of the region, it is possible to plant some quick-growing crop which can be sold for cash and thus help to alleviate whatever catastrophe might have occurred. Because there was no rain, because there would not be any rain for months, we could not plant cash crops on an extensive scale.

The vegetable garden was the best we could do. Each Friday, Iz went to the garden, and with the garden boys, pulled and cut such vegetables as were ready to eat. We had carrots, beets, and spring onions; wax, green, and lima beans; peas, lettuce, cabbage, tomatoes of several types and sizes and two colors; New Zealand spinach, squash, cucumbers, radishes, okra, and green peppers.

In the workshop I prepared a half-dozen light wooden kerosene cases with loose-fitting lids. Each of these Iz packed with whatever vegetables were available and sent them off to the mission and to Marla. She received half a crown, about forty cents, a box. It was cash, and as the good Lord knew, we needed cash.

To help out further, I killed and butchered a small pig, a sheep or a young ox each week, and we sent off chops, roasts, fillets, tongues, liver, kidneys and chunks of fat with the vegetables. We packed the meat in layers and layers of newspapers and ice cubes from the kerosene-burning refrigerator, so that the meat arrived in good condition. The meat brought in additional cash, so that in a month we earned between eight and ten pounds. It was a pitiful sum —the pound had depreciated to around $3.60—but it helped. The vegetables and the slaughtering also, of course, provided us with food, and whenever there was any surplus, we divided this among the boys as best we could.

Those of our boys who had wives started gardens of their own along the river, where they tried to grow mealies, pumpkins, and beans and melons. These were not too successful because of the locusts and the hippos. Whenever the native women needed help to defend their patches of grain or to fetch more firewood, we allowed the men to aid them. We also frequently went fishing in the lagoons because fish were food, and in spite of the grain I had stored, we needed every morsel of food we could produce or secure if we were to survive.

Throughout the remainder of the vast Mashakulumbwe district, as throughout all Northern Rhodesia, conditions worsened steadily as the dry season advanced. In an effort to destroy the locusts the natives fired the long grass, and terrific, roaring, racing fires swept across the country and the air grew acrid with smoke and dirty with flying ash.

I did not want Ibamba burned off, so Charlie Matabele yoked two spans, thirty-six oxen, before the heavy gang disc plow and tore up a wide strip of the flats between Ibamba and the mission along the boundary line as a fire guard. The tough grass roots and the heavy soil made the work slow and difficult, and the oxen used in the morning were so tired that we outspanned them and used another two spans for the afternoon stint of work.

The fireguard helped, but the breezes and the wind generated by the fires themselves wafted burning material across the plowed strips and across the river which formed the eastern boundary, and we had to fight many fires to protect our land. It was exhausting, dirty, and unnecessary work, and the hours of fire fighting did nothing to raise our spirits.

The green shoots of grass which sprang up on the flats behind the fires were eagerly sought by the thousands of cattle owned by the Mashakulumbwe. They got little of this because the locusts ate the grass as soon as it appeared. The normally fat cattle of the villagers wandered the country as shrunken, stumbling caricatures, and hundreds died. The people ate these cattle, just as they were eating everything remotely edible, but many died. Especially the old and the very young. The experienced villagers, those who looked into the future, allowed their hair to grow long and hid seed corn in their wool to be available when planting should once again be possible. Funerals were no longer celebrated with beer drinking and dancing. Sadness and worry lay over the once-beautiful land like a heavy blanket, and the natural gaiety of the people gave way to a morose acceptance of fate.

Sheasongo sent word that he required thirty bags of grain to help him feed his people. When the messenger arrived with the request, I huddled with Charlie Portuguese and Jam and Mangineera and Isabella and we debated whether to meet the need or not. By being very careful, we had enough grain stored to last us for about seven months, or until toward the end of the next rainy season when, if the locusts spared us at all, we might expect to reap some food from the fields.

I was disinclined to send the grain. Thirty bags, six thousand pounds, was a lot to spare. Sheasongo's village was a large one. Thirty bags would not feed his people for more than four to six weeks at the most. To us six thousand pounds represented a little more than three months of food.

It was the boys who decided the matter. Was not I, Sibyunni'byunni, the *mulangamu,* blood brother, of Sheasongo, and as his blood brother, was I not bound to honor his request? They were willing, the boys said, to tighten their belts still more and shorten their rations so that I, Sibyunni'byunni, their *n'kos* and their friend and benefactor, could meet his obligation.

These earnest, devoted men made me feel very humble and mighty proud. It was a revealing measure of their pride and confidence in me that they would risk their very food so that I, their *n'kos,* should not lose stature.

We sent the messenger back to Sheasongo loaded with sun-dried meat and fish and with word to send people to carry the grain to his village. There was no mention of payment, for *N'Kos* Sheasongo and *N'Kos* Sibyunni'byunni were brothers, and what belonged to me belonged to him and what was his was mine.

chapter eleven

SITUATED as we were, a hundred and twenty-five miles from the railway, at the end of a track across the veld which, as I have tried to make clear, could not by any stretch of the imagination be termed a road, it was seldom that Iz and I had visitors, but we did have one interesting visitor at this time, a middle-aged British woman I shall call Charlotte. She was touring Africa with her husband and his secretary, and the three were our guests for a short while. It developed that Charlotte was an exceptionally fine shot with a rifle. She was not the least interested in shooting game, which pleased me, but was willing to kill crocodiles. Charlotte had her own weapon and plenty of cartridges, so I had a blind constructed on the bank of the river close to the entrance to the lagoon which gave Ibamba its name and in which we did most of our fishing. I assigned Mangineera to stay with and help her—a task which at first annoyed him because he thought it beneath his dignity to act as gunbearer for any woman other than Maseccasecca—but he reported with some amazement Charlotte's ability to shoot.

The African crocodile is a fearsome and incredibly voracious creature. It has a certain degree of low cunning, but is generally timid; it is enormously powerful when in the water, through and beneath which it moves with great speed when the occasion demands.

Crocodiles killed three to four cattlebeasts a month from our herds on Ibamba. Generally the cattle were herded to graze on a large, nearly round portion of the flats which formed the eastern area of Ibamba. This portion of the ranch was surrounded on three sides by the Kafue River, but the cattle could not reach the river to drink because of the dense growths of papyrus and the steepness of the banks. The herd boys had strict orders to try and water the cattle at any one of the many shallow pans and lagoons which dotted the interior of this round plain. But the cattle often refused to drink where we wanted. The water in the pans became almost hot from the day-long scorching by the sun and was not palatable. As the herds were driven toward the kraals in the evening, they often broke away from the herdsmen and raced to drink at the large lagoon where we fished and which was connected by open, although very shallow, water with the main river. There was some flow back and forth into the lagoon and the water was cooler than that in the pans. It was also full of crocodiles.

Few of the monstrous antediluvian reptiles remained in the lagoon during the day. They came in through the shallow water late in the afternoon. Primarily they were seeking the fish which crowded the lagoon and which they hunted during the night, but they were not adverse to seizing any unwary antelope which might come to the lagoon's edge to drink, or one of our cattle. Or, for that matter, a human being so careless as to step unguarded to the water's edge.

Before fishing, the natives beat the surface of the lagoon with rods and kicked up the water and generally created a turmoil to drive away any crocs which might be lying below the surface. Fortunately, we never had a native taken during our years on Ibamba, but the crocodiles did catch many village women and children both below and above us on the river.

Generally, a crocodile waiting for an animal watches until the beast lowers its muzzle to drink. Floating just below the surface, with only the knobby bony protuberances above its eyes and a small bit of its flat skull showing, the croc waits its opportunity. When it thinks the time is ripe, it submerges completely and without a ripple. Propelled by its powerful tail, it swims at its intended victim with almost unbelievable speed and without causing a ripple on the surface unless the water is extremely shallow. Before the drinking animal knows what is happening, the crocodile has clamped a viselike grip on its muzzle or on a leg or whatever part of the animal's body it can seize.

The first reaction of an animal caught by a croc is to stiffen its front legs, drive its hooves into the mud, and rear back to try and pull out of the crocodile's grip. The crocodile, using its grip as a pivot point, swings its body and mighty tail out of the water and deals the struggling animal a terrible blow that more often than not knocks it flat on its side.

Customarily, we had a number of steel traps set in the papyrus along the riverbank to catch leopards. These traps were baited with large chunks of meat which, after a day of heat, became pretty odoriferous. Crocodiles catching the scent of these baits often left the river and crawled through the papyrus to find the meat and invariably put one of their clumsy feet into the trap. When caught, the crocodiles just lay where they were, hissing annoyance and occasionally opening their ugly mouths and snapping their jaws together with frighteningly powerful force.

When Jam, who was in charge of the traps, or I, approached a caught crocodile, unless he or I shot it immediately, it would begin to struggle. It would lash furiously about itself with its tail, and I have more than once seen a crocodile twelve to fifteen feet long snap, with a single blow, the four-inch-thick trunk of a green and growing tree as we would a matchstick. Although a crocodile may seem awkward on the land, and when seen sunning itself on a sandy stretch of shore, to be a somnolent sort of creature, one should never underestimate their speed or their terrific power. Crocodiles are vicious, constantly hungry, prehistorically ugly, utterly repulsive, and fearsomely dangerous. I cannot think of a good word to say for them. I do not even admire the leather made from the skins of their bellies.

When a crocodile has knocked a seized animal flat, it drags the animal into deep water and drowns it. Then it tows the carcass to one of its caves beneath the level of the water.

Crocodiles are so constructed physically that they are unable to tear and rend a carcass as can a lion or a leopard or a dog. So they stuff the carcass of an animal they have drowned—and this may be a human—into the cave which they have excavated with their snout and tail and forefeet. At the end of the dry season, when the level of the river was low, we saw many of these caves in the banks.

Once it has its prey stashed away, the croc remains nearby to guard it and to wait for the carcass to decompose sufficiently for it to be able to bite off chunks.

As might be expected with so loathsome a creature, crocodiles are extremely difficult to kill. When lying on a rock or a sandbar, they are very alert, and it is difficult to approach near enough for a shot at them. If one is lucky enough to accomplish this, a croc must be shot through the head or through the spine to be sure of killing it.

In the water they float with just the eyes and the top of the flat skull above water level. Shooting over water is difficult for the best of shots. With the glare it is hard to judge distance. The target is small and flat. But Charlotte seldom missed. To my delight she would spend hours in her blind, and every so often I would hear the crack of her rifle and know another of the fearsome beasts had gone to its reward, which, I hoped fervently, was nasty and uncomfortable.

In the time she was with us I don't know how many crocodiles Charlotte killed. Her total must have been a hundred or more. Her shooting chased the reptiles away from the mouth to the lagoon while she was on Ibamba, but within a day or so of her leaving the crocodiles were back, and, or so it seemed, in even greater numbers than before.

I did learn one thing as a result of the attacks by the crocodiles upon our cattle. Not from the crocs directly but from my boys. When a cattlebeast was driven to the kraal with great rips and tears from the teeth of a croc, I at first went to great pains to sterilize the wounds and close them. My careful, painstaking work resulted in a 100 per cent loss. Every animal I doctored died.

It was Charlie Matabele who told me to leave the wounds alone unless the animal was so badly cut up that it would bleed to death. The flies would come, he said, and lay eggs in the wounds. Maggots would hatch, and these maggots would eat all the bad, rotting flesh and the wounds would heal.

I was not having any success with my methods, so I followed his advice. It was a repulsive and horribly evil-smelling process to watch, but it worked in the majority of cases. Just as Charlie had said, the flies laid in the cuts and tears and maggots hatched. The maggots, a repelling squirming mass, fed on the suppurating flesh. As they fed, a stomach-retching odor rose from the hurts, but the firm new flesh formed beneath the squirming mass and the maggots did not touch this newly forming flesh. Gradually the new flesh built up behind the maggots and eventually they fell to the ground and the wound closed.

This healing process was a ghastly procedure to watch and messy and stinking. But it was effective. Further, so far as I could determine, the animals cut up by crocodiles and passing through the maggot cure did not suffer to any great degree.

I thought back to the occasional eland antelope or buffalo which I had shot and found to have been previously wounded and to have a great suppurating wound filled with maggots. We had always cut around these wounds and thrown away a large chunk of the surrounding meat; I had never had the curiosity to cut into one of those wounded areas to see exactly what was taking place.

Nowadays, I believe, special maggots are raised in hospitals under sterile conditions and introduced into human bodies to counteract the effects of certain tissue-destroying diseases. These maggots are, I think, particularly effective against certain diseases which affect the bones or marrow.

Throughout the dry season hardly a day passed when lions were not on Ibamba, nor did a week pass during which we failed to hear lions moving close about the house. Lions killed cattle at the mission. They killed at the small village just off the boundary of Ibamba and to the north. They killed eland and wildebeest and zebra and an occasional puku or bush pig on Ibamba, and lions attacked the livestock at the huge villages of Marla and Mokobella. Sibyunni'-byunni's cattle and sheep, goats, hogs, and dogs they left strictly alone.

Why? I have no explanation. Naturally, I kept harping on my statement to the natives that because I knew lions and could talk with them and was a *matakatsi,* lions would not attack. As month after month passed and an attack did *not* materialize, I half came to believe that I *did* have some sort of unnatural power. Who could say that I did not? On the day of our arrival on Ibamba I had stated that the lions would never bother us or our cattle. Everyone, white and black alike, had laughed at me. The lions had chased every other white man off Ibamba, so why, they asked, should I be immune? I cannot explain why this was so, but I *was* immune; our immunity became a subject for violent discussion, and my reputation grew with every passing season.

Even Tweetie got into the act. Usually when she landed on Iz's sewing basket, she cooed once or twice, preened a little, and then tucked her head back into her feathers and retired for the night. The comings and goings of people, of Paddy and Mr. Thomas or Popeye, did not bother her one bit. When Paddy and I wrestled on the floor below her and the uproar became unusually loud, Tweetie would take her head from her feathers and watch us with one beady black eye for a few moments before returning to sleep. Otherwise she squatted so immobile on the basket that anyone watching her would have thought she was a stuffed bird. But we began to notice that every now and then, when Tweetie came flying in, she seemed unable to settle down. She stayed awake and kept changing her position and picking at her feathers instead of really preening them. I picked her up several times when she was acting in this way and examined her thoroughly, thinking that she might have become infested with lice or that she had been injured. I could find nothing wrong.

Reading through the notebooks which I kept and in which I set down the actions and happenings of our foster children as well as notes of general interest, I noticed that the record showed that whenever Tweetie acted uneasy and upset in the evening, lions came later during the night and stalked close about the house. Iz and I watched for this, and as weeks passed, we found that Tweetie's actions were an accurate forewarning of the coming of lions.

You may laugh and scoff at this all you please. You may say that

Tweetie's actions and the subsequent arrival of lions was pure coincidence. You might be right. When an occurrence of this sort is witnessed and recorded not once but time and time again, however, I think the happening can no longer be classed as just coincidence. That is the easy lazy-mind's explanation. I admit that I have nothing better to offer, although I keep toying with the idea that extrasensory perception, ESP, enters into this in some manner.

I can think of no logical or cogent reason why there should have been any telepathic communication of any sort between our dove and the wild lions. Lions have no interest in doves and doves have no interest in lions. Doves are strictly seed-eating birds, and nothing which a lion does on the veld helps or hinders the provisions of doves. Unlike the plover, which are ground birds and cry out whenever any animal approaches, doves roost in trees for the night and are unconcerned with the animals which pass beneath. Doves are ground feeders, it is true, and they undoubtedly fly up at the approach of a lion, but I cannot visualize a lion attempting to catch and kill a dove to eat it.

It must also be remembered that Tweetie was perfectly familiar with lions. She saw Paddy from very close every evening of her life. She knew the roarings and growls and snarls of a lion. Out on the veld, where she spent her days, it is more than probable that Tweetie had watched wild lions as they stalked proudly about Ibamba.

If Tweetie's restlessness was more than coincidence, how did she know that lions would come within an hour or a few hours at most? More importantly, what difference did it make to her? Why? I always thought that Tweetie returned to the house each evening because of association and because she felt that the house was a safe place in which to roost for the night. If our little dove felt that she was safe inside the house, why then was she concerned about the arrival of lions which remained outside?

I ask myself if I am perhaps making too much of the actions of Tweetie. Yet the actions of this bird are just one phase of the strange and inexplicable happenings on Ibamba. All of which, with exception of the invasion of the locusts, revolved in one way or another about the wild lions.

I was just beginning really to study and to speculate about the behavior and the psychology of the wondrous African animals at this time. Lions, particularly, fascinated me. As I watched them on the veld, listened to them, hunted them and raised several, I grew to understand how intelligent they are.

The vocal range of the sounds uttered by lions is very wide. Lions roar, moan, snarl, and growl. They make a rumbling throaty sound which is a kind of purr. They whistle like a bird. The voices of the males differ from those of the females, and there are variations of meaning in roars and growls of varying intensities.

There were many occasions, however, when I watched lions act in a co-operative and co-ordinated manner, during which they uttered no sound which I could hear. Yet the acts which each lion or lioness performed definitely required that it should know what each of the other lions concerned was going to do. This is particularly true when lion and lionesses have separated to carry through an attack on a cattle kraal, as I have described, or when driving game out on the veld.

Thirty-five years ago I began to wonder if at least certain species of animals could and did communicate simple ideas one to another by some form of what we, in those days, called telepathy. If they could so communicate, and no one has ever been able to present definite proof or evidence that they cannot, such an ability would explain many acts and actions which puzzled me, and continue to puzzle me and many other people to this day.

It is easy for me to understand that a certain roar or growl can serve as a summons. A closely similar sound can be a warning. The grief in the moan of a bereaved lioness is unmistakable, as is the affection evident in her purring greeting to her cubs or to a friend.

These are simple sounds, however, related to simple and single emotions or thoughts. A summoning roar means only "come." It does not mean, "Come because I have killed and you can eat." Just "come." A warning growl means "go away." Although we humans, hearing a warning growl, can read into the growl the additional meaning of, "Go away because if you don't, I will attack you," the growl as such does not say this. It is only an announcement of the presence of the lion, of its displeasure at being disturbed.

When three lions approach a cattle kraal, watch it for some time, and then separate to assume different and separate positions where, at the right moment, they act in different ways—in other words, when three lions not only co-operate but co-ordinate their actions—it seems to me that some form for the communication of ideas, of thoughts, more delicate and detailed than growls, roars, purrs, moans, or whistles is both needed and indicated.

The very early theories developed during the beginning studies of animal behavior and psychology were based, at least in part if not wholly, upon the belief that animals could not and did not use their brains to reason. The ability to reason from cause to effect was a capacity, so the earliest naturalists believed, reserved exclusively to the human animal. This belief was fostered and encouraged, even made a part of dogma, by the disciples of various and numerous religions.

Man, from the time he began consciously to think, has been engaged in a rather frantic effort to establish as a fact the hypothesis that he is a being set utterly and completely apart from all other living things. It is undeniably true, of course, that man has developed use of the brain to a far greater degree than any other animal. But that is all that he has done. Man has not changed his physiological relationship to other animals one iota. The human animal has evolved, and is still evolving, along patterns identical with those which governed, and govern, the evolvement of all other living creatures.

It is, therefore, a tenable hypothesis that the basic emotional, nervous, and physical patterns are common to both humans and other animals, although the degree, or the extent, to which these basic patterns have developed and enlarged varies from species to species.

Pursuing this line of thought, why, if it is possible for certain humans to receive or exchange messages or information by means of some force which we do not yet understand but call extrasensory perception, should not other animals, which also have brains and utilize these brains, also be able to communicate in this manner?

Humans sensitive to the reception of extrasensory stimuli or capable of utilizing extrasensory ability are rare. The percentage who can do so appears to increase among those people we like to describe as primitive. This leads me to disagree with many students of parapsychology who apparently believe that the possibility of the occurrence and use of extrasensory perceptive powers rises with the degree of intelligence and civilization. I hold to the contrary theory, which is that extrasensory perception is somewhat like the human appendix. Thousands upon thousands of years ago humans had a need for the functions carried out by the appendix. As we developed, the need for this organ lessened, until now it is only a vestigial remnant playing no part, or at most an infinitesimal part, in the function of the modern human body.

I believe that the further one goes back in the evolutionary development of man, the more important becomes the use of extrasensory perception, just as the use, or influence, of instincts become more dominant. The higher one goes in the scale of intelligence, the less need there is for instincts and, so I believe, the less need for extrasensory perception.

There must have been a period in the evolution of man, before the invention of words, speech, and sentences, when communication between one developing human and another was by means of grunts, barks, growls, or other sounds comparable to the sounds presently uttered by baboons, lions, gorillas, elephants, chimpanzees, buffalo, and other animals.

It appears to me possible, even logical, that during this period of human development extrasensory perception in some form was of great importance in the exchange of ideas and thoughts. Man did not spring suddenly into a sentient, talking being. This came only through slow evolvement. Following this line of thought, I believe that those humans who today exercise extrasensory powers are utilizing a power which is a vestige, a hangover, from our early development, and not a power resulting from the increased use and development of the brain.

If there is any substance to my thinking, the place, then, to study extrasensory perception is among the nonhuman animals. Particularly among those animals, such as the lion and the elephant, the chimpanzee and the gorilla, which both co-operate and co-ordinate.

In ESP we are studying imponderable and intangible things affecting and affected by living and ever-changing beings. By their very nature they are not things which can be reduced to mathematical formulae. The ability to exercise a phase of extrasensory perception or to receive extrasensory stimuli must, by very nature, be dependent to a great degree upon the emotional, nervous, and physical condition of whoever or whatever is concerned.

This is a field of infinite disagreement. I have, by correspondence and in person, discussed various aspects of the possible occurrence in and use by animals of extrasensory perception with such world-famous naturalists, psychologists, and behaviorists as Dr. J. B. Rhine, of Duke University; Dr. Munroe Fox, of Bedford College, London; Aldous Huxley, Frank W. Lane, Dr. Konrad Lorenz, and Dr. Karkis Osis. No two agree. Often, while they were alive, I debated, sometimes quite acrimoniously with Dr. William T. Hornaday and Carl Akeley, the questions of how animals communicate. I have talked about this with Dr. James Clark and Madison Grant and Dr. John Lilly.

Dr. Hediger, director of the Zoological Garden in Basle and author of that thoughtful and fascinating book *Wild Animals in Captivity,* appears to believe that animals communicate ideas mainly, if not exclusively, by means of the sounds which we can hear and by various and subtle movements of parts of the body.

I find it difficult to accept this explanation. Animals, at least in the wild, move about a great deal during the periods of darkness which, while never total, must make the observation of slight movements difficult. In the wild, animals roaming the veld or the forest, hunting in canebrakes or long grass, feeding among bamboo, etc., are not always within sight of one another. I feel compelled to believe that animals communicate by some means *in addition to* visual observation and/or vocal sounds.

Further, I believe that if some form of extrasensory perception is the method by which animals communicate one with another, such communication can exist only between animals of like species. In other words humans could, and some still can, communicate by means of extrasensory perception with other humans, but not with cats or chimpanzees. Lions, I believe, can communicate with other lions; elephants, with elephants; members of a herd of the same species, with other members, but not with unlike animals.

It is for this reason, I believe, that Dr. Osis and Dr. Rhine failed, and will continue to fail, in their experiments to influence domestic cats by means of thought waves which the owners of the cats endeavor to project. On the other hand, there is the remarkable power which was possessed by John Solomon Rarey to influence the wildest of horses to become quiet and docile, a feat which he accomplished over and over again without the use, so far as anyone was ever able to determine, of drugs, implements, or apparatus of any kind. Rarey just entered the box stalls of horses which no one else could approach and communed with the animals and came forth within a reasonably short time leading an entirely gentle and docile animal. On one occasion when he was secretly observed, he was seen to be lying down in the straw beside a horse which, until Rarey appeared, invariably tried to kick the brains out of anyone who came near it. Both Rarey and the horse were sleeping!

The question of how animals communicate was one of the projects we had hoped to be able to study in the research station we had intended to build on Ibamba. It was to study the development and the actions and reactions of animals that we had Paddy and Mr. Thomas, the duikers, Fwifwi, and other animals living in such intimate association with us in and around the house. We believed, and I still believe, that it is only by living with animals twenty-four hours a day, day after day, month after month, that a person can begin to even reach a glimmer of understanding as to what motivates animal behavior. One must be completely in the confidence of the animal being studied to really learn how and why it feels and acts as it does. It is a corollary, of course, that you, the student, must have complete confidence in the animal, so that you will not do anything to alter or change its normal emotional growth. Such a situation can only be achieved by securing the animal to be studied *before* it has reached the age at which its environment, its parents, or experience could influence its reactions.

Because animals develop physically very rapidly in comparison with humans, they also learn very quickly. In laboratories and in zoological parks specimens are received, usually, quite some time after birth and weaning. These animals have already begun to learn. Because students studying animals in zoos or in a laboratory cannot know to what outside stimuli their specimens may have been subjected and what reactions, as a result, may have been developed in the animals, their experimental studies are based upon insecure foundations. They are, perforce, studying problems in which there must always be one very important and unknown factor present—previous experience. Animals born in zoos do offer very attractive subjects for psychological study. Unfortunately, all too often these opportunities are neglected and the zoo-born animal grows up without being observed and studied.

There is constant difference of opinion, even spirited controversy, between naturalists, especially field naturalists, and those who do their studying of animals in laboratories or under other controlled conditions. In a way this is most unfortunate because each school has something to contribute to the other.

In recent years it appears to have become fashionable—among certain cliques in several of the larger cities and centers of learning—to deprecate the reportings of field naturalists and to consider the findings of students of animal psychology working in museums, zoos, and universities with animals under controlled and wholly unnatural surroundings, as the final word. On more than one occasion I have had reports concerning my observations of wild animals in their natural state, which had been submitted for consideration to the nature editor of some publishing house or of a scientific journal, returned with the comment that, while very interesting, they could not be included in a particular journal or be considered for inclusion in a book because my work was "exploratory," that I lacked the check of "control animals." The implication was that my observations had not been conducted in a sufficiently scientific and detached manner to be worthy of serious study or appreciation.

This attitude, this development, is probably an outgrowth of the tremendous emphasis placed in this country upon specialization. We no longer have physicists, but specialists in certain narrow areas of physics. The general practitioner, the good old family or country doctor, is only a memory. Today, if a person falls ill or is injured, he or she must first be examined in an effort to pinpoint the location and type of trouble and then must go to some doctor who has specialized in bones, or hearts, whiplash, or ingrowing toenails, the bladder, the liver, or the lungs. This confining, narrow specialization extends in almost every field of science.

It is especially true in the study of animal psychology and animal behavior. Yet in their natural state of existence animals are constantly subject to and affected by all manner of stimuli: changes in barometric pressure, humidity, and temperature. Climatic changes affect them both directly and indirectly through the effects of such changes on the growth of grass, the presence or absence of water, and so on. Every species is affected, in one way or another and to varying degrees, by the presence or absence of other creatures.

The true naturalist, although he or she may be more interested in one species than another, nevertheless must, if he or she is fully to understand the whys and wherefores and hows of the life of the particular species of interest, take into full consideration the climate, the environment, and the behavior of all the other creatures—insects, reptiles, birds, mammals, and fish and even the micro-organisms, the bacteria, the protozoans—with which it is surrounded and in hourly and daily contact.

The naturalist, especially the field naturalist, works in an enormously broad area. Field naturalists should have some grounding in geology, in botany, zoology, biology, immunology, climatology, parasitology, veterinary medicine, psychology, and chemistry. Without at least some knowledge in these various fields of study the field naturalist, the behaviorist, cannot bring the total picture of the life, of the behavior, of any particular species into clear and understandable focus.

It is this necessity to have as encyclopedic, although not necessarily specialized, knowledge as possible that separates the field naturalist from the men who work and study within the confines and restrictions of a single specialty. The graduate student who devotes all his energies to becoming an authoritative taxonomist or the man who devotes his life to becoming an ichthyologist or zoologist is not, *ipso facto* because he is working in a field which can be included under the broad term natural history, a naturalist. Neither does such specialization entitle the specialists to look down upon the field naturalist as a jack-of-all-trades and master of none. The true naturalists are, perhaps, closer to understanding the wellsprings, the whys, the hows, the whens, and the reasons of all life than any other group.

As Dr. Hornaday has said, referring to the study of animal psychology and the animal mind, "The principle of determining the mind of a wild animal *along the lines of the professor* is not the best way. It should be developed *along the natural lines of the wild animal mind.*" The italics are his, not mine.

This was the basic thought behind Isabella's and my intention and hope to establish an animal research station on Ibamba. To study the animal mind along natural lines was the guiding principle underlying all our observations, and it motivated all our associations with animals.

chapter twelve

JOHN and Florence Price used to come and visit with us every so often during the dry seasons. John was fond of Paddy and not a bit afraid of her, but Florence was almost terrified. Once, when Paddy was quite small, weighing about sixty or seventy pounds and only as large as a springer spaniel, Florence and John had come to visit, bringing with them the trained nurse who was stationed on Kasenga.

We were all sitting in the living room when I saw Paddy's round head appear by the corner of the parapet which separated the living room from the conservatory. As I watched, I saw Paddy carefully note where each of us was sitting, and then she disappeared. Within moments I heard the soft pad of her feet as she came galloping through the conservatory, down the two steps, and rushed into the living room. In one bound she lit in my lap, knocking me over. Springing off my tummy, she bounced into John's lap, sending him to the floor, and then into Florence's ample lap. Florence screamed and fell sideways, and Paddy bounded onto the nurse and then onto Iz. To put it mildly, she created quite a sensation. Enjoying the confusion and excitement, which she had planned to the utmost, Paddy sat down in the middle of her scrambled, upset humans and curled her black lips in an impish grin of satisfaction and devilment.

Although I leaped to help Florence to her feet and Iz tried to calm her and the nurse, I couldn't help but laugh. Having watched the beginning, I knew the whole thing had been conceived by Paddy as a joke and to secure attention. I was about to give her a good cuffing, but her expression was so smug and so pleased I laughed some more instead.

Lions, particularly young lions, are extremely playful and full of tricks. One has only to watch a litter of cubs in a zoo to see how many mischievous pranks they can think up to play upon one another or on their long-suffering mother. Florence, however, did not appreciate Paddy's performance, although her husband laughed as hard as I. From then on she eyed Paddy with a very jaundiced eye.

On subsequent visits it both fascinated and horrified Florence, when she was sitting in the living room with Iz, with Buncher crawling about on the floor nearby, to see Paddy, who was growing very big and strong, come stalking into the room with the slow, majestic pacing swagger so typical of a lion.

The moment Buncher would spot Paddy, she would start toward her, toddling on her chubby little legs. Throwing her short arms around Paddy's thick neck and grasping an ear, Buncher would lay her face against the cheek of the lioness and crow and gurgle with pleasure.

Paddy would flop to the floor and Buncher would crawl and swarm all over her lioness, pulling back her lips to see her teeth, twisting her furry ears and poking her in the eye. Paddy just loved this, and would rumble and grumble and roll onto her back. Buncher would shriek with glee and hurl herself onto the soft, pretty fur of Paddy's stomach, and the lioness would hold her with her mighty paws.

Everyone who saw this performance was certain that our child was about to be disemboweled and eaten before their horrified eyes. But Buncher never sustained so much as a scratch. Paddy was so devoted to our baby and so careful with her that it never occurred to Iz or me to worry.

If you have ever been so fortunate as to raise a good lion in your house as a companion—in the same way which you might raise a puppy—you will know how wonderfully intelligent, how docile and placid and how completely devoted they are. I emphasize the word "good" because there *are* bad lions, just as there are bad humans.

Young elephants are lots of fun but a trifle cumbersome to have about the house, and I once had a little black rhinoceros which slept under my camp bed and was as amusing and up to as many tricks as a whole barrel of monkeys. The nearest animal to a lion, as far as companionship goes, is probably the tiger. I have met many tigers but have never owned one. Those who have assure me that they are exactly like lions, if not even a bit more wonderful.

In case, however, that my enthusiasm for lions might induce you to rush out and buy one, let me add one word of caution. There should never be any reason for you to be afraid of a lion which you have raised unless an accident happens and the animal becomes badly hurt or terribly frightened. But one must always remember that a lion, or a tiger, is an enormously powerful creature and that it is armed with fearful weapons. A lion or a tiger can, when it wishes, move or strike with such speed that the human eye has difficulty following the movements.

It was about this time that Paddy discovered that she could get a better view of whatever was going on in front of the house by leaping onto the parapet which enclosed the veranda, where she sat on her haunches like an enormous dog. This was fine, except that in her eagerness to see everything, Paddy leaned her great weight against the mosquito netting. Too often, as a result, she burst the fragile wire.

If I had had some half-inch mesh hardware cloth, or even stout chicken wire, I could have stretched this inside the fine copper mosquito screening and protected it. Not only did I not have any such wire, but we were very short of mosquito screening. Whenever Paddy burst the screens, we were confronted with a serious problem as to how to patch the wire so that the mosquitoes, which would come in hordes with the rains, could not invade the house more easily and in greater numbers than they did even when the wire was intact.

Why Paddy did not just go out to watch whatever was going on, we never knew. She came and went as she pleased. Because she sat on the parapet most frequently when either or both Iz and I were out of the house, we couldn't break her of this habit.

We were taking every precaution we could to prevent Buncher from being bitten by mosquitoes. The Mashakulumbwe district was heavily infected with malaria, and we hoped to be able to avoid having Buncher contract the disease. While seldom fatal, at least in the Rhodesias, malaria is a nasty disease which can hang on for years and which is very uncomfortable and quite debilitating. Her bursting of the mosquito netting was the final reason for our deciding that Paddy would have to be moved to an outdoor paddock.

We had a few bags of cement left. One or two had gotten quite hard, but there was enough usable material left for my purposes. We also had a number of rolls of heavy stock fencing. These rolls were 330 feet long, with a width of 4 feet. The mesh was six inches and the wire number eleven gauge, which is very strong. This was hinge-joint fencing, and I had used it during the motion-picture expedition to enclose captured buffalo and found that it withstood the charge of a full-grown animal.

So that we could utilize a full roll without cutting the wire, Iz and I, with help from Mangineera and other boys, and with Popeye, Fwifwi, and Paddy getting in the way, laid out a kraal which extended from the wall of the laboratory building 120 feet. The kraal was 60 feet wide, with one side or end being 30 feet of building wall and 30 feet of wire. We knocked a hole in the laboratory wall 6 feet from the end of the building, and set a door in this 5 feet high by 3 feet wide, through which Paddy would be able to enter her quarters inside the building and immediately adjacent to the office portion where I worked.

Along the lines of the kraal the boys dug a trench 2 feet deep and 18 inches wide. While this was being done, Charlie Portuguese took a crew to the western end of the ranch and cut a number of tall mopani trees 8 to 9 inches in diameter at the butt and as straight as possible.

In the trench we laid a brick and cement wall to a height of a foot above ground level, leaving a space 2 feet long every 10 feet. The long mopani poles were trucked in and stripped of their bark and treated with hot tar for a length of 4 feet from the butt end. This was to discourage the white ants and rot. We then set the poles upright in the openings left in the foundation of the wall and poured concrete around them. When the concrete had set, which took about five days, we hung one length of the heavy wire from the poles, drew it as taut as possible by means of a block and tackle, and set the lower edge on the brick foundation and built up the wall for another six inches so that the wire was firmly cemented between the bricks.

I mention these details so that you will understand how strong Paddy's kraal was. Later this wire enclosure was subjected to some pretty severe strains, and you might wonder, if you did not know how the kraal had been constructed, why the fencing did not collapse.

Inside the enclosure and near to the north fencing we built a long pool, using bricks and cement about six feet by three, which could be filled easily from the outside through the mesh in the wire. This was to serve as both a drinking and a bathing pool for Paddy.

The wire fencing was hung on the outside of the poles and was fastened to them with lashings of malleable iron wire rather than nailed. Hanging the first two lengths, which rose to a height of seven feet above the low parapet in the ground, did not present much difficulty. But it was a devil of a job to put on the top length and to haul this tight. A roll of heavy stock fencing 330 feet long weighs close to 300 pounds, and is balky and unco-operative. With the help of most of our boys, whose number had been reduced to about twenty by then because of the necessity to economize in every way possible, we got the wire up. I installed a heavy gate near the pool, and we had an enclosure, the wire walls of which towered eleven feet into the air.

Lions are reputed to be able to leap fourteen feet in the air, although I have never talked with anyone who ever actually saw a lion jump this high. For added security, however, we strung two lengths of barbed wire a foot and two feet above the top of the stock fencing. The barbed wire helped to stiffen the upper portions of the mopani poles.

Inside the south end of the laboratory building we laid a concrete floor and constructed an inside apartment for Paddy. Three sides of the apartment were brick; the two walls of the building and the wall between the apartment and my office working space. The fourth wall was of stock fencing in which was a door, or gate, and there was a space some six feet wide between the fencing and the opposite wall of the building. These were pretty elegant quarters which could be flushed down with water and be cleaned easily; they were cool and dim and easily accessible from the outdoor paddock through the door in the wall. We felt so unhappy at having to move Paddy that nothing was too good for her.

Paddy was a little miserable when we first moved her, but we let her out frequently so that she could come to the house, and I talked to her while I was working in the office either through a window or over the wall between us. Gradually she became accustomed to the new living arrangements and settled down.

The locusts were still with us. All over the district, all over the entire territory, the enormous swarms passed and repassed, searching for food wherever they could find any growing things struggling to survive in the dry, parched land. Only on the moist flats was there any green grass. For this the great herds of lechwe, which often numbered as many as several thousand antelope, the herds of zebra and buffalo, the scattered sitatunga, reedbuck, oribi, duiker, and impala antelope, the wildebeest, and the thousands of cattle belonging to the natives as well as the flocks of goats and sheep, contended with the locusts. Wherever the villagers tried to raise a few mealies on the riverbank, the hippos invaded the lands, crushing or eating the grain, and the locusts finished what remained.

Hardly a day passed that Iz and I, watching the sky and the distant horizon, did not see the moving clouds of locusts sweeping in their millions across the flats, to disappear behind the Luiri Mountains or flood across the bushveld. Travelers, stopping to rest in the compound, told us that the devastation and depredations of the locusts covered the land in all directions. There was no area which had not been hurt; throughout the territory starvation was rampant and cattle and other livestock were dying of hunger.

In some villages the old people had been sent onto the veld to fend for themselves and to live as long as they were able on what roots, bark, and bulbs they might be able to find. Few survived for long.

This might seem a cruel and heartless practice, but it was one which the natives had learned was necessary for survival of a tribe. When a year was bitter because of drought or excessive flooding and crops failed and the food supplies of a village dwindled, so that there was not enough for all, it was the custom that the old people—the men and women who had lived their lives, who were past the days when they could work and breed—should leave the village and go forth to die on the veld. Only by following such drastic measures could the survival of the tribe, of their race, be insured, and the old people went forth without protest. Those who remained in the village watched them go with sad eyes, but there was no wailing, there were no recriminations. Natives were, and are, fatalists. What will be will be; a man's destiny is ordained at his birth, and nothing he can do will alter it. Starvation was one of the hazards of life, and when and if starvation came, it was accepted as a manifestation of nature and something beyond the control of man.

Pete Cavadia managed to secure several hundred bags of grain, which he stored in a galvanized building at Pemba. He sold us a hundred bags, which I trucked out to Ibamba and added to our hoard, thus insuring that our people would have food until at least the end of the next dry season, twelve months, if the corn did not rot or mold and was spared by the mice and weevils.

Thinking that, if we managed to stick things out, we might be able to pump water from the river and irrigate at least a portion of the cleared lands and grow grain during the winter months, we started digging a large reservoir on the high land behind the house. The earth which we dug out we piled around the sides of the excavation, so that when, as we planned, we finally lined this with brick and cement, at least half the water inside would be three or four feet above ground level. We would then be able to lead the water through trenches onto those portions of the fields which lay on the slopes reaching down from the bushveld portion of Ibamba to the flatland. It was an ambitious undertaking which only resulted in creating an unsightly accumulation of raw earth and a large hole because we were never able to complete the project.

While we were digging the proposed reservoir, we also kept plows moving in the fields to turn over the soil and expose the egg clusters left by the locusts. It was an unending, thankless job which sapped both the spirits and the strength of the men and cattle. Although we undoubtedly killed millions of eggs which would otherwise have hatched into hoppers, other millions escaped the plows. Hoppers crawled and squirmed and hopped endlessly across Ibamba. When we could, we beat, burned, and buried the hoppers in the trenches we had dug, but this meant that we had to begin all over again and clean out the trenches to trap new hordes which hatched into life seemingly overnight. Charlie Portuguese, Charlie Matabele, Mangineera, Jam, and all of us worked and fought ceaselessly, but there was no joy in the work; no expectations that our labors could do more than stave off an eventual reckoning. In the evenings when, during our first years on Ibamba, the compound had sounded joyously to the singing and dancing and tom-tom beating of the natives, the huts huddled silently in the night. Although the fires flickered and threw their glow in pools of light before the doorways, our people sat on their stools or went about their tasks depressed and worried. A weariness which ate into our bones and joints, which banished restful sleep, pervaded the ranch and engulfed us all.

Working in the office, I often found myself staring out the window across the flats or at the area around our house, wondering what lay ahead. With the coming of the rains we would plant, of course. But would we reap? Would we receive enough money to be able to stay and fight? Would there ever be an end to the swarms of locusts? If they stayed for another year or two years, what would happen to Rhodesia? Already most of the settlers were close to bankruptcy, and because of the business depression trade of every type was slow. Had some evil outside force intent upon the destruction of the white man throughout Central Africa planned the onslaught of the locusts, whoever this was had certainly timed the invasion perfectly.

Alone, working and thinking in the office, I talked to Paddy across the wall. She always answered. Often I opened the door to her apartment and let her into the office, where she leaped to the stout bench beneath the windows and sat watching me and watching the activities outside. When she became bored, or because I had not spoken for some time, she would reach out a great paw and tap me gently on the head. I would grunt acknowledgment and for a time Paddy was satisfied that I knew she was there. Then another pat. If I failed to acknowledge this, the pats became harder and harder until Paddy walloped me strongly enough to snap my head on the end of my spine. Then I would give up what I was doing, put my arms around her, and we would tumble to the floor to wrestle for a moment and try each other's strength. That was what she wanted, and after a wrestle she would be good and sit for a long time without bothering me. Like Mr. Thomas, Paddy was something of a prima donna. She wanted attention and the spotlight. So, actually, did all our foster children excepting the placid little duikers, who were content to mosey through life in their own quiet way. Paddy, Tommy, Fwifwi, Jane Emmeline John, and even Garbage were jealous of any attentions shown to the others. Each wanted, insisted upon, a maximum degree of personal loving and attention.

Both Tommy and Popeye missed Paddy. Popeye would often wander over to Paddy's cage and stand staring at her with mournful eyes, as much as to say, "Why you poor old thing. What happened? Were you naughty, or something?" The lechwe also paid Paddy visits, but probably the most interesting visitors were the great male lions which came up out of the *saka* and rubbed against her wire and talked to her.

Tommy was getting bigger and bigger and was as heavy as a large cocker spaniel. One night Iz heard a terrific racket on the veranda. I was worn out after a long day fighting the locusts and was dead to the world. She got up, and taking a flash, went to see what was going on.

Tommy was stalking up and down the veranda, growling and hissing, with every hair stiff and erect. Not seeing anything else right away in the weak light, Iz called me and I got up and went to see. When Tommy acted that way, it meant something. Flashing the light, I explored the veranda gingerly. There was the ever-present danger of a snake.

Sure enough, that was what it was—a good-sized ringhals, a spitting cobra. One of the really mean and nasty kind.

This one was a good cobra. It was dead. Tommy had not only fought it, he had succeeded in grabbing it and had cut it into three pieces. We pushed the pieces together and the snake was some four and a half feet long and nearly two inches thick. He was very proud of himself, as he had every right to be, and responded with purrs and clucks to our praise and petting.

The next morning we fed the pieces of the cobra to Garbage, who liked snake for breakfast. Usually he got them all in one piece and had to spend some time swallowing several feet of snake. To have his food cut up for him was quite a treat.

Paddy began to call at night. A lioness calling emits a low, sweet moaning sound which never rises in volume, but which has tremendous carrying power. She would begin this song after the sun had gone, but while there was still some light. Working or talking in the house, we would not be aware of the sound at first. Gradually it beat into our ears and consciousness.

This calling brought huge lions and, sometimes, lionesses from the great *saka* and the flats. One evening, just about dinnertime, a lion suddenly wound up and began to roar not more than three hundred yards from the house. We heard the preliminary mutterings just before he let go. The sound poured in the open windows, reverberated under the iron roof, and bounced from the walls. Wild lions have far more powerful voices than those in the zoos. On a damp night, when the air hung heavy and close, I have heard a lion a full eight miles away. This may sound impossible, but I happen to be positive. The lion roaring was one of mine, and I knew not only where he was, but where I was.

Four or five times the big brute outside roared; then ended on the funny grunting noises lions utter at the end of a roar.

Isabella and I hurried into the bedroom as the tremendous sound poured into the house. Buncher had just been tucked in and we had hoped she was asleep. Not at all. She was lying on her back, gurgling and pointing with a chubby finger.

"Oh, that's just Henry," I told the baby.

"Henoo, Henoo," gurgled Buncher, using her own name for the great lion. From then on he was known as "Henoo," not only by us but by the natives.

The next morning I went out early to see what had happened during the night. Henoo had come along the road which led from the back of the ranch and along which we hauled logs. He had stopped at the edge of the clearing behind the house, and standing there, had surveyed the situation. Paddy, of course, was calling to him all this time. It was right there that he had sounded his challenging, bellowing roar. Then he had come closer along the logging path, turned into the road leading to the compound, pushed through the barbed wire, and circled down to the tomato garden near the dip tank. He had left some mane hairs on the barbs of the wire. They were fine, long, yellow and black; some were six inches in length. The pug marks were round and deeply pressed into the dust and soil of the garden. The stride was long. Truly a fine great lion.

Henoo had lain down in the garden and crushed a number of fine tomato plants and mashed some fruit, which somewhat annoyed me. Later, after having studied Paddy and her kraal from the garden and listened to more of her coaxing, Henoo had approached her paddock and pushed against the strong wire. His weight was so great that he had bent the stout wires inward. I noticed that there was a big hole in the ground near her water trough. It was about ten inches deep and two and a half feet in length. There was loose dirt on the parapet which held the base of the wire and a lot of loose dirt outside. There were lion tracks in the dirt.

I could only conclude that, after talking with her visitor, Paddy had turned around and scratched dirt in his face. Which seemed a very rude gesture on her part.

Henoo became a regular caller on Paddy. Once, twice, sometimes five times a week he would come down the road, stop at the edge of the clearing, roar and roar again, then go through the vegetable garden and up to the kraal. Other lions came up, some bringing their wives. One night we had five or seven walking about, grunting, moaning, and sniffing. The ladies stayed away from the paddock, walking under the trees, across the lawn, and through the flower beds. One lay down in a bunch of love-lies-bleeding. Possibly an appropriate place. I am sure that, here, someone is going to correct me and say I mean bleeding heart. But I don't. There *is* such a plant as love-lies-bleeding. It is coarser than bleeding heart, grows like a weed, and has the coloring and substance of cockscomb. In America, I believe, this plant is more commonly known as the chenille plant.

Once two males, one of which was Henoo, met outside Paddy's paddock and enjoyed a terrific battle. The scrap woke us up and caused us to stand at the window, with a gun in my hands and Iz holding Buncher in her arms. It was a terrible fight and lasted almost half an hour. Then all was quiet, and we could hear Paddy sounding her gentle moan again. We guessed that Henoo had won.

The wire on the paddock became badly bent inward and we straightened it and pulled it taut. One strong pole was broken loose from the foundations, and we reset it firmly. Regardless of this constant visiting, Henoo was making no progress with his lady. Night after night she scratched dirt at him until she had a hole beside her bath three or four feet long and nearly two feet deep. I don't know whether Paddy was afraid of Henoo or not. Maybe she knew somehow that wild animals, and birds, too, will usually kill any of their own kind which join them carrying the smell of man on their coats. We had seen this happen once or twice.

During all the months of the dry season the killing of other people's cattle went on all around us. Our friends in the villages began to complain a little, stating that we were harboring the lions and giving them a safe refuge to which to retire because no one was allowed to shoot on Ibamba. But as the lions continued to do us no harm, I could not see why we should shoot at them.

During all the months we had, by then, been living on Ibamba, not a single lion had even looked cross-eyed at one of our domestic animals. Lions crossed and recrossed the ranch; they traveled the roads and paths and lay up for the noonday heat in the great *saka,* or in the tall reeds by the river. We seldom saw them, except at night by the light of the moon or our big searchlight. Yet every morning the dust was marked with their tracks, and every night we could hear them roaring and grumbling as they returned from water or prepared for their nightly hunting. During the dry season, game was abundant on the ranch, and the lions could always find a fat zebra. They left the roan and sable alone, probably realizing how dangerous their sweeping horns could be. So far as I know, they never killed a kudu, but they did kill an occasional eland, wildebeest, reedbuck, and bush pig to vary their diet.

Henoo, however, began to ask for trouble. He infringed upon our hospitality. He began coming earlier and earlier, scarcely waiting decently for the shadows to lengthen. Sixpence and Lavison and Lubin refused to stay and serve supper and clean up afterward. They were afraid that they might meet Henoo on the road to the compound. Although so far Henoo had bothered neither the animals nor humans, if he came suddenly face to face with natives when he was between the lines of barbed wire on either side of the road, there was no telling what he might do. Quite evidently, close association with humans had developed a certain contempt in him for us.

Reluctantly we decided that Henoo would have to die. It was a hard decision to make because we had grown fond, in an indifferent sort of way, of the big noisy bum. But in addition to terrifying the natives, he was becoming more and more insistent and bold with Paddy. The paddock suffered heavy damage, and while we did not mind if Paddy got out—she would only come to the house—we didn't want to risk Henoo's breaking in to her.

We had a choice of three methods to get rid of our boisterous visitor. We could try to spotlight Henoo from the kitchen veranda using the electric searchlight, and shoot him before he could jump; we could build a machan in the big fig tree and shoot him from there; or we could put out our heavy and powerful traps. We finally decided on the traps because there was always the chance of a bad shot at night, which could only mean the extremely dangerous business of following Henoo into the great *saka*. Alternatively, if we shot him right in front of Paddy, we could not guess what her reaction might be. There was also the somewhat remote danger of hitting her in the excitement if anything should go wrong.

Having made our decision, I took the truck and drove out to the back of the ranch and shot a zebra. With the help of some boys we got it, whole, into the truck, and brought it back. We dumped it not far from the big fig tree and near a thickish bunch of bushes which concealed the bait from Paddy.

We didn't put too much effort into building an elaborate zareba of brush around the zebra. Henoo was familiar with the scent of man and metal and expected to find these near the house. So I set four traps, one in each entrance of the circular barricade and one by the neck and one by the rear quarters of the zebra. Each trap was fastened to a heavy log with ten feet of trek chain.

The final act was to slash open the zebra's stomach, cover the traps, and to spill a little blood around. We didn't expend much effort on the set. My heart—I can't speak for the natives—wasn't in the job. I really didn't want to catch Henoo.

He came that night, just as we had been afraid he would. As usual, he stopped at the edge of the clearing, on the timber road, and sounded his roaring challenge. Then there was silence and we knew he was walking down the road, making his way through the barbed wire and going on to the vegetable garden. Paddy was uttering her siren moan, which made us feel even worse. It was as if we were luring Henoo to his death with love songs.

For minutes we stood at the kitchen windows, listening. Not a sound except from Paddy. Henoo apparently was being very careful. We guessed that he had smelled the zebra, something new, and was estimating the situation. Then, without warning, a terrible roar burst forth simultaneously with the clanking of chain. Henoo had put his foot into a trap.

That was the beginning of one of the most frightening and terrible nights we ever spent. The great lion outside was only twenty-five yards or less from the house. The sound of his fight for freedom poured in the windows and echoed through the house. All our little animals woke and crowded into the living room, where we had built up a fire. Buncher woke, and Isabella cradled her in her arms as I stood guard by a window. There was no telling what that lion, in his pain and fury and fright, might do. I could tell that he had dragged the trap or traps away from where we had put the zebra, and that he was much closer to the kitchen. We could hear his panting breath, the grating sound of his huge teeth as he bit at the steel and tore the log and bushes. Shattering roars rent the night. Paddy joined in, whether from sympathy or fright, we shall never know, but Ibamba ran to the sound of the battle. Beyond, in the compound, I could hear my natives shouting. They knew what had happened, but not one would venture forth.

All night we sat in the living room, listening to that epic and fearful battle. With the coming of the first faint light of dawn I stole into the kitchen and slowly opened the back door and eased myself, rifle in hand, out onto the stone flags. I was in my bare feet so as to make no sound. We hadn't heard from Henoo for nearly half an hour, and I was not certain whether he had finally managed to escape, or if not, where he was.

As the light strengthened, it showed a scene of ruin. I could see the zebra lying much as we had placed it, but most of the bushes were uprooted and smashed and tossed about. A small tree had been chewed off about a foot above the ground. Nearer, another thick clump of bushes was a tangled, torn mess. The ground was torn up as if someone had run amok with a plow. Paddy was quiet, and there were no other sounds. Even the doves were silent.

I stared hard at everything, but could see no sign of Henoo. Crouching on the cold damp stones, clutching the rifle, I coughed. Instantly the mass of bushes nearest me shivered and a great bloody head rose up from their midst. Henoo! I raised the rifle, and the motion caught Henoo's eye. Slowly he turned his massive head and snarled at me. The look in his eyes was terrible to see. Hatred blazed from them. Balefully he stared at me and I stared back. He made no move beyond turning his head, but just sat there, glaring his pride and fury. We were scarcely fifty feet apart.

Slowly—and oh, so reluctantly—I brought my gun to my shoulder and drew a fine bead. Then I squeezed the trigger and the heavy blast echoed across Ibamba and rolled over the river. Henoo dropped. It was over.

Instantly, at the sound of the shot, wild yells issued from the compound and the natives came running, brandishing spears and knobkerries. They were elated and jubilant, and screamed and sang their joy that Henoo had been removed. I left them to get the body out of the traps and the bushes and returned to the house. I didn't want them to see that I was crying. I felt like the very lowest of humans that morning.

Henoo, as we had suspected, turned out to be an exceptionally large and powerful male. I guessed he was just over his prime, and was about eight or nine years old. He was very heavy and fat, and boasted a gorgeous black and orange mane.

We repaired the damage as best we could, cleaning up and planting new shrubs and bushes. Paddy did not seem to be at all affected, even when, out of curiosity, I took her out and let her wander around the places where Henoo had put up his tremendous battle. She was, as always, loving and docile, wanting to gambol and play games.

For the remainder of that dry season ranch life on Ibamba went on just as it had before. Lions came and went and the three paid us their periodic visits. Paddy continued her siren calling in the evenings and called more visitors from the veld. For weeks and weeks we lived, at least during the nights, surrounded by huge, magnificent wild lions. It was fascinating.

For some time Iz and I had been discussing the debatable question of whether a lion raised as Paddy had been would turn savage if allowed to kill her own food. All the experts, of course, said that she would. We had been told innumerable times that once Paddy got the taste of hot fresh blood, she would no longer be trustworthy and would become very dangerous.

I doubted this. Since she had been as big as a large pointer dog, Paddy's diet had consisted almost entirely of fresh raw meat and bones. Some of the meat had been very bloody and still warm. This had made no difference that we could see in her attitude toward us or toward little Buncher. And Paddy always licked the warm blood from any scratch she inflicted on me during our wrestling matches.

To try to find an answer to the question of whether letting Paddy kill her food would change her disposition, I got a small pig and turned it loose in her paddock. It was cruel, but this was an experiment.

At first Paddy just tried to play and gambol with the pig. It was frightened, and squealed and tried to get away. Paddy put a big paw on it to hold it down, and the pig squirmed from under, but not before Paddy's claws had cut in and brought blood. Paddy sniffed the blood and went after the pig. She kept looking at me, watching from outside, and I tried to encourage her. It took quite a while, but eventually Paddy got the idea that the pig was for her, and she killed it and began to eat.

When she was well into it and her face and paws were slathered in blood, I opened the door to the paddock and walked in. Paddy was feeding on the farther side. I called to her, and she answered with a snarl. Oh, oh, I thought, maybe the experts were right. I called again and approached closer. Paddy snarled again, and I walked a little nearer. When I called the third time, she suddenly leaped up, dropped the pig, and rushed me and knocked me down.

She weighed well over two hundred pounds. For a moment I was pretty badly frightened. But Paddy only wanted to play. We rolled around, growling and yelling and tugging and pulling; then Paddy dashed off, grabbed the pig, and started to gallop. I managed to grab a hind leg, and we had a tug of war with the pig between us. I got covered with blood from Paddy and the pig, but this made no difference to Paddy. We had quite a time yanking and wrestling and fooling about.

I tried this same procedure on two subsequent occasions, using goats. Paddy killed the second goat quickly and neatly, but otherwise the action was much the same as the first time. Killing her own meat made no difference which we could see in Paddy's attitude toward us, and, of more importance, it did not seem to change her feelings toward the lechwe and Popeye, who continued to visit, or toward the dogs.

The actions of one lion cannot be taken as a criterion for all, but a tame lion, or a tame leopard for that matter, has yet to hurt me deliberately. I have been scratched and bitten by many animals, sometimes fairly seriously. With the exception of a monkey (on all of which let here be a curse), no tame animal which I have raised has ever hurt me deliberately.

Mr. Thomas did once slash his beloved foster mother. We were in bed, and Thomas was asleep around Iz's head. Just what happened, neither of us knows, but Tommy suddenly slashed out and split Iz's eyelid. It was enormously fortunate that he missed her eye, or she would have lost it. What caused the action remained a mystery. Possibly Iz rolled on Tommy in such a way as to hurt him and, being asleep, he wakened and lashed out. It might have had some basis in his jealousy of Buncher. Animals will resort to some peculiar tricks to draw attention to themselves. Or Tommy might have been dreaming.

That Tommy was fearfully jealous, we were well aware. But we were not prepared to gauge the lengths to which he would go.

We were sitting on the veranda having tea one afternoon. Iz was holding Buncher in her arms. The baby's basket crib stood on a bridge table near the veranda parapet. We were sitting quietly and not talking when Tommy came onto the veranda. It was unusual for him to be up at that time, and we watched, saying nothing. He spotted the basket immediately, and walked under the table, sniffing. Then he jumped onto the parapet and stalked the basket, his back hair raised and his long tail held stiff behind him. Whether, because of his poor eyesight in daylight, he didn't see us, or whether he was so absorbed in his opportunity that he didn't care, we don't know.

Anyway, Tommy got to the basket and jumped onto its strong wide edge. He balanced there precariously for a moment and stared into the depths and sniffed at the baby smell. Then he turned about, raised his tail, and deliberately defiled the basket, jumped down, and returned to the bedroom.

It is possible, of course, that he realized the child was not in the basket. But he certainly chose a most effective way to show us what he thought of the, to him, interloper who was taking so much of his foster mother's time and affection.

That the act was deliberate and meant as contempt, there could be little doubt. Tommy, as I have said, was one of the cleanest of animals, and had never before dirted except into his basin of water.

chapter thirteen

AS the rainy season approached, we forced ourselves to resume preparations for planting and for the battles we knew lay ahead. We watched the incredible numbers of locusts settle and then rise to pass and repass across the flats. In all directions, in Northern and in Southern Rhodesia, Nyasaland, Portuguese East Africa and Angola, in Bechuanaland and the Kalahari Desert and the Transvaal, swarms similar to those we watched cluttered the sky. Wherever they settled, they laid eggs, and hoppers emerged and added their destructiveness to that of their flying progenitors.

An area three-quarters the size of the entire land area of the United States was literally being eaten alive. Other swarms, remnants of the migration of the locusts down the eastern portion of Africa which had originated in faraway Iran, Iraq, and Saudi Arabia, were still wreaking destruction in Tanganyika, Kenya, and Ethiopia. Coupled with the ever-deepening business depression, it is a tribute to the tenacity and courage of the people who lived through those years that the territories came through and survived as entities, to enter into the last terrible war and later to develop into the flourishing countries we see today. Truly, the decade between 1930 and 1940 was a period of intense trial and tribulation for the inhabitants of East and Central Africa and the northern part of the Union.

Fortunately, there were relatively few bush pigs on Ibamba. Neither were we bothered by baboons. Both species, especially the baboons, are chary of becoming trapped by men, predatory animals, or floods, and realized that an island such as the bushveld portion of Ibamba could be a dangerous place.

Bush pigs are particularly destructive to such ground crops as peanuts and potatoes, although a herd can raise cain in a cornfield. Baboons, coming as they do sometimes by the hundreds, lope along the rows of mealies, stripping off the cobs to take one or two bites and then move on to despoil still more. In an hour a hundred baboons, which are animals weighing up to sixty pounds when full-grown and equipped with longer and stronger teeth than a leopard, can devastate a ten-acre patch of grain completely.

Adult male and female baboons will turn and fight when pursued by dogs. Armed not only with frightful teeth but with hands as well, baboons seize the legs of dogs and bite through the tendons, hamstringing them. Then they literally tear the dogs to pieces.

The crafty, sinuous leopard is a constant foe of baboons as well as monkeys. More than one of the spotted cats has met its death, however, beneath a swarm of shrieking, barking, fighting baboons. If there had been even one troop of baboons on Ibamba, we would not have been able to let our dogs run loose as they customarily did.

Although the leopards, of which there were quite a few on Ibamba, occasionally caught and made away with a dog, the dogs were protection against the incursions of pigs and antelope. At one period we had as many as twenty-eight great Danes, plus a good many other animals which could only be described as dogs of uncertain parentage.

The Danes were not the finest examples of the breed. But they were large; they had fine deep husky barks and they made an impressive show. Many nights when the grain was tall and ripening —which, of course, was before the locusts—we heard the dogs barking and racing through the mealie fields, chasing and fighting with the bush pigs. Usually, when this happened, either I or Charlie Portuguese, who was allowed to keep a shotgun in the compound, would get up and fire a shot over the field. As the boom of the shot rolled through the night, the barking of the dogs rose to a crescendo, and then we would hear the sounds fade as the dogs pursued the pigs onto the veld.

When the lions came to visit Paddy, the dogs grew frenzied. Probably this was because the visitors were always somewhat noisy, in contrast to the trio of lions which came regularly on their inspection trips. At night, because the boys had made pets of this one and that and fed them tidbits from their cooking, the dogs stayed mainly around and in the compound. Often the first notification we in the house had that the lions were nearing or actually visiting Paddy was the sudden barking from the compound. The sounds the lions uttered were usually too low and gentle to attract our attention. Listening, we could hear the barking come nearer and nearer along the road from the compound. The dogs, however, always stopped about halfway. Whether this was because from that point they could see the lions or because the strong, somewhat putrid smell which always surrounds a wild lion became too strong, we could never determine.

Only old Spottie, the old half-breed ridgeback, would dare to approach closer. I could follow her progress because I recognized her bark, but the moment always came when Spottie's nerve gave way and she let out a howl and fled to rejoin the others. We never found any indication that the lions ever chased the dogs. I think the lions just stood rather contemptuously watching the lesser animals, and then whoofed at them or growled. A good whoof from the deep chest of a large lion is warning enough for most creatures.

Anticipating the ordeal which we were certain lay ahead if we were to reap any crops at all, we abandoned certain of the areas we had cleared of bush. With the reduced number of natives in our employ it would have been idiotic to have tried to defend more than the acreages close by and to the west and north of the house. Before the rains came down, and so that we could devote all our efforts to planting, cultivating, and battling the locusts, we hauled great quantities of dead wood for the fires and stacked many large bundles of grass where we could reach them quickly. We no longer had any old tubes or tires or tar with which to make smoke. Such things had all been burned in the previous struggles.

Financially crippled as we were, we had to cut back expenses in every way possible. Kerosene was much too expensive to be used as lavishly as before to start the fires, so we stored dry grass in the space where we kept the laboratory equipment piled. I zealously hoarded our supply of gasoline against emergency, and we used oxen for every possible hauling or pulling task.

I have always enjoyed working with oxen. Oxen are such patient, powerful animals, and the better ones are quite intelligent. Charlie Matabele was an excellent ox trainer, and the spans which he developed were a joy to work with.

In America it is seldom that one sees—*saw* is perhaps better, because oxen are used so infrequently nowadays—more than two oxen in the yoke at one time. Throughout Rhodesia we used oxen in spans of sixteen or eighteen animals. The eight or nine pairs pulled in yokes bound to a long wire rope or a chain. At the head of the line were the two leaders, each of which had, and knew, its name. The driver, walking beside the plodding animals, shouted the name of the leader on the right if he wanted the oxen to swing to the right, or of the leader on the left if he wished to turn the other way. With the pistol-like crack of the long rawhide whip which was fastened to a pole ten or twelve feet long, the driver shouted and yelled and talked to his oxen and they swung obediently to his commands.

Whenever the going or the pulling was exceptionally hard, the long line of straining animals went to their knees, throwing their weight against the yokes, heaving and struggling until they succeeded in moving forward.

Often when we had an exceptionally heavy log to haul to the saw pits, or a tough, recalcitrant stump to pull, or the four-furrow disc plow stuck in heavy soil, Charlie would hitch up two and even three spans, thirty-six or fifty-four oxen, in one long line. It took at least three drivers to control such a number, and the uproar as the men yelled and shouted and cracked their whips echoed across the land. More than once, when bound to something too heavy, the oxen surging together snapped the chains, and once they pulled a heavy steel wire rope apart.

Because of the heat in the middle of the day, Charlie Matabele and the other drivers inspanned their oxen very early in the morning—often around three-thirty or four, when the first light of dawn chased the night from the flats and off the ranch. The oxen were worked for perhaps five hours and then outspanned and driven off to graze and drink and rest until about four in the afternoon, when they were inspanned and worked through until shortly before sunset. Watching the oxen work or walking beside them, they seemed slow; but as furrow after furrow rolled over, it was surprising how much plowing was accomplished in a day.

As the arrival of the rains drew nearer and nearer, we completed most of our preparations. Great piles of dry firewood lay stacked all about the fields. Where necessary, fence posts had been replaced and the barbed wire pulled tight. The ditches to hold off hoppers were cleaned and the sides squared. The soil in the fields was leveled and made ready to receive the seed. We renewed the grass which had been laid on the iron roof of the house to deaden the noise of the pelting rain and cleared the drainage troughs dug to lead excess water away from the foundations. The mosquito wire on the windows and doors and the verandas was carefully examined, and wherever there was a hole or a split, repairs were made. Iz did some repainting inside and had our clothes carried outside to hang for a final sunning and airing before the wet weather. We made a careful and detailed inventory of our supplies, and I made a last trip to the railway to bring out the few necessities we could afford. All the way in and out to and from Choma I drove through locusts. The insects were not so numerous as on previous trips, but there was not a mile when locusts were not beating against the windshield or flying into the cab.

Then the lightning came and great bolts jarred into the ironstone ridge on which the house was built and the winds moaned and whistled from out the flats. The air was filled with fine ash from the enormous fires which had burned away the grass, and with sand and dust. The zebra, the wildebeest, the roan and sable, the wart hogs and the impala, grew restless and began their annual retreat from the lowlands westward toward higher ground. At night the heavy humid air resounded to the snorting and honking of the small herd of hippos in the river, the grunting coughs of hunting leopards in the papyrus, and the royal roaring of lions stalking the herds of antelope.

In defiance of the locusts the dry crowns of grass once again sent forth green shoots and the trees and bushes budded and readied to leaf in anticipation of the rain. The burned, seared veld blossomed with small, delicate wildflowers and the wild orange trees in the great *saka* dropped their yellow fruits.

The land, vibrant with quickening life and eager to blossom forth, lay waiting for the life-giving water to fall. In the villages the emaciated people watched the skies, noting the swarms of locusts with despairing eyes, and bent to their hoeing and the preparation of their gardens. The thin cattle grazed eagerly on the new green shoots of grass which gave them scours. The blades were short and far between, and none ever filled their bellies.

Because the meat of cattle, even thin, scrawny cattle, was and is food, deaths among the older and larger owners of cattle increased markedly. The Mashakulumbwe worshiped cattle and would not kill one, no matter what might be its suffering, except to mark and celebrate its owner's death. It was their belief that the spirits of cattle killed at a man's funeral would accompany him into the next world. Because of the dire shortage of food not a few of the deaths which occurred among the cattle owners were brought about by the judicious introduction into food of some poisonous concoction prepared by the village witch doctor.

To us, waiting and watching on Ibamba, trying to calculate our chances of reaping a crop of mealies or of peanuts, the odds seemed stacked against us. The promise of the land was there and we had our seeds ready. The fields had been fertilized and cleaned of weeds and prepared as thoroughly as we knew how. The planter had been oiled and oxen trained to pull it and to walk in straight lines so that the rows of planted grain would look straight and parallel.

But every day swarms of locust flew between us and the sun and the shadows of their passing swept silently and ominously across the veld, crawled soundlessly up the sides of the house, and passing over the roof, flowed away onto the flats or were swallowed in the bushveld. Often the insects flew so low that the dry rustling sound of their wings filled the air, seeping into the rooms in the house and into the office for an hour or two hours or more as the locusts fluttered over. The boys and I, working in the fields, watched and cursed the locusts, using horrid native words.

The brilliant and often deafening electric displays quieted down and the winds changed to gentle breezes. The rains came, and we brought out the farm machines and put seed corn and peanuts into the ground and stood by to watch and fight.

It was rapidly becoming an endless and a hopeless struggle. As before, we concentrated on protecting the vegetable garden, and succeeded in this fairly well. The entire garden did not occupy an acre. The corn and peanuts shot up from the ground; for a time they prospered, and we found courage and hope in the sight. The plants looked so young and strong and healthy and were of such a beautiful green. When the new shoots were some ten inches high, the locusts came pouring in low over the trees like water plunging down a waterfall.

Again battle was joined and Ibamba reeked of smoke and resounded with horrible noise and confusion. Again and again, bone-weary, heart-sore men and women dragged themselves to the compound at the end of the day, so tired and discouraged many hoped aloud that the next day would never come. For Isabella and me the days were tragic. With every lost battle we saw our hopes of founding the research station shrink toward nothing. As the weeks and months wore on and the locusts never ceased their attacks, we began seriously to wonder whether we would ever be able to save enough in money and possessions to leave the territory and begin life again some other place.

Sometimes events can start out in the most deceiving way. It was a perfectly normal spring evening about three weeks before Christmas. Iz and I were finishing supper in the dining room. Buncher was asleep in the bedroom and Sixpence and his picanin were washing up in the kitchen. Lavison was clearing the last of the dishes from the table when he stopped, and then stepped to one of the casement windows to listen to some noise he had heard outside. It was raining gently, and the air was close and heavy.

"*N'Kos,*" he told me, turning away from the window, "there's some *skillum* (bad actor) after the chickens."

I got up hurriedly, and with Lavison, stood listening at the window. It was a pitch-black night, as heavy rain-laden clouds obscured the moon and the stars. Iz joined us. We couldn't hear much. The rain, gentle as it was, made a pattering sound on the metal roof. We moved to the kitchen and stood in the doorway.

There was trouble, all right. We could hear hens fluttering about the run and an occasional squawk. Something was after them. The hens should have been dreaming on their perches inside the henhouse, generating eggs for the morning.

I sighed. I loathed night-time excursions. Usually there was nothing much to worry about. But there were always possibilities. I hated, and still vehemently dislike, possibilities. Such as finding a leopard grinning at me in a henhouse or having a ringhals cobra spit at me from the thatch. In any case I'd just finished a large supper, and I should have rested for digestion's sake.

The chickens came before my digestion. I walked down the house to the back veranda and found my rubber boots and pulled them on. I got a shotgun and loaded one barrel with fine shot—in case of a snake—and the other with a charge of heavy buckshot. That would be handy, heaven forbid, in the nasty event that a leopard was waiting to make things unpleasant for me. Such encounters are always a toss-up as to the outcome. Which was one reason I didn't like them. I'm a sure-thing gambler.

I picked up a kerosene lantern by the bail. Lavison had thoughtfully lit it for me. He was staying in the house, although I must admit he would have accompanied me if I had asked him. I took a small flashlight in the same hand as held the lantern, and carrying my shotgun in the other hand, fared forth to rectify whatever situation existed. Moodily I brooded on how helpful people were, and how quick to assist some poor devil out into the wet dark when *they* were staying in the warmth and comfort of a house. It *was* dark. The light from the lantern only reached a few yards. And it was wet. The cold rain soaked first through my shoulders and then trickled down my back. Drops hit the hot glass of the lantern and sizzled.

I clicked on the flash with my thumb and swung the beam about. I knew the way perfectly, but I had to pass the woodpile, and there was always the chance that the wood boy had left a chunk in the path against the possibility that I would have to come out during the night and would trip and fall on my face. That would have been good for a laugh even if he had to pay for the prank by taking a cuff beside the ear. It is always a hilarious situation when the boss-man hits the dirt. It's why little boys leave banana peels on the pavement.

The outside wire for the hens ran parallel to Paddy's kraal, but a distance of thirty feet separated the two. As I made my way along the path, cussing under my breath, I threw the beam of the flash into the paddock. She wasn't outside. During the day, when it was warm and the sun would come out eventually, Paddy liked to lie in the rain and get wet. But not at night. I didn't call to her, as I wasn't sure just what lay ahead of me. The less noise I made, the better. So I scuffed along in my awkward boots, trying to make as little commotion as possible.

I flicked on the flash again as I neared the corner of the chicken run and just caught a glimpse of a tawny shape dashing into the chicken house. The animal moved so fast and the rain obscured the light so much that I couldn't determine what it was. But it was big. It was yellowish. And fast.

I pulled up short. Standing there in the dark, in the middle of a small circle of flickering lamplight, I suddenly felt very alone and very silly. I hefted my shotgun and that gave me a little courage. Suppose that was a leopard I had glimpsed? It could have gotten in easily, as the top of the chicken run was not fastened very securely. Leopards, especially when cornered inside a coop, are not the friendliest of animals. They dislike very much being interrupted when dining on chicken.

I debated what to do. I could retreat and call for reinforcements from the compound, which would have been the wisest thing to do. But I was never noted for wisdom. Or I could maintain my reputation as a great hunter and go it alone.

I advanced. Cautiously. I was, and am, cursed with a vivid imagination, and could see myself stretched out on the floor of the chicken coop with my interiors spewed among the feathers and a leopard sitting on my chest! I could almost smell the lilies being laid on my grave.

In spite of my horrid vision of my coming demise, I kept on. I made my way along the chicken run and around the corner of the laboratory building to the door to my workroom. There I stopped and battled with myself again. To open or not to open the door? Was there a leopard waiting inside? If there was, would it choose to do battle with me or would it scoot out the door the chickens used and over the outside wire? If it was inside, would I have time to see it, raise my gun, and shoot it before it began a personal argument?

I opened the door as carefully and as slowly as I could. A burglar couldn't have done it better. Fortunately, because it was the rainy season and things rust, the hinges were well oiled.

It was black as pitch inside the office. Slowly I brought the lantern forward so that its light splashed inside. I saw at once that the door between the workroom and the chicken house was open part way. Either I or one of the natives had neglected to close it tightly. That night I blessed whoever it was who had forgotten to close the connecting door. At least I wouldn't have to open it, with the possibility that there was an angry or frightened leopard behind it in the dark.

I shoved the flashlight into a hip pocket and eased myself into the workroom. Duck bumps prickled on my arms, and the chill which played across the back of my neck made the short hairs rise. It was the silence which frightened me. There wasn't a sound. Not a hen clucked or cackled. There was no rustling. Beyond the feeble circle of light the darkness was forbidding and blacker than it was outside. My hand, gripping my gun, was wet, and it was not all rainwater. I set the lantern down gently and looked about for something I could toss into the darkness in the other room. If there was a leopard there, that might startle it so that it would make a noise and I would know where it was. The object might make it angry, too, and bring it out in one terrific leap. If there was a leopard and it came out, it would have to come over the lantern and through the door. I hoped I would be quick enough to hit it squarely with the charge of buckshot as it sprang. Leopards don't die easily.

Backing out of the circle of light as cautiously as I could, I reached my workbench and found an old broken kitchen knife I used to scrape deposits from crystallizing dishes. It had a heavy handle. I moved back toward the half-open door, took my gun by the forepiece in my left hand so I could raise it quickly, and tossed the knife into the blackness of the room. It hit a crate and clattered and bounced on the floor.

At once there was an answer. A long-drawn-out mushy-sounding *ek-eow*.

Paddy! It was Paddy who was in the chicken coop! I shook so with relief, I nearly had to sit down. I had really been scared up to that point.

When I had made my way through the outer door, I had concentrated so on the half-open door to the chicken coop that I had never thought to look at the door to Paddy's apartment. I did then. It was open. So she had just come out, crossed the workroom, and finding the henhouse door open, gone in. She'd wanted to play with those lovely white chickens for a long time.

Muttering uncomplimentary remarks about pet lions and those idiotic enough to love them, I set my gun down, and picking up the lantern, placed it so that part of its light shone into the hen coop, then walked boldly in. There were some feathers still flying in the air. They drifted through the glow of the lantern like yellow snowflakes. Paddy was inside the coop, lying in a corner and facing me.

Chickens lay all about. If they were all dead, she had really cost us heavily with her spree.

Paddy grinned at me, curling her lip and showing one of her huge canine teeth. As I stepped toward her, chickens suddenly began to come to life. They'd been playing doggo. Paddy, too, came to her feet, and as several chickens charged out the door to the outside pen, Paddy took after them. I took after her, bending low to get out the door. Birds flew clumsily about the long run and Paddy had wonderful fun batting them down on the fly and rushing madly after one and then another. She moved so quickly, and I, with those blasted rubber boots on, so slowly, I couldn't catch her. If I could have gotten hold of her someplace and then reached her collar, I might have been able to stop her. As it was, her hide was slippery with the rain and I could not grasp her firmly.

Then she ran into the coop after a chicken and I got there fast enough to block her exit. Feathers and chickens and dust and bits of bedding were flying all about the small enclosure. The dust got in my throat and up my nose. I crowded Paddy into a corner and made a leap for her. Got my arms around her neck, but she struggled so I couldn't get hold of her collar. She dumped me off and started after the big rooster. He tried to take off, couldn't, and disappeared under Paddy. She stopped for a moment to pick the rooster up in her mouth and I caught up with her and grabbed her tail.

My hanging onto Paddy's tail didn't faze her at all. She just dragged me about the henhouse floor, filling my rubber boots with rubbish and dirt and rolling me in chicken manure, chips, straw, and the Lord knows what. I couldn't hold her. I did slow her down, and she began to pay me some mind. She dropped the rooster and let me work my way hand over hand up her tail and seize her collar. Then she wanted to play. Down we went, wrestling. I hollered at her to quiet down, and she growled and whoofed as she always did whenever she fussed with me or with the baby. Frantic hens added their squawks to the uproar. Anyone who didn't know what was going on and who heard the ruckus would have been certain that I was being gutted and torn limb from limb.

It was hard on my shirt and shorts. Paddy certainly made a mess of me that night. The floor of a chicken house, while fairly soft, isn't exactly the cleanest place to roll around. Paddy lay on me and pushed me into the mess, then she licked my face, taking off some skin with that rasp of a tongue and leaving me all sticky and gooey so that the feathers and dust stuck.

I finally managed to get my heavy rubber-booted feet under me and straightened up and horsed Paddy to her feet. I had a firm grip on her collar and had her by the tail with my other hand. Using my knees, I pushed, shoved, and tumbled her toward the door. Just as I almost had her out a chicken, playing dead on the floor, decided that was the time to take off for other parts. Paddy lunged for it as it squawked and flapped away, and down we went again to roll and tumble and wrestle around.

I was tired. The rubber boots weighed a ton each. We'd been at this wrestling business ten minutes or more, and you can take my solemn word for it that ten minutes trying to pin a lioness to the mat—or to a chicken-house floor—is equal to the full half of a hard football game. Not one played in the two-platoon system, either.

Paddy decided to become more amenable. She'd had her fun. I got her to her feet again and shoved her out the wire door and into the workroom. Lions are the most unpredictable animals. As soon as I had kicked the door shut behind us, Paddy quieted right down, rubbed against my leg, and ek-eowed mushily, as much as to say, "I'm sort of sorry, boss. But wasn't it fun?" Just as nice as pie she walked into her apartment, said good night, and let me shut her in.

In the chicken coop, surprisingly, I found only four dead hens out of the forty that had been there. The rooster looked weak, and he died the next day, but, considering, the damage was slight. If she had had a mind to, Paddy could have slaughtered them all.

I picked up my lantern, closed the door firmly, took my gun, and made my way back to the house after securing the outside door. Isabella and the houseboys were waiting in the kitchen. Just before I got to the door, I took a couple of deep breaths and tried to swagger along like a guy who'd just accomplished something wonderful.

I didn't realize what a sight I was, with feathers sticking to me all over, streaked with dust and dirt and other things.

My bluff didn't come off. Lavison took one look at me, let out a yell, and fell to the floor, howling with laughter. Iz's eyes widened, and then she, too, began to laugh. She laughed so hard, she couldn't talk. Just pointed at me and then made washing motions and pointed toward the bathroom.

I was never so humiliated in my life.

Christmas was coming. The boys, of course, knew that there was not enough grain in the storehouse to permit the making of beer. Because of the locusts they had done without the previous year. Mangineera, however, came to the office one rainy day when I was working there and squatted on the floor to discuss things.

I swung around in my chair to smile at the blocky little man crouched before me. He stared back at me solemnly, then looked at Paddy, who was sitting on her haunches on my workbench. His wondrously wide grin parted his lips and showed the two rows of sharp filed teeth. The grin forced the tip of his mutilated nose upward, deepening the crease lines in his pock-marked cheeks. The thought flashed through my mind that to others Mangineera probably looked ugly, even ferocious. An impression which would have been right in one way, although in my eyes my gunbearer was handsome and appealing in a rugged, disfigured sort of way. That spontaneous grin gave him away. Behind his façade of bravado and swagger Mangineera was kind and gentle, devoted, and one of the most utterly reliable and honest persons it has been my privilege to know.

"Would the *N'Kos,*" Mangineera asked, "permit his people to make a little beer for Christmas if they used grain saved from the rations issued?"

I pondered the question while my little man anxiously watched my expression. I thought of all the hours he and the people in the compound had spent racing up and down the fields in the disastrous and unending battle against the locusts. I thought of their acceptance of the reduction in their rations and the fact that not one had been heard to complain. I thought, too, of the fact that we would, if we made beer, be setting a bad example. John Price, the government officials, the traders, everyone, was urging the natives to conserve their grain by every means and to forego the making of beer even for funerals. For us to celebrate, however modestly, hardly seemed the thing to do.

I mentioned this, pointing out that Ibamba was, in a way, the showplace for the district. It was to us that natives came to watch plows work and to learn how to handle one before parting with oxen to purchase a plow from Cavadia. It was on Ibamba that natives were taught to make bricks, to become carpenters and masons and sawyers. It was by watching us work and participating that the village natives came to appreciate the value and use of available fertilizers such as wood ashes and cattle manure; the need for cultivation of crops to insure maximum yield; and it was from us that this one and that secured small quantities of improved strains of hybrid corn to grow.

Slowly nodding his head, Mangineera acknowledged the validity of what I said. It was true, he agreed, that we taught and helped many. It was also true, Mangineera argued, that our people were tired—which was an understatement if I ever heard one—and he rose and walked to the open door and pointed outside, where I could see the shimmering yellow and red bodies of locusts fluttering above the ground.

"They," he said, referring to the locusts, "have beaten us. The spirits of the people have died within them. In the villages where our sons and daughters live, where live the old people who gave us life, death walks from hut to hut. Although here, because the *N'Kos* is great and has money, we have not yet starved; but we know of the things which have been happening all around us and our hearts are sad. The people no longer have the will or strength to work as they should. A little beer would help."

Why not, I thought? Our people certainly deserved something in the way of extras, and we could not afford to hand out Christmas "bockes" that year. I visualized the stacked bags of grain in the storeroom. A portion of the grain, I knew, had become infested with weevils and a considerable poundage had become almost inedible. I say "almost" because under the conditions the people would eat anything.

"Can you make beer," I asked, "using only broken grain and grain which may have been eaten badly by insects?"

Mangineera's face brightened. His quick mind grasped at once my line of thought.

"It would not be so good as other beer," he told me. "But the women can clean the grain and beer can be made."

"All right." I made my decision. "Send Charlie Portuguese to me and I will show him what bags you may pick over and clean. The broken grain, the grain with weevils, you may have to make beer. The rest must be returned and be bagged and stored. There must be no cheating."

"It is good," stated Mangineera.

He rose to his full five feet and stood looking at me and at Paddy for a moment. She curled her lip and showed one great canine tooth in a leonine smile of condescension. Mangineera pursed his lips and made a rude noise in return, and the smile vanished. The lioness and the little giant of a man were friends, but he always insulted her.

At the door, as he left, Mangineera turned and spoke softly: "There will be no cheating, *N'Kos*." Then he was gone, and I heard him shout to Charlie Portuguese. I got up and returned Paddy to her apartment, shut her doors, and walked to the storeroom to show Charlie what grain he might use.

The throbbing of the tom-toms sounded unusually loud Christmas Eve because the air was heavy with rain and because we had not heard them for so long. Iz and I had finished decorating the tree and sat in the living room admiring it and listening to the shrill voices of the women singing in the compound. Later, as we wrapped a few little presents for Buncher in gay paper saved from previous Christmases, we tried to hide the depression and worry which gnawed in each of us and tried to joke and smile. Neither of us fooled the other. The tragedy of the locusts, the hopelessness which had been engendered by the business depression, weighed too heavily on our minds, as indeed they did on the minds and spirits of everyone, black and white, throughout Northern Rhodesia.

Throughout Central Africa, Christmas and Boxing Day were passed battling against the voracious descending swarms of locusts. For many of the whites it was their last Christmas in the territory. With the coming of the dry season hundreds abandoned their farms and ranches or ceased searching for nonexistent work in the mines and left for "home." For once, the hard, boisterous, self-sufficient settlers cast their eyes and thoughts heavenward, and not a few prayed earnestly for guidance and deliverance.

It was six weeks after Christmas, the middle of February, when Mr. Thomas disappeared. We were frantic. Just what happened, we shall never know. When we first suspected that he was gone, we searched every nook and cranny of the house. Lavison and the other boys turned every closet inside out and searched through all the linen, the storeroom, and all the shelves and bookcases. Tommy was a fair size, measuring nearly five feet from tip of nose to tip of tail. He needed a good-sized place in which to hide.

When a complete search determined that Tommy was not in the house, I summoned everyone from the compound and we put them all to work searching the grounds. A reward was offered, and children crawled under all the bushes, the tomato vines, and through the woodpile. As the first day passed and we found no signs, the search was widened and men beat through the longer grass in rows and groups. Nothing.

We passed a restless and unhappy night. Several times Iz got up and walked the veranda, calling. She called from the windows of the living room. Until then Tommy had always answered her with his soft cluck-clucking noise. She got no replies.

In the morning Mangineera and Jam found marks which showed that a small cat—the tracks looked like those of a civet—had been around the house during the night. We tried to follow, but the animal was too light to leave marks in the grass which we could decipher. Whether it was Tommy who was around that night we never found out. If it was, I do not understand why he did not answer his foster mother.

We searched all the second day, the hunt spreading farther and farther afield. Everyone felt that going too far was useless, as no one believed that Tommy, who loved his comfort so, would venture far. Certainly he would hide during the day, if only for the reason that he would not be able to see much. There was plenty of food available; locusts cluttered the ground everywhere, so he would not go hungry. But the second day passed without any results, and we sat, heavy-hearted and weary and forlorn, in the living room after supper as we tried to reconcile ourselves to the fact that we had lost our foster child. We missed him terribly. Every chair and every corner in the room had its dot of civet where Tommy had backed up and deposited it. A faint civet perfume could be detected in the air. The big bed seemed sort of empty without that long black shape curled on a pillow.

The next morning one of the boys who looked after the traps we often put out for leopards came running in, all out of breath, with the news that a large civet cat was caught in a trap near the big *saka*. This trap was nearly two miles from the house. The native said, between gulps for air, that the civet looked like Mwaming Thomas so he had not killed it. He added that it was badly cut up as a leopard had come along later to get the bait, found the civet cat already in the trap, and had fought with it, or vice versa.

It didn't seem likely that Tommy would, or could, have wandered so far, but on the chance that it was he, I got the truck and filled the tank with some of our precious store of gasoline and drove out.

Leaving the truck near the *saka*, I followed the native to the set. It was a shambles. In one of the traps—I used four at one set—lay a civet cat, caught high up on a rear leg. It was covered with dirt and matted blood. I could see jagged rips across its head where the leopard had swatted it with its claws. But the little fellow had fought back. The ground was all torn up. Bushes were bitten and chewed, and I could see blood on the chain and the jaws of the trap where the cat had fought and bitten the metal. Leopard tracks were all about in the dirt, and the big cat had eaten some of the bait. The remainder filled the air with a stinking sweetish taste.

It was easy to get the civet out of the trap. There was little fight left in it. We wrapped it carefully in a couple of stout grain bags and carried the poor broken little fellow to the truck, and I drove as fast as possible to the house.

Iz was waiting in the kitchen as we carried the civet and laid it on the metal top of the table. It was impossible yet to tell whether it was Tommy or not. The cat was barely alive, and made no resistance as I stretched it out and gently began to probe and feel the wounds. It was terribly hurt. The heavy trap had smashed the hind leg. The gaping cuts around the head were the worst.

Sixpence brought warm boiled water. We had disinfectants, needles and sterile gut, cotton and bandages. Carefully and slowly we sponged off the wounds, getting out the dirt and the bits of leaves and the dried blood. Jam, Mangineera, and Charlie Portuguese and Lavison helped, and the kitchen door was jammed with natives worried about Mr. Thomas. All the time we worked, the beaten cat just lay still, its chest rising and falling with its heavy breathing. Iz kept talking to it and calling it by name, but there was no response.

For nearly two hours we labored. Our eyes were wet with tears, because even though it might not be Tommy who lay on the table, the poor little chap was in such terrible shape, it was heartbreaking work. It was dreadful to see what the leopard had done. How the cat lived at all was a wonder.

Finally we had done everything we could. While we were working, snipping off ragged flesh, cutting off matted hair and shaving places to get them clean, and pulling gaping cuts together with gut, the cook had been baking a custard. We hoped that if it was Tommy who lay on the table, he would show some reaction to the smell of his favorite food.

Bandaged and clean, the civet cat lay on a fresh towel. Its eyes were closed and its breathing barely discernible. Iz took a tablespoon of custard and held it under the civet's nose. For a long moment, while I am sure everyone in the kitchen held their breath, there was no reaction. Then the little black nose quivered. Iz spoke urgently, cluck-clucking. The head moved a trifle, and then one eye, badly damaged, opened a trifle.

It *was* Tommy. Iz broke down and wept. A hard lump swelled in my throat, and tears trickled down my face. The cook cried a little, and even the hard, impassive faces of our hunters worked with emotion. It was apparent to all that even in his dire extremity, Mwaming Thomas knew his foster mother and reacted to her voice as it reached him in his daze of pain and fear.

Unless you have lived with, cared for, and loved an animal, you will not understand the grief we felt or the pall of gloom and unhappiness which fell over Ibamba. The tom-toms in the compound were quiet that night. Iz and I were quiet and preoccupied and soft in our movements as we put Buncher to bed and took care of Thomas lying in a carefully padded box. We did get a little warm milk, much sweetened, with some nux vomica, into him during the long night by pulling his lip gently away from his gums and pouring the mixture with a teaspoon. It was mighty little. It was very difficult for Tommy to swallow, his throat and the muscles covering it were so badly torn. But he tried.

For two days we battled to bring our pet back. But our efforts were to no avail. Tommy tried to co-operate. He seemed to know that we were trying to help him in every way we knew. And beyond any question he recognized his foster mother. Which made it so much more heartbreaking.

During the third night Tommy died. Quietly, while he seemed asleep.

We buried Mwaming Thomas Sibyunni'byunni Mashonto, in his box, reverently, at the foot of a tall palm up which climbed one of the beautiful flaming red vines which were so conspicuously a part of Ibamba during the rainy season.

chapter fourteen

DURING all the years I hunted and captured animals professionally and for study, I used dogs to help me. These were not of any special or chosen breed. If we had any preference, it was for mongrels. There were exceptions, but generally speaking pure-bred dogs lacked physical stamina; they were more susceptible to disease than the mongrels and they lacked heart. The mongrels were far smarter than their elegant companions and much less highly strung and nervous.

In addition to the protection which having dogs about brought to a camp, the dogs were used for two purposes. To chase after, stop, and surround some swift young animal which we were trying to catch, or to pursue a wounded animal and bail it so that it could be shot and put out of its misery. Use of dogs saved hunters miles and miles of running and tracking and insured that only the minimum of animals escaped to die lingering deaths.

It was never the function of a dog to fight or savage an animal. All that we wanted, or expected, was for the dogs to catch up with the fleeing quarry, surround it, and bark to bring us quickly to the spot. We did not want a captured animal injured in any way. If the animal had already been wounded by a bullet, a dog was more apt to frighten the animal even more by biting it and thus drive it farther away than if the dog circled at a moderate distance and just barked and made threatening moves.

Brave dogs, dogs such as the English bull terrier, which like to dash in close and get a grip with their jaws on an animal, seldom lasted long. Wild animals are fast and quick in their movements, and most are armed with efficient weapons of one sort or another. Wart hogs and bush pigs could, and sometimes did, rip a pack of dogs to pieces with their razor-sharp tusks; sable and roan, when bailed, lie down, and can protect every portion of their bodies with sweeps and thrusts of their strong, needle-sharp horns. Even lions have been killed by sable and roan. The great eland antelope can kick with sufficient force to cave in a dog's skull, and zebras both kick and bite ferociously.

I learned the value and use of dogs from Harry and Mackie Walker, who taught me hunting shortly after I first went to Northern Rhodesia. They bought their dogs, in lots of fifty to a hundred, from the pound in Johannesburg.

In the nineteen twenties it was possible to write to the pound and arrange to buy all the dogs which were brought in over a period of, say, a month or six weeks. At the end of this period whoever was buying went to the pound and looked over the collection. As might be expected, it was motley. I have been offered a selection running from a beautiful pair of great Danes, which had been picked up as being too savage, and a racing greyhound, through collies, bulldogs, pointers, spaniels, and poodles, to run-of-the-mill mongrels of every color and size.

The buyer paid the food bill for all the dogs which had been collected and held for the period specified. This was never large because the dogs were fed mainly on horse and donkey meat, and old horses and donkeys were common and cheap in and around Johannesburg. Having paid the food bill, the buyer then made his selection. For those chosen he paid a shilling apiece—twenty-five cents. Those which were not chosen were put to sleep.

It can be a bit of a problem to transport a hundred dogs for a distance of twelve to fifteen hundred miles. I solved this by hiring two railway box freightcars or, as they are called in Africa, goods vans. The cars were not as large as the American freightcar; they were made of wood, and each had a large door in the center on each side.

A few of the more pugnacious dogs and the smaller ones were put in crates. The rest were fitted with inexpensive collars and chains. The crates were stacked at one end of the car, and along each side we ranged the other dogs, stapling the free ends of their chains with a stout double-nail to the floor in such a position that one dog could not reach another. Food and drink pans and a fifty-gallon drum of water were loaded aboard. The native who was to ride with the dogs and tend them put a cot at the end of the car opposite that where the crates were stacked, and hung a water bottle on a nail. With sandwiches, precooked food, and a little cash he was all set for the four to five days' journey.

By paying a small premium above normal freight rates, the dog cars were attached to the end of a through mail train. While the owner of the dogs rode in comfort in a compartment, the yipping, barking, howling cargo snapped along at the tail end of the train, and the turmoil and hubbub floated away and was lost in the plume of dust following the rattling cars. During the day the native attendant usually rode sitting in the open doorway of the car with his bare feet dangling over the edge, and suffered the uproar. He was paid a bonus.

At the base camp, or ranch, the dogs were sorted out and soft collars of rawhide were fitted loosely around the necks of each. Each native working with the dogs was given a long thin length of rawhide with a small loop in one end. This loop was slipped over the thumb and the length of rawhide passed through the collars of two dogs and the end brought back to be held between the thumb and index finger. A native handled four dogs; two on each side.

When it was time to let the dogs go, the dog-native dropped the loose end of the length of rawhide and yanked, whipping the leash free through the collars so that the dogs could run. The dogs loved to hunt, and when they heard a shot and the native holding them did not release them promptly, they turned on him and nipped him.

One curious fact developed from our use of dogs. No matter what species of animal was captured, more often than not with help from the dogs, the dogs never bothered it once it was brought to camp, quieted down, and released. No matter what the uproar and excitement of the chase may have been, after an animal was installed in camp, the dogs paid it only the most casual interest.

Paddy associated constantly with our dogs on Ibamba, and occasionally shared with them when Mangineera or Charlie Portuguese was dividing meat. During the day the lechwe, the duikers, Fwifwi, and Popeye came and went without any interference from or fear of the dogs. In fact, they often seemed to play together, chasing one another round and round. But when darkness settled over Ibamba, the mood of the dogs changed. They seemed to know that during the hours of night they were to be on guard.

The intelligence, the behavior, the friendships of animals are, to me, fascinating to watch and study. There was once a big lion in the Johannesburg Zoo whose constant companion was a whitish mongrel dog. The two were so devoted to each other that a small opening was cut in one corner of the bars on the lion's cage just large enough to permit the dog to go and come.

Regularly, at certain times, the dog, whom everyone in Johannesburg knew by sight, would leave the cage and trot out of the zoo and go visiting along the streets, begging for handouts of food. Satisfied, it always returned to the cage, entered, and slept curled up beside its tremendous friend. When, after many years, the dog died of old age, it was only a matter of a month or two before the lion died also. Those who watched said the lion never seemed to cease grieving for its pal.

There have been many horses which have had dogs for companions, or sheep or a goat. Unless these animals were shut up with them in their box stalls, the horses were too nervous to rest. On Ibamba, Jane Emmeline John and ugly duckling Garbage gave every sign of friendship one for the other. Fwifwi and Mr. Thomas loved Isabella particularly, and Buncher and I were the special pals of Paddy. Dogs, lion, white people and black, civet cat and antelope, dove and crested crane and hornbill, we all lived together in perfect harmony. If this is against all the teachings and tenets of the naturalists and animal psychologists, I cannot help it. That was the way life was on Ibamba.

The many species of wild animals that inhabit this earth live together, relatively speaking, as peacefully as they do mainly, or so I believe, because no single species wishes to dominate all other species as does man. It is this need, this will, to dominate that has made man the greatest killer, not only of all other animals but of his own species, which the world has ever known. I have often wondered why, with our vaunted wisdom, we have not taken a leaf from the wild creatures' book and tried to fashion our world community living after the pattern existing among the other and "lower" animals.

For many years I have carried the thought that someday I might write a book to be titled, "Why Don't We Behave Like Animals?" Such a book would probably offend the sensibilities of too many people to become a success. But it would be fun to write. There are so many parallels between the actions of human and other animals.

In March and April what grain we had been able to save from the attacks by the locusts began to mature. Having pulled in our horns and reduced the acreage and prepared fully for the battle, we were able to save more than had been possible in the previous years, although the cost in outlay for wages and fuel and physical and mental exhaustion was high. There were actually enough tall stalks standing to make the fields look green and deceivingly prosperous. Deceiving, because where the stalks had not been eaten down, the corn had tassled nicely, but the insistent nibbling by the insects prevented full development and pollination was inadequate and spotty. As a result the plants which rose so tall and green and were so pleasing to look at set comparatively few cobs and the yield per acre was low. The fact that we reaped anything at all cheered us up and buoyed our sagging spirits.

Isabella, of course, each week sent off her boxes of vegetables and meat. When we pulled the peanuts, we cleaned enough nuts to fill some twenty bags and sold these to the *boma* to be used to feed prisoners held awaiting trial. But we were desperately short of cash, and there were several occasions when we were unable to meet our wage bill and had to ask the boys to wait until we accumulated funds.

Going without their pay involved very little hardship on the men. They were being fed and they were housed and doctored. In more affluent times they usually spent their wages on beer brought in from the villages, for women, for gaudy blankets and lengths of cloth or for tidbits to liven their menus. It was the exceptional native who looked to the future and invested his wages in a young ox or heifer or some goats or sheep.

As the rains began to peter off, Iz and I discussed the possibility of making a trip for a couple of months into the region west of Sheasongo, which I had named the "Home of the Lion." This was an area about a hundred miles wide and two hundred long which stretched between the Batonga and Mashakulumbwe tribes on the east and the Barotse on the west. It was a sort of buffer zone and was almost completely uninhabited by natives.

The Home of the Lion had been visited by only a very few white men. I think that the Walker brothers and myself were about the only whites ever to have seen the country at that time. This was not because the area was inaccessible. It was a tsetse fly area into which it was certain death to take any domestic animals. The tsetse carried the trypanosomes of nagana, which is the type of sleeping sickness which affects only livestock. Except for the unpleasantness of being bitten—the bite of a tsetse fly is like that of a horse fly only worse—human beings were not in danger. Presence of the fly discouraged native settlement. Both the Barotse and the Mashakulumbwe were great cattle-owning people. They would not settle in an area where they could not maintain their herds. Although the Home of the Lion was well watered, with many large pans and numerous water-holes, the soil was sour and would not grow good crops. Another reason why natives avoided the area.

As a result, the Home of the Lion had become an undeclared game refuge. The herds of sable, roan, hartebeest, wildebeest, zebra, eland, kudu, waterbuck, and impala were both exceptionally numerous and large in numbers. There were many tremendous herds of buffalo, and elephants ranged over most of the region, although, during the dry season, they were infrequent visitors in the northern portion, which was where we discussed going.

As was to be expected in an area so thickly populated with game of every description, Carnivora abounded. Lions were everywhere and leopards very common. Packs of destructive wild dogs roamed and raced across the veld and hyenas whooped and moaned throughout the nights. There were cheetahs and servals, bush cats and civet cats, an occasional lynx and innumerable jackals.

Because our cash was so limited, we could not continue building or fitting up the laboratory. During the dry, or winter, season, until a month or so before the rains came again, there would be little which we could do on Ibamba except to watch the locusts come and go. For a month or two the boys would be perfectly capable of taking care of things, so Iz and I decided that we would go out to the Home of the Lion and try our luck hunting. Maybe, we thought, with a bit of luck, we would be able to earn a few pounds.

So we wrote to a couple of the better known curio dealers in Johannesburg, inquiring as to their interest in maned lion skins, good heads of horns, leopard skins, and such. These were items which could usually be sold for fair prices to the dealers, who then, in turn, sold them to tourists or to hunters who had failed to secure trophies by their own efforts.

The dealers wrote back to tell us that there were very few tourists because of the depression; those that came through had no money, and that hunters were almost nonexistent. However, they said they would be able to use a few lion skins, leopard skins, and maybe a trophy or two if unusually good. Buffalo heads with a wide, even spread of horn were most in demand. The prices offered were low, but better than nothing.

On the trip we would also be able to make riems. These are the thirteen-foot-long rawhide ropes made from game hides and used to handle oxen. Every working ox has a riem which is used as a lead rope and is also tied to the trek chain. A buffalo hide could be cut into forty riems, and each one sold for a shilling.

In addition to skins, hides, riems, and strops there would be great quantities of meat and fat. The meat, such as was not eaten by our boys, could be salted, sun-dried, and tied in bundles to be traded later for grain, if any could be found, or sold for cash. The fat from the game could be tried out carefully, be strained through cheesecloth, and then stored in five-gallon tins thoroughly cleaned of the kerosene they had once contained. This fat could be sold at the railway line for both cooking and to make soap. Florence Price, I knew, would buy at least ten tins. She was always making soap. A lot was used around the mission. Lion fat, of which one sometimes got a surprising quantity from a fat old rascal, was in much demand among the East Indians, who rubbed the stuff on their aching joints, much as our ancestors used bear grease and goose fat. Lion fat commanded a price of five pounds a pound and was often worth more than the skin.

We would not even have considered such a trip except that we had a rather plentiful supply of cartridges and shells on hand. We had not done nearly as much shooting as we had thought we might, and ammunition deteriorates fairly rapidly, particularly during hot and humid weather. If we had had to purchase ammunition—some of which for my heavier rifles cost as much as forty cents a cartridge—it would have been impossible for us to go.

We discussed the idea with our boys, and they were enthusiastic. They loved the excitement of hunting and camping, and the thought of all the fresh meat they would have to eat made their mouths water. Reluctantly, Charlie Matabele agreed to remain on Ibamba to oversee care of the cattle, and Shamakembie, after we promised to send meat back to him whenever we could, said he would stay and look after Paddy. In consultation with Charlie Matabele, Shamakembie would kill a small cattlebeast or a goat periodically to feed the lioness and such of the dogs as we left behind. As well, of course, as himself.

Jam left to inform Sheasongo of our intentions and of our impending visit. Eight days later he returned with word from the chief that the land was still too wet to allow us to get into the Home of the Lion, that we should wait until the moon was full again, and that he was glad his brother was coming.

I made a trip to Choma to return the empty gasoline drums which had accumulated during the rains and to get four full ones and bring out a list of supplies which Iz felt we would need on the trip. Jam and Mangineera and Charlie Portuguese cleaned the heavy protective grease from the guns, oiled them, and put them into shape for use, and overhauled our various traps. Shaluma made boxes to hold the canned goods, tins of flour, and sugar and other edibles. The moon waned and waxed to the full and started to shrink before we were ready to load the truck and leave.

Because the truck would be so heavily loaded, we sent most of the boys who were to make the trip ahead on foot to wait for us at Sheasongo's village. Mianje would ride in the cab to help hold Buncher, who was, by then, a scrambling handful. Mangineera, Charlie Portuguese, Lavison, Mianje's husband, Shaluma, and Sixpence, the cook, would ride on top of the baggage.

Both Shamakembie and Charlie Matabele were apprehensive at being left to care for both a lioness and the livestock. Despite the fact that wild lions had never attacked since I had taken over possession of Ibamba, they were afraid that they might do so during my absence. I assured them solemnly that this would not, could not, happen. The lions knew, I stated positively, that the livestock on Ibamba belonged to Sibyunni'byunni, and regardless of the fact that I might not be in residence, they would respect my rights. I hinted that I had already spoken to the lions and sent forth the word that they were not to become bothersome just because I was away on business.

The two listened intently and nodded their heads and gloomily agreed that it was true nothing *had* happened. Still. . . . They brightened when I told them I would allow them to keep a rifle in the compound provided they showed it to no one and kept the weapon hidden unless it might be needed. I would leave five cartridges as well. My agreeing to leave a gun did more to brighten their spirits than my assurances concerning the lions. It was against the law, of course, but justifiable, and I was as certain as a man could be that they would keep the gun so carefully hidden that the magistrate could never find it should he suspect and come to look. I was almost certain the gun would not have to be used.

Driving across the veld where there were no roads of any sort, or even native paths, put a tremendous strain not only on the vehicles used but on the driver and, especially, on the tires and tubes. Due to the high cost of gasoline and the necessity to extract the last ounce of use from every gallon, we invariably overloaded. At best, which was when for a mile or two we could drive down the dry, relatively level bottom of a shallow vlei, the going was merely rough. A vlei is a shallow valley between rolling tree-covered land and is carpeted with grass of varying height and usually studded every few yards with small but very hard gray-colored anthills from six to eighteen inches high.

Through the bush country we drove, winding among the trees, swerving to avoid deep ant-bear holes and fallen trunks and logs; passing under branches so low, they swept across the top of the cab and brushed against the load behind. When we came to a donga, which is a dry stream bed, usually with a sandy, rocky bottom, we searched for the best place to cross; then, with picks and shovels, we chopped out ramps so that the truck could inch down and out again, using the lowest and most powerful gear. We drove right over small trees and bushes, and the crankcase became polished to a bright luster.

Cross-country driving was hard on tires. The thornbushes, which were everywhere, bore innumerable thorns from an inch to three inches long. These were needle-sharp, extremely tough and hard, and penetrated right through the thickest tire casing. If a thorn failed to penetrate to the tube when first run over, it broke off and the lengthy tip remained in the casing and gradually worked through until the inside of a tire, after a month or more of such driving, felt as prickly as the back of a porcupine. It was impossible to repair a tire in such condition. We had to throw them away because the points of the thorns, working constantly as the wheel revolved, cut into the tube and let out the air. We tried all sorts of expedients to overcome this. Some cut old tubes in half around their length and used these to reline the tire. We tried lengths of soft tanned antelope skins, and I even sandpapered the inside, hoping to blunt the thorns. Nothing was satisfactory.

Fortunately, I had negotiated an arrangement to test tires for the General Tire and Rubber Company, and was well supplied with spare tires and tubes. Excellent as these tires were, we used them up at an alarming rate.

For those of you who have never organized a trip into a region in which you could not obtain supplies of *any sort,* except the meat which you shot, the water from a pan or waterhole, and firewood, it may be of interest for me to list the major items we loaded on our truck. This list, and the conditions we faced, may also help to explain to the curious why an average hunting safari in Africa is so expensive.

Each drum of gasoline weighed close to 400 pounds. That meant we put 1,600 pounds, three-quarters of a ton, aboard as a starter. We had 20 gallons of kerosene for lamps; 20 gallons of oil and 10 pounds of grease; 4 new spare tires and 8 tubes; a tire and tube-repair kit and an extensive box of tools followed. To these were added several extra leaves for both front and rear springs; a spare universal joint; spring shackles and a soldering kit in case the radiator burst, and spare hose; wire and spark plugs and an extra timer and a new needle valve for the carburetor.

On Ibamba I made our distilled water for the battery and we filled two gallon jugs and put these on the truck with a spare coil, spare condensers, gasket cement, hose clips, and valve inserts for the tubes.

With the anticipated needs of the truck taken care of, the remainder of the load was made up of Buncher's folding mosquito-proof crib; camp furniture; food boxes; two hundred-pound bags of grain for the natives; cooking utensils; an eighteen by twenty-four foot green tarpaulin which was very heavy and bulky; steel traps; eight gallon drums in which to carry and store water; ammunition boxes; duffel bags of clothes and bed linen; plates and cups and knives and forks and spoons; hurricane lanterns; electric torches and searchlights, with replacement batteries; picks, mattocks, shovels, axes, skinning and meat-cutting knives; our large medicine chest; binoculars, cameras, notebooks and, of course, the guns. Even with the helper springs to support the load, the chassis sagged so close to the rear axle, I knew we would have to proceed exceptionally carefully if we were to reach the Home of the Lion safely.

After a tearful good-by to Paddy and Fwifwi, Popeye, Jane, and Garbage and the duikers, we took off early one morning, and driving to the western end of Ibamba, turned onto the track leading to Namwala.

Beyond Namwala the track across the veld deteriorated terribly. Between Ibamba and the *boma* we had driven for the greater part across clayey ground which had dried and become firm under the wheels. As the track continued toward Shaloba's village, we left the edge of the flats, climbed to slightly higher ground, and drove among scattered trees. The soil became very sandy and light.

Shaloba was, perhaps, the richest of all the Mashakulumbwe chiefs. I doubt if even he knew how many cattle he owned. His village was enormous, containing, so it was said, five hundred huts. I never counted them, but the circle in which they stood was very large in diameter, and the people and cattle that lived there numbered in the hundreds and thousands.

Every day the cattle were driven out to graze, and many traveled along the track which we had to traverse. Dozens and dozens of other beasts were walked to Namwala to be traded with Cavadia. The hooves of these animals cut the ground and pulverized it so that the track became a continuous sandy waste; to get over it, we had to shift into our lowest gear and move at a pace of only a few miles an hour. Clouds of fine dust and sand rose from beneath the wheels, and because we moved so slowly, swirled about and into the cab. It was hot, and we sweated, and the dirt stuck to our faces and hands and necks.

It was only some sixty miles from Namwala to Sheasongo, seventy-four from Ibamba, but I did not want to stop at the village even though Shaloba might think me rude. We had everything we needed aboard the truck should we have to camp beside the track, but I wanted to avoid having to do this if possible and to reach Sheasongo before dark. So, as the huge village opened before us, I turned and drove around the circumference while people poured from the huts to shout and wave and call inquiries to the boys riding in the back. How anyone could distinguish who was who in all the dust I could not fathom, but I heard names shouted back and forth.

We found the continuance of the track and passed beyond the churned-up land which surrounded the village for a great distance in every direction. As I drove along, we watched the bushveld roll past. There was not a great deal of game, but we did see a herd of roan antelope, several duikers, and a few baboons loping among the twisted trees. I could see occasional tire markings in the earth and guessed these had been made by the small pick-up truck from the Nanzilla Mission, a couple of miles distant from Sheasongo's village.

About halfway between Shaloba and Sheasongo, the Nanzilla River comes in a slow curve from the southwest, to meander through a wide arm of the flats on its way to join the larger Kafue River. Here the track was rutted and badly cut. Great cracks had opened in the surface of the ground as the moisture was sucked out by the sun and the clayey mixture contracted and caked. I stopped, and Mangineera got off and trotted ahead of the truck to find the best and easiest way. The track led in among many trees, and for a time we drove along the edge of a dense *saka*. The *saka* covered a very large area, and its tangled growth offered a haven to many buffalo, lions, and kudu antelope; in it they could escape from the relentless sun and hide from hunters.

The sun had sunk so close to the horizon that its rays, filtering through the branches of the trees, struck blindingly into the cab. We were hot and dusty and thirsty, and Buncher was beginning to fret. She cried a little, and Mianje crooned to her.

The bushveld thinned and became more open. Long stretches of dry, heavy sand blocked the track. On each side I could see long marks where vehicles from the mission had turned off onto the veld, attempting to drive around the sand. I did the same, and we wove back and forth from one side of the track to another while the engine growled and protested and boiled, trying to pull the heavy load through.

Suddenly, natives in groups appeared beside the track on both sides. The women were keening in their high, shrill voices, and we heard the music of *olimbas.* Children raced beside the truck, leaping and calling. Buncher leaned from the cab to watch, and Mianje became so excited, she nearly let the baby fall. I had not realized we were so close to Sheasongo's village. It was several years since I had last been there.

Driving slowly and carefully as the people crowded close to the route, I saw Shamoanna beating furiously on the *olimba* hanging from his neck. There were other musicians, and the grinding of the truck was drowned in the music and the cries of the villagers. It was indeed a royal welcome, and we were very proud and happy as we emerged from the bushveld and drove across the wide open vlei, at the head of which we could see the huts of the village.

The boys whom we had sent on ahead, and the dogs, were waiting for us beneath a spreading mabunga tree. Sheasongo had seen to it that they, with assistance from his own people, had cleared a large piece of ground of all rubbish and dirt and built a camp surrounded with a fence of grass six feet high for privacy. Pots and pots of water waited for us, and there were piles of firewood. My brother had even remembered that I preferred a grass bed laid on the ground to a canvas cot, and large bundles of clean dry grass stood waiting for Mangineera to fashion into beds for me and for Maseccasecca.

After a decent interval to allow us to unload what might be necessary for our stay and for us to wash up and relax, Sheasongo sent a number of women with pots of beer, small baskets of dried fish and meat, a pumpkin, and a little basket of peanuts. There was also a young goat to supply meat. Later, when the cattle had been driven in and the cows had been milked, there would be fresh milk.

So we came to the village and the people to whom I was, because of my blood brothership with Sheasongo, a chief. Our welcome had been fine and one befitting a chief; tired from the arduous trip, we relaxed and were content.

After our supper Sheasongo sent word that he would like to visit for a while; he came, and after the formal greetings we sat opposite each other and talked of other hunts and he told me of where he thought it would be most advantageous for us to go when we left for the Home of the Lion. Sheasongo told me that he was sending Shamann'yati with me, and I was glad. That grand old hunter knew more about the ways and manners of the wild animals than any man I have ever known.

While Isabella and I talked with the chief, Mianje watched Buncher fall asleep in her crib and Mangineera and Charlie Portuguese made up our beds. These were made by laying two six-inch logs on the ground parallel to each other and some four feet apart. Then they laid long grass across from log to log, another layer lengthwise, one crosswise, and so on until they had built up a springy mattress twelve to fourteen inches thick. For one night this made a wonderfully springy, comfortable bed. As grass was abundant, a new bed was built each night. It was far roomier, warmer, and more comfortable than a canvas cot—even one with a mattress.

After Sheasongo had returned to the village, Iz and I retired. Our beds were close to the fire. The dancing lights glanced across Buncher's cot, which stood close by and illuminated the soft features of the sleeping child. On the opposite side of the tree trunk our natives crouched and lay beside their fires and the odors of roasting meat and fish wafted to us on the gentle breeze. In the village the tom-toms throbbed and pulsed and the singing of the dancers drifted to us. What reason they had to celebrate, situated as they were in the midst of the locust-devastated land, I could not guess. But the drums throbbed on as the singing rose and fell, and we fell asleep with the sounds beating in our ears.

chapter fifteen

EARLY the next morning Sheasongo came. He was particularly interested in the fact that I had inoculated the dogs which were to go out west with trypan blue. It was believed by many that trypan blue acted as a prophylactic against the development of trypanosomes when introduced into the blood of an animal by a tsetse or other biting fly. We knew that by taking the dogs into the Home of the Lion we were subjecting them to the risk of death from nagana, but I wanted to discover whether inoculation with the dye was effective.

Tsetse flies occur within sharply defined areas which are called "belts." It is possible to ride a horse or drive oxen within a few yards of the boundary of a fly "belt" without having an animal bitten. The reasons or causes determining the boundaries are not understood, but nevertheless they are sharp and definite.

If the tsetse remained permanently within the boundaries of the belts, the situation might not be so grave, although the total of the square miles closed to domestic animals by reason of the presence of the fly is enormous. Unfortunately, and for reasons which no one has yet been able to fathom, tsetse-fly belts suddenly move or expand. The movement may be in any direction and it may be restricted to only a few hundred yards or a mile. Because of the danger of such movement no rancher or farmer wished to take up land which could, however remotely, be considered as in danger from a fly belt. Once tsetse flies occupy a piece of land, there is no known way to eliminate them; and no feasible, sufficiently economical inoculation has been developed to control or combat the disease they carry.

The occurrences and the causes for the movements of tsetse flies were subjects which had long been of deep interest to me. Perhaps because of my training as a geologist at Harvard, I was inclined to think that the moisture content of the soil might be one of the factors determining whether the tsetse moved or remained stationary in any particular belt. In the early and middle thirties, we knew that the fly was very particular about where it laid its eggs. The condition of the laying area had to be just right, and I hoped, while in the Home of the Lion, to find some clues which might help unravel the mystery.

The dye injected into the dogs had turned their skins blue. Sheasongo was intensely amused by what he called our blue dogs. The color was not noticeable until one parted the hair and looked closely at the skin, and the chief examined one dog after another, chuckling at the color.

As a cattle owner, Sheasongo was as interested as I in the question surrounding the tsetse fly and their belts and movements. He was extremely intelligent and a fine observer. When I expounded on my thoughts concerning the fly and what I hoped to find, he listened carefully and made helpful suggestions. It was continually surprising to me to learn how quickly his mind not only received and followed my fairly technical remarks, but how thoroughly he understood. The chief was also interested in conservation. Not only of the game but of the soil, and he and I discussed these matters at great length on many occasions.

Jam, who was in charge of the dog boys and the advance party, came to say that he was ready to leave. Shamann'yati, old as he was, insisted on walking with Jam. He loathed riding on the truck, for which I could not blame him. Unless he could ride, as befitted his age and dignity, in the cab with me, I was never able to persuade him to avail himself of the truck or car. The advance party would camp out the first night and then move on to a special place near a series of pans which we had decided upon as our first hunting base. If Isabella and I got started early the coming morning, we would probably arrive at about the same time as Jam and his men. The pans were about forty to forty-five miles from Sheasongo. There was not the faintest trail or path to mark the route, but we knew where we were headed and how to get there.

Nights on the high Central African plateau can be quite cool during the dry winter months. Once or twice I have found a thin film of ice covering the surface of buckets of water set to cool the evening before. Isabella and I wore sweaters as we bustled about preparing to leave, and Buncher was wrapped snugly in her blankets. Mangineera and Charlie Portuguese and the assembled spectators from the village had gay trade blankets pulled about their shoulders against the chill of the early morn. The sun was just peeping over the trees as we finished breakfast and waited for the cook and his picanin and Lavison to clean up and place the utensils and dishes aboard the truck. Sheasongo arrived to wish us good luck and safety, and then we pulled away from the camp and headed for the west.

A few miles beyond the Nanzilla River, which we crossed by driving over dry sand and rocks exposed between the pools which were all that remained of the river at that time of the year, it became apparent that we were entering a different type of country from that through which we had passed coming from Namwala. The land was a series of gently rolling swells, the slopes and crests of which were covered with tall trees and bushes. It was open country, much like an old abandoned apple orchard in appearance, and we could see through the trees for long distances. Most of the grass had been burned off. Some of the fires which had swept over the country had been started by people hunting for honey or medicinal roots or meat. Others had been started many miles away outside the tsetse fly area by cattle-owning villagers and had swept across the land for dozens and dozens of miles before reaching the Home of the Lion. During the dry season every year, throughout Africa south of the Congo, vegetation which had grown during the rains was burned off and the territories were covered with palls of smoke and fine ash. This annual destruction of material which should have fallen to the ground and rotted to add humus to the soil was one of the reasons Africa was drying out and year by year eroding away and becoming less and less fertile.

Between the gentle swells lay the long, shallow vleis. Many of these were already carpeted with green grass although the ground was hard and firm. Driving along or across the vleis was pleasant and we made fairly rapid progress, having only to avoid the numerous small gray anthills which dotted the surface. As we penetrated into the area, game became more and more abundant. The animals were unafraid and curious, and the herds stood for long periods, watching us approach. It was only when the swaying, grumbling truck came within a hundred yards or so that the animals ambled away. We passed herds of reddish hartebeest and dark sable with their beautiful curving horns. Wart hogs raised their skinny tails and the long mane hairs on their backs and scurried ahead of the truck. Iz laughed with glee, watching the little ones imitate their parents and race after the larger wart hogs with their tuffed tails stiffly upright. Now and then a series of lines of round holes about four inches deep marked the surface of a vlei to show where elephants had crossed while the ground was still wet and soggy.

The boys behind shouted and pounded on the top of the cab to draw our attention to this herd or that. There was so much game around, however, that I would not stop. We did not drive a mile that we did not see impala leaping and bounding across the veld; see duikers or oribi or reedbuck, a herd of roan or eland or stately waterbuck. Wildebeest, with dark heads, heavy manes, and slate-blue bodies, raced parallel to our route. Accompanying the wildebeest were striped zebras which, we realized suddenly, presented us with a problem. The problem, of course, was Mianje, who was not supposed to see one of the animals because of her bewitchment.

Buncher loved to watch the running animals. Zebras, with their vivid coloring, were her favorites. But Mianje could not watch the trotting, running animals, and crouched down on the seat and tried to hide her face. Buncher would have none of this, and struggled to pull her nurse's head up and turn her face so that she, too, could watch the animals which gave the child so much enjoyment.

Mianje's husband, riding on the load behind us, realized his wife's predicament and kept shouting loudly to her whenever he or the other boys spotted a herd of zebras. At the warning, Mianje would cower down and cover her eyes with her hands, letting go of

Buncher, who was leaning far out of the window. Iz had to lean over Mianje and take a firm hold on the seat of Buncher's pants to prevent the child from tumbling out.

At first, amused and somewhat worried for Mianje, we put up with her shenanigans. Then we began to notice that, in spite of her pretense of not looking, Mianje was actually peeping from between her fingers or from the corner of an eye and watching the zebras just as interestedly as Buncher. Iz spoke sharply to her then, pointing out that we would probably be surrounded with zebras for most of the day and that unless she wanted to crawl onto the load behind and ride with her face covered, she had better sit up and make the best of the situation. Which, after considerable mutterings and touching of the amulets hanging around her neck, she did.

We had covered perhaps twenty-five miles when we stopped for a bit of lunch on a rise not far from a small pan in which the water was covered with lilies. We decided to give Buncher a chance to have a nap. Her cot was unloaded and set up in the shade, and after eating, she lay down and slept for an hour or more while Iz and I relaxed in deck chairs and watched the cranes and storks hunting frogs and insects beside the pan. There were tsetse flies about, and every so often we were bitten. The flies lit so gently on our skins that we were not aware of them until they dug their probosces into us. The bites felt like stabs from a hot needle, but they were relatively infrequent.

Camping in Rhodesia was a fairly luxurious way of living. Whether we traveled on foot, by ox wagon, or with a truck, we always had folding canvas deck chairs and demountable camp furniture; a portable folding wooden table, china and glass and silver, a wide array of pots and pans for cooking all manner of dishes and making bread; canvas washbasins mounted on folding stands, a canvas bathtub, and cots and mattresses if one preferred these to grass beds.

There was no need for tents, which can be hot and smelly. From the end of May until the end of September no rain fell, and one perfect day followed another so regularly as to become monotonous.

When we camped, the boys quickly chopped down small straight trees and set these in the ground and bound long thin poles to the tops to form a roof on which long grass was laid to serve as a shelter from the sun. Walls to insure privacy around the bath or elsewhere were quickly fashioned with poles and grass. A dozen natives could build a truly luxurious camp in a matter of a few hours. The only danger in such a grass camp was from fire, and we took precautions against an outbreak. For a more permanent type of camp we often stretched a large tarpaulin tentwise over poles and ate and worked beneath this. It was cleaner than a grass roof and kept off the sun nearly as well. The height of luxury was to construct a grass roof above the tarpaulin, leaving a space of a foot or eighteen inches between for the circulation of air.

All our camps were wide open. That is, we did not surround them with barricades of thornbushes. I could never see much point in doing this. Unless one piled the thorns to a height of eight to ten feet and pushed them very tightly together, the barricade—it was usually called a zareba—would not keep out any wild animal except possibly hyenas. Hyenas, attracted by the scents of hides and meat and cooking which always emanate from a camp, often tried to sneak in under cover of darkness, hoping to find an old boot, a piece of hide, a discarded bone or some other tidbit which they could snatch. Dogs kept the hyenas away quite effectively.

Leopards will, very rarely, try to spring or rush into a camp to snatch a sleeping dog. Except for lions, which are prompted by their intense curiosity, no wild animals will approach a camp if they can avoid doing so. Lions quite often stalk through a camp at night and look at the sleeping men and dogs, leaving their pug marks as evidence of their visit. But I have never heard of lions, except in a small area in Portuguese East Africa where there were several man-eaters, disturbing anything or anyone during their nightly visits of inspection. When they come, lions move so quietly and so carefully that it is unusual for even a dog to wake. When a dog did wake, I think it did so because the putrid scent of the lions stimulated its nostrils to message the brain, and not because the dog heard a sound.

When Buncher woke up, we reloaded the truck and resumed our journey. Already, in spite of the minor discomforts in the crowded cab and the bouncing and jouncing of the rough going, we were beginning to relax from the strains and worries which had beset us on Ibamba. There were locusts about, but somehow, away out in that uninhabited region, the locusts did not seem so horrible and terrifying as they did on our ranch. They were just as destructive. We could see where the insects had stripped the trees and bushes of all leaves and where they had eaten off the grass. We drove across occasional swarms of hoppers. But in that enormous open country the destruction seemed puny and ineffectual when compared to our ravaged corn and peanut fields. The game we could see was fat and strong and healthy, showing that they could find forage and survive where domestic cattle might have perished or at least become emaciated and weak.

The animals among which we passed were unafraid and beautiful. There was a feeling of peace and quietness and solidarity to the country which was missing from the regions inhabited by men. It was a big land across which the herds wandered and grazed, stopping to breed and to give birth to young and, sometimes, to die. Lions and leopards, cheetahs and wild dogs, hunted the country killing for their food, but this was natural and did not disrupt the over-all peaceful live-and-let-live pattern of existence. There was never any wanton killing and no species fought with other species for exclusive rights to a waterhole or an area of grazing. The herds of mighty buffalo, the members of which all wore perpetual frowns, shared water with the slim, graceful impala and the impish, utterly absurd-looking wart hogs. The cranes and storks, the ducks and spur-winged geese, moved about the pans while wildebeest, waterbuck and zebra drank and splashed.

Until the late thirties the Home of the Lion was probably more truly representative of what Northern Rhodesia was like before the coming of the white man than any other area in the territory, with the possible exception of the region on the north bank of the Zambezi where the Kafue joined that mighty river and a portion of the Luangwa River valley. We knew that we were intruders into this kingdom of the animals. It really was not right that we should enter the region to hunt and that the crashing reports of my heavy rifles should roll across the veld to frighten the animals, many of which would never have heard the crack of exploding powder before. If we had not been so desperately in need of cash, cash which could be earned through the sale of meat and hides and fat and skins, I do not think I would have gone. To hunt, at least. I might have gone, under happier circumstances, just to look and study or to make pictures, as we had done during the motion-picture-making expedition. But not to kill.

Because our trip would not last longer than two months, I knew that so far as the animals were concerned, my hunting would be only an episode of short duration. But as a result of my shooting there would be many creatures who would learn for the first time that man was dangerous; a lesson none would ever forget; and many would die. The instincts of the killer-hunter were never strong in me, and I could never understand what justification there was to kill an animal just to secure a trophy. Unless the hunt of some particular animal involved real and acute danger to the hunter, required the exercise of great skill and the use of much knowledge, and tested the stamina and strength of the hunter to the limit—so that the odds in favor of the hunter coming out alive were no better than fifty-fifty—I could never understand how a man could point with pride to some stuffed trophy hanging on the wall and say, "I killed that." Whenever I have heard men say those words, I have always wanted to ask them why.

There was a sudden terrific banging on the roof of the cab. I stopped. Charlie Portuguese appeared beside the cab and stood on the running board. He pointed to the lower end of the vlei down which we had been driving, where I could see circles of bare ground surrounding three large pans. No water was visible because of the lush growth of grasses and reeds and lily pads which gave the pans the appearance of three fat emeralds shining in the brilliant sunlight and surrounded with mounting of dull-gray platinum. The platinum,

I knew, was exposed trodden ground from which all grass had been eaten and trampled by the hooves of countless animals coming to the water to drink and bathe. A quarter of a mile beyond the pans a spur of the bushveld jutted into the vlei. A group of fine tall trees rose on the spur, and Charlie said that this was the spot where we were to camp and where Jam and his men would join us.

It was a beautiful spot, and the game trails which radiated in all directions from the pans were proof that this was a center for game of every description. As the truck moved slowly across the trails, I tried to see the spoor which marked them. Many of the tracks looked large and splay enough to be those of buffalo, and there were a few of the patty-cake droppings buffalo leave scattered here and there. But the large tracks might have been those of eland. It was hard to tell from the height of the cab.

I drove among and under the trees and stopped. At once Mangineera, Charlie, Lavison, Sixpence, and Shaluma hopped off and began to untie the ropes which held the load. Buncher rolled and tumbled on the ground and toddled here and there, disrupting proceedings and happy to stretch her chubby legs. Iz and I walked about the site and decided where we wanted our shelter to be put up and where the kitchen and the bath enclosure should be built. I marked a spot for the digging of the latrine.

Firewood was collected for cooking and the night campfires. Mangineera took a sickle and departed to hunt for grass with which to make beds and Lavison fashioned a broom from dry branches and swept a large area clear of leaves and debris and set up the table and chairs. Stones on which to set the pots for cooking were nonexistent, so Sixpence trotted down to the vlei and collected a number of small anthills. They would eventually crumble from the heat, but would serve for several days. Shaluma untied one of the eight-gallon drums and a carrying pole, borrowed Mianje, and went to the pan to fetch water. The man-and-wife team returned quickly with the eighty-pound load of water swinging from the pole between them.

The shadows cast by the trees were beginning to stretch out and cover the edge of the vlei when we heard a dog bark, and hurrying to the edge of camp, saw Jam and the advance party trudging down the open country toward us. Soon they arrived, and the hustle and bustle increased as everyone strove to make things ready for our first night.

It was wonderfully pleasant and cool as Iz fed Buncher her supper and Lavison began to lay a cloth and set the table. From the direction of the kitchen fires the gentle breeze brought the tantalizing odor of rich meat being basted, roasting sweet potatoes, and hot new bread which was baking in the Dutch oven. The soft chatter of the natives grouped about their little fires blended into the background, and one by one stars came out to shine far overhead through the trees. The kerosene lanterns spread pools of yellow light through which the dark forms of the natives moved gracefully and soundlessly. The warmth of the fire was welcome, and Iz and Mianje adjusted Buncher's crib so that she would have the benefit of warmth without any smoke. With the coming of darkness the tsetse flies retired and there were no mosquitoes. A few hard brown beetles flew stubbornly against the globes of the lanterns, trying to knock themselves unconscious, but they were harmless insects.

At the upper end of the vlei down which we had driven a zebra stallion neighed loud and clear. He was suspicious of the light and the camp of men which had appeared near the waterhole since his last visit. It would be an hour or more before the zebras would make up their minds that it was safe to approach and drink.

Then the lions began to talk. First from the south, to be answered by a troop passing to the north, then from the west of us and from the east. Grunting, whoofing, mumbling lion language, the kings and queens, with their retinues of princes and princesses, stalked the veld to find water to drink; to stampede and kill antelope or zebra or, perhaps, to tangle with an angry buffalo cow whose calf had lagged behind the herd to suddenly find itself attacked by lions. Every so often a lion or a lioness roared and the magnificent sounds rolled through the darkness, sweeping over us listening in camp, to die away in the immensity of the land.

A hyena whooped, dismally and forlornly, as it tagged along behind a party of lions, hoping that they would kill and, after they had eaten, leave some scraps behind. Only such a misbegotten, ugly creature as a spotted hyena could utter so mournful and apologetic a cry. Scavengers, hyenas are the garbage collectors of the veld. As befits their lowly social status, they skulk at night and are despised by men and the other animals alike. Endowed with a certain low cunning and with the frantic courage born of constant hunger, hyenas can be dangerous. I have seen a number of natives who had been bitten on the face, a hand, or a foot by a hyena while sleeping outside their hut or on the veld. The bites were severe in the extreme because, in proportion to its size, a hyena has the most powerful jaws of any living animal.

In the quietness of the night, as the murmuring of the camp died down and tired men dozed off to sleep, a black-backed jackal added its high yipping bark to the chorus rising from the veld. Faintly, we could hear the occasional gentle splash of water and knew that some animal, braver or more in need of a drink than others, had come to the pan to drink. As more animals came, emboldened by the first, low snorts and huffings floated to us as the animals came to the hot scent of man on the trails the boys had trodden going and coming from the water.

Then, suddenly, it was morning; we woke refreshed, and lazily stayed in our grass beds while Lavison made early tea and brought it to us; we played with Buncher, and she tried to help Mangineera revive the fire. Mingling with the smell of roasting meat, the sweetly pungent odor of boiling corn meal drifted beneath the trees as the boys prepared their breakfasts. Pots and pans rattled in the kitchen, and we heard the slap and pound of Sixpence's hands as he kneaded dough on a board in readiness for the day's baking.

I did no hunting near the pans at which we were camped. Instead, accompanied by Jam and Mangineera, Charlie Portuguese and Shamann'yati, the dogs and others, I left camp early each morning and walked several miles before I would consider shooting at an animal. Wild animals, unless there are no alternatives, do not defile their nests or homes. We, I felt, could scarcely do less.

Although the success or failure of my hunting was of vital importance to us, I do not propose to recount my adventures in detail in this book. With my wonderfully skillful trackers and hunters I hunted coldly, methodically, and heartlessly. When, after hours of patient spooring, we approached a herd of buffalo and I fired, we ran beside and even amongst the stampeding animals, and whenever the opportunity arose in the clouds of dust, I fired at a galloping animal. With Mangineera racing beside me, passing me my second rifle and then reloading the one I had used to be ready for another chance, I killed as many as nine buffalo in one encounter. Returning along the route we had run, we hunted down the animals I had dropped but not killed and despatched them as quickly as possible. Jam backed me up with his rifle, and when we were charged, as we often were, both of us sometimes fired to stop a raging, furious animal.

It was dangerous work which taxed our strength to the limit. Each day we walked from twenty to thirty miles. The sun beat on us and dust clogged our throats. The heat sucked the juices from our joints, so that when we halted to rest, it was painful to move again. In khaki shorts rolled far up my thighs, a sleeveless hunting jacket with seven loops for cartridges at each breast, a light pair of crepe rubber-soled shoes and an old felt hat, my skin burned to the color of dark mahogany and my legs and arms were crisscrossed with a network of scratches and tears from the catnail thorns through which I ran or forced my way.

It was professional hunting—skin hunting, as we called it. Whenever I made a large kill and the disjointed meat was too much for the boys who accompanied me to carry, we either sent to camp for more men or Isabella brought out the truck, with Mianje and Buncher bouncing on the seat beside her. Iz had to have pillows piled behind her so that she could sit far enough forward to reach the clutch and brake pedals and the throttle and see over the engine hood. How she managed, driving straight across the veld, to avoid the ant-bear holes and the fallen logs, to drive over the small trees and thornbushes and to pass around sandy patches, I never fully understood. Not once did she get stuck and have to send for help.

Steadily the hides piled up and we began to cut them and make them into riems. Lion and leopard skins were carefully cleaned of all fat and blood and lightly salted and dried in the shade and then dusted with arsenic powder to discourage the bacon beetles. During these weeks of intensive hunting I had a few pleasant and interesting interludes while with my natives I watched a badger and a honey-guide bird, or a buffalo playing with a vulture, or came unexpectedly upon some baby antelope lying waiting for its mother on the veld.

The Kasha Pools lay about eight miles to the northwest of our camp. There were several of these pools ranged in a rough line beneath and surrounded by tall trees. The water was deep and dark and cool and originated deep in the earth from springs. For a wide area about the pools the ground was bare, and deeply worn game trails converged on the water from all directions.

In spite of the barrenness of the ground, which was broken here and there only by a few clumps of bushes, the trunks of the trees, and scattered stunted palms, the pools were beautiful to see in a land which, for months at a time, suffered from a scarcity of water. There was only a trickle of overflow from the pools, and this was absorbed within a few feet by the thirsty soil. The flow from the springs was just enough to counterbalance the loss from the surface by evaporation and consumption by the game.

With my hunting boys I visited the pools a few days after establishing our first camp. From the spoor on the trails it was easy to read that many species of antelope came to drink at the waters, as well as zebra, wart hogs, an occasional leopard, and numerous small animals. There were few cranes or storks because the pools were too deep for wading and the edges and bottoms dropped steeply to the springs far below. The depth of the pools was the reason they were seldom visited by buffalo. Buffalo like to wallow and to wade in the water and eat lily pads and water grasses, and the Kasha Pools offered no opportunities to do these things.

Lion spoor abounded. As we circled the pools and studied the trails, it became evident that a number of lions came to the pools to drink. We found the tracks of a single lion which, from the length of its stride and the size of the pug marks, was of unusual size. It was very evident that this was one place where we should put down at least one set of lion traps, so Charlie Portuguese sent a native back to camp with a note scribbled on a bit of paper asking Isabella to send us four lion traps, clamps, wire, four trek chains, and a set of pliers.

While we were waiting for the men to come from camp, Jam and Charlie and Mangineera and Shamann'yati and I strolled about, studying the situation. Shamann'yati spent a long time examining the spoor left by the big lion, and as I watched him moving along the tracks, I could see that a frown creased his black forehead. When he glanced up at me, his face was anxious, as if some thought was bothering him. Jam and Mangineera, too, wore solemn expressions, and their eyes roved about and stared thoughtfully across the veld as they turned this way and that. It became more and more evident to me that my hunters were worried about something of which I was completely unaware. If I had not known each so well, I would have thought them frightened.

It was when I pointed to a spot beside a young palm and stated that I thought that would be a good place at which to construct a zareba for the bait and traps that Shamann'yati spoke.

"This is not a good place," he told me, gesturing with his hand and spear to include the whole area about the Kasha Pools. "This lion"—Shamann'yati lowered the spear so that the tip of the blade rested on one of the big lion tracks—"this lion is a *matakatsi, N'Kos*. He is not as other lions, for the spirit of the Chief Shechambia lives in him." The old tracker paused to stare about as if fearful that the lion might be close enough to hear what he was saying. "This is not a good place, *N'Kos*. You can see that no one has stayed here when passing through this region. There are no ashes, no burned pieces of wood. It is said that if a man stops here for the night, the great lion, which is not a lion but is Shechambia, comes and speaks to the person and this is terrible. So terrible that the person flees into the night to escape this place and to escape the lion which talks like a man and that thereafter the man is never again as he was before he came to this place."

The dog boys and others with us had crowded close about as Shamann'yati spoke. Looking into their dark, earnest faces, I could see that they believed completely in what the old man had said. Which was not surprising. From infancy, each had grown up surrounded by elders who not only believed utterly that by taking certain medicinal preparations before they died, witch doctors and chiefs could insure their reincarnation in animal form, but talked about such happenings much as we might discuss the latest gossip or political shenanigans. Throughout their lives the natives lived so close to the animals of the veld that they spoke of them more as people than as animals differentiated from themselves. Many of the more spectacular creatures, such as certain elephants, rhinos, hippos, crocodiles, and lions had names, and when these creatures were spoken of, it was by name. To the native all living creatures possessed a spirit. Even the despised hyenas. It was a completely acceptable thought to them that the spirit of a departed person should reappear in the body of an animal. As I looked into the eyes of Mangineera and Jam, men whose courage and intelligence I respected, and saw the belief, the knowledge, that what Shamann'yati had said was true, glowing in their eyes, their sincerity flowed over and was communicated to me and I felt a faint chill of fear.

I fought the feeling down and argued that I, too, was a *matakatsi,* that, as they knew, I could talk with lions. Had they not witnessed many examples in the past, and was it not true that, despite all the prophecies to the contrary, the lions on Ibamba had not attacked my cattle? They shuffled their bare feet nervously in the dust and held their eyes downcast and mumbled that while what I said was true, and no man could deny this, no man could catch or shoot the great lion which was Shechambia. If I pointed my gun at him and pulled the trigger, water would come from the barrel instead of a bullet. The lion, which was not a lion but a man, thought with the brain of a man, and it was impossible to trap him. Only great trouble and danger could come if I persisted.

Their very uneasiness and nervousness piqued me. The challenge to match my wits and cunning against those of the great lion whose tracks I stared at was one I could not ignore. I gave orders that the men were to cut thornbushes for a zareba and four heavy logs to which the traps could be attached. Reluctantly, because I was Sibyunni'byunni and a *matakatsi,* they prepared to obey, but they would not go afield to cut the thorns and logs unless Jam and Mangineera, each with a rifle, accompanied them. While the men dispersed, because it is inadvisable to chop and cut near a place where traps are to be set, I sat with my back against a tree and the dogs tied nearby, reviewing what I had been told. Alone, I confess that I grew uneasy and kept glancing continuously about me. Although I could hear the chunk of axes biting into wood only a few hundred yards away, I became conscious of a feeling of menace, of danger. There was nothing which I could see to account for such a feeling, but it was there and it was very real. As the boys came and went, bringing the thornbushes and the logs, the feeling lessened somewhat while they were close, but it did not disappear completely. I could see that every man felt just as I did, and I knew that had I not been there, they would have fled.

As I sat, waiting and watching, Shamann'yati came and hunkered down nearby. Somberly I studied the ancient, withered native crouching motionless on his heels. His short-shafted long-bladed stabbing spear resting with one end on the ground pointed backward, with the polished blade rising across his right shoulder. Around his right wrist he wore a leather bracelet to which was attached a tiny pouch which contained some "medicine" prepared by a witch doctor and supposed to help and protect him in his hunting. He was naked except for a narrow breechclout of soft hide, and his skin was covered with a thin film of dust. The tight little curls of hair on his head were flecked with gray. I knew Shamann'yati to be one of the wisest men in the ways of animals and the most skillful of all my trackers. His disapproval of what I intended to do was so strong and so evident in his face and in the way he held his body that I seriously considered calling the matter off.

As I looked at Shamann'yati, I got a glimpse of movement on the veld beyond the trees surrounding us. As the old man turned his head toward me to speak, I saw that a herd of zebra was approaching.

"This is not a good thing which you do, Sibyunni'byunni," stated Shamann'yati. "It is true that you are a great hunter and that no man has caught as many buffalo nor so many lions alive as you. People say that you can talk with lions and that you are a *matakatsi*. I am old, and you will forgive an old man when I say that I, Shamann'yati, do not know if what the people say is true. But I tell you that Shechambia was a great chief, greater and with more cattle than Sheasongo, and that this lion is Shechambia and only trouble can come from what you try to do."

"There is truth in what you say," I admitted, for in the presence of Shamann'yati I was more pupil than chief, and his understanding of human nature was as wide and deep as his knowledge of wild animals. "But this is a thing which I must do. And perhaps the gods who watch us are favorable toward me, for see, zebras come, and zebras are the favorite food of lions."

Shamann'yati slowly turned his head and watched the zebras as they came cautiously toward the pools. There was little danger, I knew, that the other men might frighten the herd away. Constantly watching the veld as they always did, they would have seen the animals and knew that I would see them, and they would remain motionless, waiting for the sound of a shot.

A large fat stallion was leading the herd. He was nervous, as wild creatures always are when they are exposed in the open and approaching water where other, and possibly dangerous, animals might be waiting. The stallion snorted and neighed and the herd wheeled, ready to dash away. But the need for water was great and the stallion calmed and resumed his approach. I let him come to within two hundred yards and then shot him behind the shoulder. He dropped, never knowing what had happened. The other zebras dashed madly away, raising a great cloud of dust.

The boys bringing the traps came, and we hauled the zebra in bodily from the veld and placed it not far from a small low palm. Around it we built a thick barricade of thornbushes, pushing the bushes tightly together so that the branches interlocked. Two openings were left in the barricade, opposite each other, so that a lion approaching either could look right through and over the zebra and see the open veld beyond. Lions are extremely reluctant to enter any enclosure from which they cannot see a way of escape.

The ten-foot lengths of half-inch chain were wired to the heavy lengths of log and the opposite end to one of the powerful Newhouse traps. Mangineera and Jam affixed the clamps to the double springs and screwed these tight, compressing the springs so that the jaws of the traps fell open and lay flat on the ground.

Carefully we dug excavations just the right size to hold and conceal the traps, digging one hole by the hindquarters of the zebra, another by the neck, and one in each entrance. The traps were placed in these and fine balls of soft raveled grass were placed beneath each of the pans so that dirt would not seep beneath and prevent the pans from falling and triggering the traps. The chains were buried and the wire binding them to the logs was smeared with mud.

Cautiously the clamps were released, and the traps lay ready except for a final dusting with dirt and broken leaves and tiny bits of twigs. When, to the human eye, there were no traces to show the traps lay hidden, we stood off to look at our work. The zareba was innocuous-looking but of deadly construction. As they stared at their work, the natives shook their heads, and behind my back I heard them murmuring to one another.

Quickly, for the sun was sinking toward the tops of the trees across the vlei, I stepped into the zareba and with my knife slashed open the bloating stomach of the zebra. A great rush of sour wind issued and tainted the air; I reached in and pulled forth handfuls of the partially digested grass and scattered this around and over the traps and dropped small heaps in my footprints as I stepped out. As I stooped at the edge of the pool to wash my hands, a sharp smell flowed across the dark water. With it was mingled the hot scent of blood.

Mangineera took a small dry bush, and using this as a broom, swept the area all about the zareba. This would do nothing to hide the smell of men which would linger around the spot. It was done so that we would be better able to read the story left in tracks the next morning should any animal come to the bait.

As we trudged toward camp, I fingered and examined a few long hairs that Jam had plucked from a thornbush beside one of the trails on which we had found the big lion's tracks. They were mane hairs plucked from a lion as it brushed against the thorns, but they were unlike any I had seen previously. The manes adorning most of the lions in Rhodesia were of an orange-yellow color interspersed with black. Sometimes the number of black, or dark, hairs outnumbered the lighter ones and the lion became a black-maned animal. In others the black hairs were few and the mane was of a golden color.

The few hairs which Jam had given me were neither black nor orange. They were so few and so fine, it was hard to be sure, but it seemed to me that they were grayish-fawn in color, somewhat like the body color of a lion or lioness but with a faint tinge of green. Whether the hairs had come from the mane of the lion which had left the large spoor, none of us knew. Many lions traveled the trails about the Kasha Pools. It was even possible that the lion which was Shechambia did not have a mane at all. There were such lions.

Contrary to the usual practice, the natives were silent on their walk to camp. The pace they set was faster than customary at the end of a day, and when we strode into camp, the sun was still throwing a fanfare of red and orange above the horizon like a gigantic fan. As I turned away after standing my rifle against the rack near my bed, I saw that Isabella was watching me curiously from her chair and noticed that the camp seemed unusually quiet. Even Buncher was subdued, and Mianje, sitting on the ground beside the child, glanced at me and then turned her eyes quickly away, as if I had suddenly become something on which it was unhealthy to look.

"What on earth have you been up to?" queried Iz as I sat down and accepted a cup of tea from Lavison. "Ever since you sent the boy in for the traps everybody has been going around as if the end of the world was coming."

So I told her about the spirit lion which was not a lion but was the chief, Shechambia, and about what Shamann'yati had said and how the boys had reacted. Iz listened solemnly, for she had been worried by the sudden change which had come over the camp. She did not believe, any more than I did, that people who died could return to earth and live again in the bodies of animals. Nevertheless, the profound uneasiness of the natives on whom we depended so heavily and for many of whom we had so much respect and affection was very disturbing.

I tried to talk with Lavison and, later, with Mangineera. All I could get out of them were monosyllabic grunts and a few short evasive words. I retired, puzzled as to whether the natives were genuinely fearful of the wrath of the lion which was Shechambia or whether they were frightened of the impending clash between two *matakatsis* and that I, their *n'kos,* might be the loser.

We were up and away very early the next morning. As we approached the pools, we slowed and fanned out so that men could look ahead from various angles in order to overlook nothing which might indicate what lay in store for us. While still a hundred yards distant, I could see that the zareba had been demolished. As we drew closer, we could see that the thornbushes had been flung and knocked all about, and then we saw that the zebra had been taken from where we had left it and was lying a few dozen yards out on the veld.

Gray, ugly vultures had already discovered the bait and were feeding on and squabbling over it. Several others perched in nearby trees, their heavily beaked heads turning on their naked necks as they craned to see us. We walked boldly forward. When there are vultures on the ground, it is almost certain that there are no lions nearby.

I went first to the remains of the zareba. There were lion tracks all about. Big ones. There were also scratches and marks in the ground, as if the lion had torn at the soil. Each of the four traps had been sprung. They were so covered with dirt and debris it was impossible to tell whether they had been sprung when the lion smashed the thorns about or when it dragged the zebra out. Although they did not actually say so, I could see from the way in which Mangineera and Jam studied the marks in the ground that they were debating whether the lion might not have turned its back on the zareba and scratched dirt onto the traps to spring them. However it had managed, the lion had gotten the zebra out of the thorns and then feasted on it at its leisure.

We dragged the remains of the zebra back to the site of the zareba and piled the thorns all over it to keep the vultures away and then moved on farther to resume hunting until it was time to return and rebuild the barricade and reset the traps.

When we did, the stench from the zebra, which had by then been dead for more than twenty-four hours, was nearly overpowering. Quickly we built up the zareba around the remains and set the traps, brushed the surrounding ground, and headed for camp. Although there was little chatter, there was more life in the men, and I guessed that their spirits had risen because of my failure to have come even close to trapping the big lion.

The next morning was a repetition of the first. The zareba had been broken and tossed all about. The bait had been dragged out and lay on the veld. All the traps had again been sprung, but there was no indication that we had come close to getting the big lion to put a foot in one. The lion was clever. Apparently it either had had experience with traps before, or it smelled the steel hidden in the earth and recognized that this meant danger. The boys found a few of the curiously colored mane hairs dangling from the thorns, which showed that the lion which left the large pug marks was the one which possessed the odd-colored mane.

The boys could barely conceal their relief that the lion had again beaten me. They pointed out that it had eaten only a few mouthfuls from the remains of the zebra, and interpreted this as showing the lion was more choosy than others as to what it ate. Another indication, so they said, that the lion was not really a lion but a man.

We covered the bones and stinking meat and left for our hunting. On our way back in the middle of the afternoon a reedbuck jumped from a patch of tall grass a mile or so before we reached the pools and I shot it. The boys hung the carcass from a pole and carried it in and we used it as bait, placing it on top of the remains of the zebra, which by then could be smelled a mile or more downwind. I reset the traps, changing their positions somewhat and concealing them as carefully as I could.

The third morning the zareba was again flattened and destroyed. The lion had picked the reedbuck up bodily and carried it onto the veld, where it had consumed more than two-thirds of the animal. The traps had been sprung, but what both intrigued and annoyed me and confirmed my boys' belief that the lion was Shechambia was that the lion had gone to the trouble of seizing and carrying away the rotten remains of the zebra. These it had left in a heap not far from where it had eaten the reedbuck, and it had methodically and completely defiled the remains by defecating all over them.

This gesture of contempt and defiance was all the boys needed to convince them as to the lion's true identity. Who, they asked, ever had heard of a lion doing such a thing before? Was not the defilement the sort of gesture which a man might make? The lion had eaten none of the rotten zebra, so why should it have gone to all the trouble of carrying the revolting mess onto the veld? Unless it wanted to tell us what it thought of us and of our attempts to trap it?

The challenge was too obvious to be ignored. And, I confess, the needling which my boys gave me got underneath my skin. I determined that I would trap that lion, and in my flustered and angry state of mind, told the boys that I would not only catch the lion but catch it that coming night.

At which statement their faces darkened and the solemn, frightened looks returned. I really had no business devoting so much time and effort to trapping that particular lion. After all, the big lion was just another although very clever lion, and if I succeeded in catching and shooting it, would be only one more skin to add to the pile in camp.

But my prestige among the natives not only as a hunter and trapper but, more importantly, as a *matakatsi* who could talk with lions had become involved. My attempts to trap the lion had become much more than just a contest to see which of us was the more clever. In the minds of the natives the contest had become a struggle between two witch doctors, two *matakatsis,* one of whom was the reincarnation of a great chief in the form of the lion with the peculiar mane.

Part of the fear which obsessed the boys originated, I am convinced, in their uncertainty as to where their loyalties lay. Most were devoted to me and immensely proud of my reputation. They did not actually want to see me defeated. At the same time, all their training, all their centuries-old traditions and beliefs, told them that it must be the lion who was not a lion but Shechambia which would win the struggle. Should I win, the natives' dilemma would be almost catastrophic. It would mean to them that I, a white man, had met one of their great witch doctors and defeated him at his own game and on his own battleground. During recent years they had paid lip service to the fact that I had some mysterious power over lions which enabled me to prevent them from killing my cattle on Ibamba. I knew, however, that they held reservations as to just what my powers might be. Our natives basked in my reputation as a witch doctor of lions and helped to build and foster this. In their hearts, I am sure, they hoped I would never be placed in such a position that I would be forced to recant or back down. When I sent men back to camp to bring more traps and chains and wire, the gloom which enshrouded us deepened and the boys who remained seemed to avoid passing close to me. This may, of course, have just been my imagination.

While we waited for the boys to return with the additional traps, I had them dig a hole with the digging ends of their stabbing spears and bury the remains of the zebra and the reedbuck. Then I set them to collecting new thornbushes for a zareba and logs for the traps.

My luck was in. While we were eating our lunch and sitting with our backs against various trees, I saw and watched a small cloud of dust moving down the vlei along which we traveled to and from the camp. Within a few minutes I made out that the cloud was being stirred up by a herd of zebra coming slowly and nervously toward the pools. The zebras were approaching up the wind, and it was only a question of time until the scent of man would become too strong and they would gallop away.

Choosing my single-barrel rifle and signaling to Mangineera to follow, I left the pools, and traveling in a semicircle, stalked the now stationary herd. In ten minutes I was within long rifle range, and steadying myself, fired at the plump zebra nearest to me. It dropped, kicked a few times, and then stretched out. Mangineera ran to it to be sure it was dead, and then he and I returned to the pools; there he collected all the boys except Shamann'yati to haul the carcass back to us.

The old hunter watched me silently as I moved along the game trails. Carefully, using sticks, I measured the stride of the lion and measured the distance between its front and rear prints when it had stood for a time staring at the zareba before approaching it. I found a few mane hairs hanging from a bush beside the trail and tried to estimate the shoulder height of the lion. There was no question that it was big and long-bodied.

When the zebra was hauled in, I had it placed where the first had been. We constructed another zareba a little higher and denser and larger in diameter than those we had built before. I dug excavations for the traps at the hindquarters and the neck as previously, and in each entrance. Except for Shamann'yati, who I think had begun to figure what I intended, the boys were puzzled that no apparent change had been made in the trap arrangement.

As soon as the natives arrived with the additional traps, I set to work with my measuring sticks. Although the lion was suspicious of and careful about the traps, he was apparently not frightened by them. When he came, he would expect to find the traps, and he would step over them as he had done previously. I did not agree with the natives that the lion had scratched dirt at the traps until he had snapped them.

On my hands and my toes, without touching my knees to the ground, I approached the zareba just as I expected the lion to do, and advanced first one hand and then the other over the trap in the entrance. In this semiprone position the distance between my hands and my toes was approximately the same as that between the front prints and the rear prints of the lion.

The boys crowded close about, watching me anxiously and with deep concern. I leaned as far forward on my hands as I could and tried to bring my face close to the zebra. Unless I moved my hands closer to the bait, I could not reach it with my mouth. There was, however, a trap not far in front of my hands and close to the neck of the zebra which I would have to avoid if I was to seize the animal, as the lion would wish to do.

I could only move my hands forward a certain minimum distance if I was to stay out of the trap. The lion, I hoped, would be confronted with the same situation. So near to having his meal and yet so far away. At this point the lion might, stepping very carefully, back out of the entrance and go around the zareba to try at the other side. I intended to lay the traps in the same way there so it would again be confronted with the same situation.

The lion, I hoped, would be hungry and want the zebra badly. The hot smell of the fresh meat and blood would be tantalizing, and I guessed the lion would circle around the zareba, seeking an opening several times before it would decide to attempt one of the entrances again.

When the lion did this, it would find, as it had before, that it could not reach the zebra by stretching its neck and shoulders forward and straining above the trap beside the neck. The only way by which it would be able to move close enough to seize the zebra would be by moving its forefeet six to eight inches closer to the animal. This, I hoped most fervently, it would finally decide to do in spite of the menace of the trap, which would be lying right under its nose. If my measurements and thoughts were correct, the lion would not be able to move its front feet forward without first bringing its back feet closer. If it did bring up its back feet, then, and only then, would it be able to sway and thrust its shoulders and jaws far enough forward to grasp the meat. I was banking heavily on the lion's appetite to assist me here.

When, pretending to be the lion, I moved my hands closer to the zebra and then brought my feet forward, the natives suddenly realized what I planned. One gasped, and I heard them murmuring excitedly, but I was too intent on my measurements to look up.

Satisfied at last, I backed carefully out of the zareba—I did not want to get caught in one of those powerful traps—and marked the last position of my feet. There I dug a hole and laid down a trap and concealed it carefully. I did not think the lion would overlook it when it came. My expectation and hope was that when it decided to try for the zebra and found it could not reach it without moving its forepaws closer, it would forget the last trap which I had set and bring its hind feet forward to increase its reach. When it did this, if my measurements were close to being correct, it would place one of its hind feet squarely onto the trap.

It took some time to work this all out and measure and place the trap and hide it. It required just as long for me to set the stage in the other entrance to the zareba, and the sun was close to the trees when I announced myself as satisfied. After a final look around, we set off for camp.

The camp was enveloped in tension that evening. Except for one or two, I did not think the men were actually frightened. But they were torn emotionally. The experienced hunters among them, Mangineera, Shamann'yati, Jam, and Charlie Portuguese understood the trap I had laid for the great lion. Knowing lions even more intimately than I, they fully comprehended the danger to the animal, and it was terrible for them to have to face the fact that I might be about to destroy the spirit lion, Shechambia. If I succeeded, my triumph would mean that I had destroyed one of the many gods, or spirits, which inhabited the nebulous world of their beliefs and traditions.

As was my usual custom, after supper and before retiring I walked about the camp to check and see that everything was as it should be. The men, huddled about their little fires, pulled their blankets a little tighter about their shoulders as I passed and hung their heads. Shamann'yati sat alone, staring into the darkness in the direction of the Kasha Pools. He failed to wish me good night. Only Mangineera, the closest to me of all my men, looked up at me. He did not speak, but a thin, devilish grin curled one corner of his lips.

Twice during the night I rose and walked about in the dark. Shamann'yati had not lain down. He had not bothered to unroll his sleeping mat, which rested beside him as he sat unmoving, listening to and watching the night. The second time I got up, I saw a dark figure silhouetted against the faraway star-studded dimness of the sky. The figure—I recognized it as my half-pygmy gunbearer—faced in the direction of the pools, and I knew that Mangineera was listening. Had he heard some sound which had escaped the others? His hearing and his sense of smell were marvelously acute. I did not disturb him, and if he heard me, which he must have done, he chose to ignore me. When I lay down on my grass bed, I tossed and turned, unable to sleep. I could hear Isabella rustling on her bed, and knew that she, too, was awake. But we did not speak.

The chill which had come with night seemed to deepen as dawn flushed the sky and the half-seen shapes and shadows of the darkness solidified. I listened to Sixpence rattle his pots as he boiled water for our early tea, and lay on my back staring up at the branches above. I waited patiently for Lavison to bring my cup. There was no hurry now. I knew, and from the changed feeling which pervaded the camp I knew that everyone else knew, that we had caught the great lion.

Do not ask me how I knew this. I could not tell you. But I was certain. Mangineera may, perhaps, have heard some sounds, for the night had been very still and on such a night sound carries far, and his ears were very sharp. If he had, he did not tell me, but when he came to check the rifles, I could see his knowledge on his face.

Excitement surged through the camp. Instead of the gloom and silence which had enveloped us the night before, the natives chattered and talked. Lavison relented sufficiently to wish me a pleasant good morning and was unusually solicitous in his attentions to Isabella. Mianje was her old grinning, cheerful self. The change in attitude was extraordinary. I could only explain it by guessing that the men brought themselves to accept possible capture of the spirit lion because of their fatalistic beliefs. The downfall of the spirit lion, of Shechambia, would be an act of destiny, a fate which had been ordained by the Great Spirit who had created man and animals and who governed all their actions. I could only surmise, because natives were reluctant to discuss such matters, that if the great lion was caught and I shot it, they would accept the fact and install me, or at least my image, in its place.

I asked Iz if she wanted to go along, and she said she did. We could not leave Buncher alone in camp with just Mianje, so I decided to take the truck. As soon as the boys learned I planned to drive, everyone wanted to go along. I took them all except Sixpence and his helper, who had bread to bake.

As I drove out of camp, we looked like a war party starting on a raid. Every man standing in the back was armed with three or four spears, the polished blades of which, held upright, shone in the increasing sunlight. Mangineera, holding my favorite falling-block single-shot 500/450 rifle, stood on the running board on my side of the cab, one arm locked over the window's edge. Jam stood on the other running board with a double-barreled rifle, and Charlie Portuguese and Shamann'yati stood immediately behind the cab and leaned on the roof to peer ahead. It was the first time Shamann'yati had consented to ride anywhere except on the front seat.

Isabella sat between me and Mianje, who was holding Buncher. The excitement and expectation had communicated themselves to the child, and she chattered and pointed and bounced up and down, and reaching forth, pulled at the leather thong with amulets which hung around Jam's neck.

As we approached the pools and the tall trees which surrounded them, the natives fell silent. Every eye was straining to see what lay ahead. As I drew closer, I could see vultures perched in the trees, but none on the ground. Two low palms obscured the view. Then, abruptly, the area where we had built and left the zareba came into sight. A thin cloud of dust swirled gently above the spot where I had set the traps.

The zareba was a torn and tangled heap of brush. I saw the green of two freshly broken palm fronds lying on the earth nearby. My gaze fixed on the scene, I drove to within fifty yards, and then the heap of thorns exploded and a huge maned lion swayed to its feet and stood, the remains of a thornbush balanced on its back, snarling and growling and glaring at us with furious eyes.

At sight of the tremendous lion a loud shout went up from the natives behind. The lion roared, and blood flew from its lacerated mouth. The pile of thorns in which it stood heaved and shook as it struggled to free itself of the steel and chains. Its eyes glowed and changed from red to green as fear and rage surged through its body. The cheers of the natives died in their throats, and the only sound was the growling of the lion and the light, childish voice of Buncher who was pointing at it.

Mangineera dropped to the ground and waited for me to descend from the cab. Jam, on the opposite side, moved forward close to the front fender and stood with his rifle ready.

I took the rifle from Mangineera and walked slowly forward to stand some twenty-five yards from the straining, snarling lion. Unlike any other lion I had ever seen, it was all one color. The mane, which was long and thick and now matted with blood and dirt, was the same tone and color as its body. The lion was magnificent, and I felt ashamed that I had tricked it and terribly, terribly sorry that I had to kill it.

I raised my rifle and aimed for the spot between the neck and shoulder behind which lay the mighty heart. As my eye lined up the sights, I looked into the face of the lion and into its eyes. Never have I looked at such a blaze of defiant fury and, I think, contempt.

Then it was all over. As the crash of the rifle rolled away across the vlei, the great animal crumpled and fell and lay on a bed of thorns. A wave of nausea and emotional exhaustion engulfed me, and I walked to the truck and sat on the running board to recover.

The lion, we found, had been caught by one hind and both front feet. With the heavy traps and chains pulling it down and hampering every movement, it never had a chance. Even so, it had bitten the low palm completely through, torn the bark from a nearby tree, and ripped up the ground in a great circle. Its battle throughout the night must have been horrible and terrible.

We freed the lion of the traps and carefully and respectfully carried the body to the truck and laid it on piles of grass. After the first great shout there had not been much noise from the boys, and they gathered the traps and chains and wire and loaded them silently. My triumph was complete, but it was hollow and unsatisfactory. I was not pleased, and did not fail to notice that my hunters failed to congratulate me as they had always done before when I killed a lion.

chapter sixteen

WE stayed at our first camp in the Home of the Lion for a little over four weeks. Periodically, in accordance with arrangements made with Sheasongo, carriers came from the village, and by these we returned large quantities of dried meat to help feed the villagers, and also sent loads through to Ibamba.

About once a week the mail boy brought out the letters and magazines which had arrived, and also news from Shamakembie and Charlie Matabele. Paddy, they sent word, was in fine shape, but the wild lions were becoming bolder and bolder and the wire surrounding her paddock was being tested to the limit. The lions had not bothered any of the cattle or other livestock, but the crocodiles were bad. Hoppers, the mail boy reported, were very numerous all along the edges of the flats and were causing great destruction. Ibamba was crawling with them, and swarms darkened the skies day after day.

The carriers taking meat to Ibamba reported that sight of the long dark bundles of food on their shoulders had aroused talk and envy among the people in the villages through which they had to pass. They had become so afraid they might be attacked by the hungry that they applied to Sheasongo for protection. The chief sent four men with each group of carriers as guards. In spite of this the carriers said they were afraid to pass close to a village and followed roundabout routes through the bushveld.

No matter how successful I might be in my hunting or how many animals I shot, it was manifestly impossible for me to feed the hundreds, the thousands, of natives who did not have enough to eat. I discontinued sending meat to the ranch to avoid trouble and sent a message to Shamakembie that he and the others would have to make out on what I had already sent them, plus the meat from the animals they killed to supply food for Paddy.

The men left on Ibamba had grain. Although the daily ration was slim, it was more than many of the other inhabitants of the Namwala district had. Unless they had been unusually generous handing out dried meat to friends and relatives, the supplies we had sent should carry them through until our return. We continued sending to Sheasongo.

During the fifth week of our stay in the Home of the Lion we moved our camp thirty miles farther into the area, to a spot beside a series of flat pans lying in a row several miles long and connected by a wide, dusty vlei. Animals of every species were, if that was possible, even more abundant than around camp one and the Kasha Pools. Many, such as waterbuck, hartebeest, and wildebeest, were of no interest to me as a hunter. The meat of waterbuck was tough and rank, and their hides were not good for the making of riems. Neither were the hides of wildebeest, hartebeest, or zebra.

Such zebras as I did shoot we either used as bait for lions and leopards or we ate ourselves, saving the hides to be tanned for floor rugs. The drying zebra hides caused Mianje considerable distress, as did the zebras which were almost constantly in view from camp. She succeeded in arriving at some sort of a compromise with the devil which bewitched her, and avoided the fits which had seized her every now and then while on Ibamba. Iz and I, discussing Mianje's condition, speculated as to whether or not she had been subject to a form of epilepsy when young, and might, perhaps, have grown out of this as she matured. It was our guess that when, as a child, Mianje had had her first fit, a witch doctor had been called to try and effect a cure. It might well have been that the child had eaten zebra meat just before her seizure or that her father might have brought zebra meat to the hut. Casting about for a cause for the child's condition and learning of the meal of zebra, the witch doctor might well have blamed the seizure on that and stated that the child had become inhabited by the spirit of a zebra. It would not have been difficult, playing upon the beliefs of the natives in the omnipresence of spirits of many types, to have developed such a firm conviction in Mianje's mind that she was possessed by a zebra spirit as to cause her to become so emotionally upset at sight of a zebra, a piece of striped hide, or a chunk of zebra meat as to bring on a seizure. Both Isabella and I were convinced that her fits, if they could be called by this name, were more mental than physical. If they were not, why did Mianje's hypnotic dance bring relief?

We put out several sets of traps for lions and leopards—some many miles from camp. Hyenas and bush cats and civet cats got caught in these as well as the larger animals. The hyenas were a nuisance. We did skin one or two, for their skins are exceptionally tough and make excellent rugs, but the process is disgustingly odoriferous and unpleasant. Generally, we shot them and dragged the carcasses away from the traps and left them to be eaten by their former companions.

The buffalo were my main interest. Herd after herd came to one or another of the pans near which we were camped. Day after day I hunted them after they had moved from the pans, and killed many. Lions followed nearly every herd, and we came upon them often. They were big lions, unafraid of man, and full of fight and confidence. Several crumpled under the smashing impact of the heavy, blunt soft-nosed bullets from my rifle. One, a lioness, came at me up an anthill and sprang in a magnificent leap over a large fallen log. My bullet caught her squarely in the throat in mid-air, and she was dead before her body hit the ground.

One evening I returned to camp from the veld to find everyone in a state of considerable excitement. Early that afternoon a great herd of buffalo had come to the pan at which we drew water for the camp. After wallowing and drinking, the enormous animals had moved slowly toward the camp. Grazing on the crowns of harsh dry grass, the buffalo covered the vlei and surrounded the camp on two sides. For an hour or more Isabella and Buncher and Mianje and the cook and work boys had watched as the powerful truculent-looking animals moved all about them.

Iz told me that at first she had been nervous. The animals were so big and there were so many of them. I sympathized with her. Buffalo have fearsome reputations, and wild animals do queer things at times. Gradually, as she saw the buffalo apparently were paying no attention to the camp and the people watching them, Iz's qualms subsided and she tried to count them. The animals moved about so constantly and there were so many that when she reached two hundred, she stopped counting.

At their leisure the herd moved away, and the dust cloud which hung above it and the white cattle egrets and the tick birds which accompanied it moved also. By the time I returned, the buffalo were several miles away and there was not enough daylight left for me to take up pursuit.

I was on the spoor at daylight the next morning. The herd had wandered in a great circle, and we covered more than twenty miles before we caught up with it. When the shooting was over, I was a trifle surprised to find that we were only some five miles from camp and that Iz had heard the reports of my heavy firing.

Wild dogs, those voracious, relentless scourges of the veld, were rather numerous. Out hunting, I saw packs of the dogs several times, and on several nights, dozing in camp, we heard the dogs chase an antelope into one of the pans. The deeper pans, those with water of a depth of three or four feet or more, were the only refuges to which antelope attacked by wild dogs could flee. If the antelope succeeded in reaching a pan with deep water, it plunged in and stood while the dogs circled, yipping and barking around the edge. The dogs would not go into water in which they had to swim, and their quarry, so long as it stayed in deep water, was safe. Eventually the dogs would abandon the chase and rush away to find some other antelope. Often they came close to the camp and yipped and growled at us. Flashing the searchlight on them, the veld suddenly came alive with a myriad yellow gleaming eyes, moving and circling in the night. Such occasions were eerie experiences, and for some reason, vaguely frightening, although there was no danger. I have never heard of a human being being attacked by wild dogs.

The most enjoyable hours during our stay in the Home of the Lion were those we passed watching the kaleidoscopic scenes around the pans and those of quiet discussion and talk about the campfires in the evenings. The pans, over which flashed brilliant green-and-yellow flycatchers, were visited by an ever-changing stream of animals. It was seldom that two species of antelope watered at the same time, for the herds were large and the thirsty animals waded into the water in such numbers as to occupy almost the complete area. When their thirst was slaked, the antelope grazed on the luxuriant, lush green sedge and grass and water lilies. As they moved, their thin graceful legs threw up sprays of water, the drops of which, catching the sunlight, shone like polished beads. Blue cranes, tall red-kneed cranes with black-and-red striped bills fourteen inches long, and egrets stalked in the shallow water near the antelope and zebras, watching for insects and frogs disturbed by the feet of the larger animals, and hurrying to seize some delicacy as it leaped or flew for safety. Tick birds often accompanied the antelope, riding on them and clinging to their backs and sides, their necks and heads, picking at the ticks. Occasional kingfishers hovered on rapidly beating wings over the pans, and then, abruptly folding them, dove into the water. Families of wart hogs drank and then wallowed in the mud at the edges of the pans, contentedly grunting and thrusting their backsides deeper into the gooey substance so that the cooling mud half covered their gray bodies.

Coming out of the mopani forest near the southernmost pan, herds of waterbuck displaced the wildebeest and zebra, and they, in turn, were followed by reddish hartebeest and big, strong, proud roan antelope with white bars across their muzzles. Sometimes buffalo came with egrets and tick birds riding on their broad backs, and they might be followed by stately, gigantic eland antelope, or sable with their long curving horns, or dainty kudu. Lions came to drink, usually late in the afternoon or early in the morning, and after drinking, paced slowly away to find a secluded place in which to sleep away the heat of the day or began their hunting.

In the evenings, when the last meal was done, Shamann'yati, Mangineera, Jam, Shaluma, Charlie Portuguese, and Lavison gathered by the central fire. They brought their carved stools with them or sat on logs and passed clay pipes with three-foot stems one to another or inhaled snuff and we talked about animals and native customs and beliefs; the locusts and the government. Mianje was allowed to join the group because she had become a privileged person by reason of caring for Buncher; and Sixpence came, and others.

Together we relived former hunting trips and thrilled again to the excitement of catching buffalo and lions alive; of tangling leopards in nets; of chasing after elephant calves. We spoke of charging animals and of men, both black and white, who had died beneath the ponderous feet of elephants, on the horns of a furious rhinos, or gone down before the determined onrush of a great bull buffalo. We listened to the lions roaring on the veld and Shamann'-yati and Mangineera interpreted what they thought they were talking about and taught Iz and me to differentiate between the voices of the lionesses and those of the lions. Each cry, each call, each sound, provoked a story, and each story was told in anecdotal form. Those were wonderful hours, during which the ties which bound us together were strengthened and tightened.

It was late in August when we moved out of the Home of the Lion and ground and boiled our way in the heavily loaded truck along the dry, sandy track from Sheasongo to Namwala and then on to Ibamba.

The boys for whom there was no space on the truck had preceded us, so Shamakembie and Charlie Matabele knew we were coming. Jonas, the bedroom boy, who had remained on Ibamba, had dusted and cleaned the house. The bed was made and turned down. There was a fire burning in the kitchen stove. The two little duikers shyly acknowledged our return, but backed away from Buncher's stumbling rush to seize them and love them. Fwifwi was on the lawn, but he was distant and aloof. Popeye came galloping up. She had grown as large as a Shetland pony, and her horns were nearly four inches long. She nuzzled us wetly and seemed glad we were back. Jane Emmeline John stalked from beside the lily pool, uttering her strident call, and Garbage waddled after her.

Paddy went nearly frantic. She had, Shamakembie told me, heard the truck long before any of the people. Nervously she had paced up and down inside her paddock, rearing up against the wire to her full height to stare along the edge of the flat between Ibamba and the mission along which we would come. When we pulled to a stop behind the house, I saw her racing around the paddock. She leaped at the wire and stood on her hind legs and mewed and ek-eowed and called and grunted for attention.

When I walked to the door into her paddock, Paddy went into a frenzy of excitement. Bounding and bouncing about like a tremendous rubber ball, she waited for me to enter. When I did, she rushed me and knocked me down and sat on me and licked me until my face was raw. All the time she uttered her rumbling throaty purring sound. I had to wrestle and struggle with her so that I could get off the ground, and as soon as I was up, she knocked me down again. Like Popeye, Paddy had grown greatly during the two months we had been away. She was a big full-grown lioness and fearfully strong and rough. It was all her way of showing how much she loved me and how much she had missed me, but she scratched me several times in her exuberance and I had to punch and slap her to quiet her down. I was afraid to let her out.

It was not that Paddy was dangerous. It was just that I feared for Iz and Buncher. Paddy was so large. She weighed nearly three hundred and fifty pounds. In her enthusiasm and forgetfulness she might overwhelm Iz and Buncher and flatten them to the floor or ground and, unmeaningly, of course, hurt them. So I did not let her out until the following morning, after Iz and Buncher had visited Paddy and given her time to work off her first violent bursts of affection by talking to and stroking her through the wire. For such a usually staid and placid creature Paddy, for a short time until she regained her dignified composure, was almost obnoxiously loving.

And love it was. Paddy's excitement and joy had nothing to do with food. Shamakembie had fed her regularly and well, but she still treated him with disdain. It was me, my presence, that she wanted, and the presence of Buncher and Isabella. We were her mother and father, her sisters and brothers, all rolled into one. We were the ones who played and talked with her, who had warmed her as a kitten and taught her to eat. Paddy loved us. There was not the faintest question of that, just as Mr. Thomas had loved Isabella. Fiercely and possessively. All the cold, scientific Md's and Phd's, the anti-anthropomorphists and the unemotional psychologists, to the contrary.

We slipped back easily into ranch life. The rains would come in six weeks or so, so the plows were greased and made ready for work. The items we had brought from the Home of the Lion were cleaned and packed, and I took them to the railway line. There I sold the fat and riems and shipped the skins and trophies to Johannesburg. We did not realize as much as we had hoped for, but any cash was welcome. I used most of the money to buy supplies to carry us over the rainy season, and trucked these back to Ibamba.

The locusts were just as numerous and widespread as when we had left Ibamba. As I tramped back and forth across the ranch, the results of the unceasing, constant nibbling and feeding of the insects were obvious on every side. When we had first come to Ibamba, the bushveld portion had been green and rank with the growths of trees, vines, bushes, and tall grasses. In spite of our partial success in preventing the veld fires from invading Ibamba, a success which should have resulted in promoting the increased growth of the plants, the land looked denuded. On the flatlands which surrounded the long, rectangular rise of higher ground there was grass. At the end of the dry season this was dry and harsh and yellow and lay in tangled windrows through which it was difficult for men and cattle to walk. New green grass formed beneath the protection of the old, and the cattle found and fed on this. But the bushveld lay bare and dry and naked to the sun and the winds. Ranging over our lands, I could not escape the feeling that a blight had fallen on the district.

Lions roared every night. Paddy called to them, and they came in the darkness and pushed and leaned against the wire of her paddock. During our absence the wild lions had snapped four of the tough mopani uprights holding the wire. Shamakembie had rigged guy wires on the outside in an attempt to hold the poles upright, but one of the first jobs we had to do was to replace the poles and tighten and straighten the heavy wire. The hole Paddy had dug near her water trough was deeper than ever, and she had started a second in the opposite corner. Scratching dirt at her visitors was, evidently, a favorite pastime.

During the two months we had been hunting in the west, Ibamba had slumbered peacefully. Now, once again, dust clouds boiled up behind the gang plows and from beneath the feet of straining oxen. The bushveld rang to the chunking sound of axes biting into dense green wood as logs were cut and made ready for piling for fires throughout the grain fields. Everyone knew that the struggle between ourselves and the locusts would be resumed and that we must prepare. The high sing-song cries and yells of Charlie Matabele and the other native drivers as they guided their spans of oxen carried far on the gentle breezes. At times the staccato cracking of the long whips sounded like a fusillade of shots.

The tensions and fears which we had been able to shed for a time in the peacefulness and beauty of the Home of the Lion returned and began to churn and mount in all of us, natives and whites alike. The business depression had engulfed the world, and in America, so our friends wrote, conditions were almost desperate. It was impossible to liquidate the real-estate holdings of my father except at fearful loss. As a result we received less and less cash. We explained the situation to our boys and gave them I.O.U's in place of pay. We still had some grain and quite a bit of dried meat. We had the cattle, a few goats and sheep and hogs, chickens and eggs, and we worked desperately to develop the best vegetable garden possible.

We would not starve. If we were forced to quit, it would be because we had no money and there was no way by which we could earn any in substantial amounts. As soon as the garden began to produce, Iz resumed her weekly shipments of vegetables to the mission, the *boma,* and Cavadia, but the money she earned was a pitiful sum.

Just before the rains came, when the dark masses of clouds were taking turns with the swarms of locusts in casting shadows across Ibamba, Popeye, galloping along the road from the compound toward the house, put her left front leg into an old fence-post hole. Flying heels over head, she broke her shoulder. The boys picked her up and, struggling, carried her to the house, but as Iz and I worked over her, I knew there was nothing we could do. I felt like a murderer when I placed a rifle against her ear and shot her and watched the light fade from her beautiful, luminous eyes. Popeye's death added to the sense of gloom and desperation which was rising within every one of us.

Fwifwi, we discovered, had not really abandoned Iz. He was absent for long periods, several days at a time; but then he would return, and in spite of being a full-grown animal, eagerly accept a bottle of milk.

He was, however, standoffish, and preferred to graze and stay at the edge of the lawn near the beginning of the long grass.

Then one evening we saw the reason for Fwifwi's absences and why he only grudgingly gave loyalty to Isabella. A second oribi appeared and stood timidly at the edge of the lawn, its lovely petal ears pricked forward and its body tense to dash away. Anxiously the new arrival watched as Fwifwi answered Iz's calling and approached her for his milk. As soon as he had drained the bottle, he bounded away and the two beautiful little antelope disappeared into the grass. Fwifwi had found a mate.

We were, of course, glad for him but sorry at our loss. I gave orders that under no circumstances were any of the boys whom I might send out hunting to shoot at any oribi on Ibamba.

The first fierce deluge of rain had swept over us when word came that Sheasongo had died. Suddenly. The news was a great shock to both Iz and me. Sheasongo, for all his tyranny and ruthless use of power, had been a fair man and a fair ruler according to the code under which he lived, and he had been a true and lasting friend to me for many years. When Jam brought the messenger to me and he and I talked with Charlie Portuguese after the messenger had been dismissed, Jam hinted that Sheasongo's death had not been natural; that he had been poisoned. Poisoning was the almost inevitable death for all the powerful and autocratic chiefs. Sheasongo, like

Mokobella and Shaloba and Chinda, had tasters who sampled his food and beer before he partook of either, but there were so many subtle means to poison a man.

One of the most common was to secure the bark of a certain bush which grew here and there upon the veld and dry this and grind it to a powder. Mixed with tobacco, the bark, when heated, released a violent poison, undoubtedly an alkaloid, without imparting taste to the strong tobacco fumes. There was no known antidote.

The death of the chief presented certain problems for me. As an acknowledged blood brother I had certain rights which ought to be considered. Talking these things over with Charlie Portuguese, Mangineera and Jam and Lavison, on whose counsel in such matters I relied heavily, I decided to send Jam to represent me at the funeral celebration; to send an ox for slaughter and to instruct Jam to tell the elders of the village that I wished to be eliminated from any considerations and did not wish to exercise my rights to participate in their councils.

The boys agreed that this was right and proper. My relationship had always been with Sheasongo the individual, the chief, and on a man-to-man basis. Although Sheasongo had at times conferred with me about certain of his problems, I had never intruded into one of the village council meetings. Jam assured me that I would continue to be able to summon labor from the village whenever I might need men and that my rather unique position would be maintained.

Jam departed with two men leading a fine fat ox about four years old. He was gone for ten days. When he returned, he reported that there was considerable dissension in the village as to who should succeed to the chieftainship. The logical heir, Sheasongo's first son by his first wife, had died as a youth—an occasion, as I have mentioned previously, on which Sheasongo was reported to have shot two of his slaves to insure attendants for his son in the spirit world. As I listened to Jam, I was glad I had decided to remove myself from involvement in the deliberations.

Late one afternoon, some weeks after Jam's return from Sheasongo, as we were completing the day's tasks and the oxen were returning to the kraals after being watered, we heard the soft, tinkling music of an *olimba.* In the quiet evening air the sound flowed to us from the direction of the track which the natives used during the dry season to cut across the flats on their way to Namwala *boma.*

As we stood near the house listening and as the music steadily increased in volume, we wondered what chief could be visiting us and who it might be who was so rude as not to have sent notice on ahead. Curious, we waited, and I could see the women and children in the compound come from between the huts and stand beside the track. As the music came nearer and nearer, I looked questioningly at Charlie Portuguese, who was standing with me. There was no doubt that only a single *olimba* was being played. I knew of no chief who traveled with but a single musician.

Distantly, from beneath the trees which closed in above the track, a single figure emerged. In the deepening twilight I could not distinguish who it was. Slowly the figure of the musician drew closer and passed the compound, and the people crowded behind and followed. Iz heard the music, and she and Lavison and Sixpence came to the kitchen door to learn what was afoot.

As we watched the man come, it seemed as if he wobbled and swayed and that his feet wandered from the path so that his course changed from side to side of the path. When the player reached and passed the corner of the laboratory building, he raised his head and I saw that it was Shamoanna, the Mankoya slave musician who had played for Sheasongo. The old man tottered on his feet. His pipestem legs moved as if weighted down with lead. But when he saw us waiting in the glow from the kitchen lamps which streamed through the open door, he steadied himself and his strokes against the wooden blocks doubled in intensity. Playing furiously upon the wide instrument which hung from his neck, Shamoanna drew up before us.

He was covered with dust and dirt. His dry black skin hung in wrinkles on his belly and on his arms. His eyes were so sunken in his head, I could scarcely see them. Reaching up to lift the *olimba* from about his neck, Shamoanna nearly fell. Charlie Portuguese and

Lavison rushed to him and helped him and half carried him into the kitchen.

There, to our dismay, the old man fell to his knees on the hard concrete floor. In front of Iz and myself he beat his forehead against the cement, crying out that he had been thrust from the village to die because he was old and a slave and there was no food. Stumbling, tottering, sleeping out on the cold, wet veld without blanket, clothes, or a weapon, he had come because I was Sheasongo's brother, and since Sheasongo's death he now belonged to me. It was a terrible and pitiful story, and we wept a little as we raised the old man and comforted him and sat him on a chair.

At Isabella's orders Lavison brought a basin of warm water and some soft cloths and Shamoanna sponged himself off and washed his face. His cheeks had fallen in from lack of food and his hands trembled with fatigue and strain.

We fed Shamoanna soup, strong with meat juice, and then a custard which the cook had baked for our dessert. Gradually a little of what strength he had left returned and he sat straighter and some of the trembling of his body eased. We wrapped him in a warm blanket from the storeroom and I told Charlie Portuguese to lead him to the compound and to see that he was made comfortable until the morrow, when we could discuss what to do.

We adopted Shamoanna. Or, perhaps, it is more truthful to say that he adopted us. Particularly Isabella and Buncher, to whom he became devoted. Iz ordered Sixpence to give Shamoanna all the special leavings from our table and occasional eggs, and to cook him broth and puddings. In no time at all—underneath his aged, wrinkled exterior the old fellow must have had sinews and bones and organs of steel—he began to fill out; his skin lost its dead, dry look and his face filled. He walked with his shoulders squared, and in his eyes, still deep in his head, there appeared a mischievous twinkle. Every evening and every morning, except when the rain was heavy, he played outside the living room and dining room, either marching up and down on the short grass or sitting on the ground.

Somewhere Shamoanna found the skin of a pied crow; he cleaned it, fashioned it into a headdress, and wore it as a hat. It did nothing to add to his appearance, but Buncher was entranced. She liked nothing better than to have Shamoanna sit on the grass with the big *olimba* before him and play for her while she listened. Then she would take the hammers and play, although not so well as he.

Shamoanna was deeply touched by the child's devotion. Gentle and patient, he would play for her by the hour. Buncher, dressed in her short white skirt and panties and blouse, and with a soft white hat on her golden hair against the sun, loved nothing so much as to sit between the naked thighs of the old musician and lean back against his bare old body while the music flowed around her. In one way they were a ludicrous pair, closely akin to beautiful Jane Emmeline John and ugly Garbage. The ancient man was separated by seventy years from the child in his lap. With his grotesque headdress and unclothed body he was anything but attractive. He could not talk to Buncher because she could not understand his archaic language. Yet the two were completely compatible. They had no difficulty whatsoever in communicating with each other.

One afternoon Mangineera and Charlie Portuguese and I, with a couple of other natives, were sorting out things in the storeroom when Shamoanna appeared in the doorway and climbed over the high step into the room. After watching us silently for a time, he clapped hands for permission to speak and I nodded to him.

To my amazement and the hysterical laughter of the boys, Shamoanna announced that he wanted me to buy him a wife. Shamoanna made his request in a very dignified manner, explaining that as I was his owner and his chief, it was my duty to provide him with a woman. Delicately he stated that he was grateful for the food and lodging and care which I gave him, but hinted that inasmuch as I did not pay him any money, he felt the responsibility for providing a wife lay with me.

Mangineera laughed so hard at the idea of such an old man wanting a wife that tears ran down his black cheeks. Even Charlie, who was considerably older than Mangineera, could not restrain his mirth, and all the natives unmercifully ribbed and teased the old man.

Shamoanna shrugged the teasing off and clung to his point. He needed a wife, he stated firmly, to prepare his food and to hoe a garden for him and to bring water from the river. It was not fitting that a man of his age should have to do these things himself. Besides, he added, he had many things to do during each day, and having to fetch his own water and prepare his food made the doing of these more difficult. Just what all these duties were Shamoanna did not explain. He had no assigned duties that I knew about. His daily concerts and his attention to Buncher were entirely voluntary.

When the laughter and teasing had died down, I questioned Shamoanna. Who, I asked, would marry so old a man as he, and where did he expect to find a willing woman?

He had answers ready for me. There was a certain woman who came to visit in the compound from a village across the Kafue River and a dozen miles away. She had stayed in his hut and he had found her agreeable. He had asked if she could be bought, and she had replied that she was a widow living with her son and that he would be glad to sell her. Her price, Shamoanna told me, was four pounds.

Realizing that Shamoanna was in deadly earnest, I agreed to think his request over, and he shuffled away after thanking me politely and saying he hoped it would not take me long to decide. When he was gone, I questioned Charlie Portuguese, and he told me that he knew the woman; that she had stayed with Shamoanna on several occasions and cooked for him. He did not know whether the woman could be purchased or not. I would have to write to the chief of the village where the woman lived and inquire. In reply to another question Charlie said he did not think the woman was just after money, nor that she would come and stay with the old man for a short while in the hope of getting goods from him and then leave.

That evening I discussed Shamoanna's request with Isabella. She was as astonished as I had been and just as inclined, at first, to laugh. Four pounds was a lot of money to us right then. Iz was disposed to spend the money, however, justifying the outlay by reminding me of Shamoanna's age, his basic feebleness, and the rough unhappy life he had led for so many years. He was overdue, she said, to receive some comforts, and four pounds was little enough to spend to give them to him.

So I wrote a letter in English to the chief of the village and then painfully translated this into native, which I spelled phonetically. I gave the letter to Charlie Portuguese and told him to send one of our men to the village to deliver it and wait for a reply.

This resulted in quite an extensive exchange of notes between myself and the chief, whose name I have forgotten but whose official rubber stamp signature was that of a large buffalo head. A stamp and pad was supplied to every chief recognized by the *boma,* with a different animal engraved on each stamp. Shamoanna was on pins and needles of anxiety with the arrival and departure of each note, and grew more and more insistent.

In the end, after several weeks of dickering, we arranged for the sale of the woman to Shamoanna for two pounds in cash, six native hoes, and a small ox with horns the length of a man's forearm. The ox was to remain on Ibamba, but the son of the woman would come to place his brand mark on it. Shamoanna was delighted, and when, in due time, the woman arrived, he marched her from the compound to show her to Iz and me. I am afraid that truth compels me to say that I had seldom seen a native woman quite as unkempt and unpleasant-looking. The day after her installment in the compound, Shamoanna played extra loudly and furiously outside our breakfast window.

It was planting time. The first rains had fallen on and been gratefully absorbed by the thirsty soil in the bare, freshly plowed fields. Dutifully, because it was the proper time to do so, we placed the seed in the ground and prayed beneath our breaths for a chance for it to grow and mature. There was no enthusiasm for the planting. Overhead the swarms of locusts searched the land from border to border for places to light and feed or to lay eggs. After our previous bitter and futile battles no one on Ibamba expected that we would reap a crop. Still we planted because it was not yet in us to call the whole thing quits and put our tails between our legs and go home: Iz and I and Buncher to the States, and the people to their villages.

Indeed, what would be the advantages in returning to the States? Ibamba was our home. Letters received from America told only of people standing on the streets trying to sell apples to earn enough to eat; of bread lines and hours and hours spent searching fruitlessly for work. In the villages the plight of the villagers was as bad, or worse, than ours on Ibamba. The entire territory was utterly impoverished. The only people who had any money in Central Africa in those days were a few of the traders; those receiving government pay; the missionaries, and a few who were drawing wartime pensions. For all practical purposes the Protectorate of Northern Rhodesia was bankrupt, if not in morale at least in cash in circulation.

Nevertheless we doggedly continued working. We just could not sit or stand still and watch everything we had worked so hard to bring into being slide down the drain. We cleaned the hopper trenches and kept up the firewood piles and raced shouting and screaming across the fields, beating tom-toms and tins. Clouds of smoke poured again into the sky, and Ibamba was hideous with the turmoil and the desperation of our struggles.

One morning, as I stood near Paddy's paddock, watching the locusts fluttering their wings to dry them of the night's dew preparatory to whirling aloft to invade the mealie fields, I wondered what would happen if the insects suddenly, for some reason, became larger than they were. Suppose, I thought, that the locusts, instead of being three to four inches long, grew to several feet. What would happen to the world in such an event?

The thought stuck in my head, and I jokingly talked with Iz about it. Out of our talks came the idea that I would try and write a book about giant insects invading the earth.

Just why, I do not know, because I had never been in Florida, I decided to lay my story there. To give the story a quasi-scientific authority, I decided to begin with a pool in the Everglades which was subject to flooding by tidal waters. The thyroid gland has a powerful effect upon growth. Iodine affects the thyroid, and iodine can be secured from seaweed. So I imagined a pool in the Everglades in which a quantity of seaweed had been trapped and left by receding tidal waters. The seaweed rotted, releasing unusual quantities of iodine into the water in the pool, and all the frogs and insects which drank of these waters grew to enormous size. The bullfrogs grew so large that, squatting, they occupied the space of an entire football field. Spreading out from the pool, mosquitoes as large as fighter planes and dragon flies as large as bombers attacked the northeastern seaboard of the United States.

With the locusts all about, it was easy to imagine such a happening, and I began to fashion a story and to write every morning in the office. As I completed the drafts, Iz read and criticized, and together we put together a story; when she had the time, she typed a final clean copy. In this way, and because it gave us something to do and took our minds off the devastation all about us, *The Thousandth Frog* came to be written. We could not devote all our time to writing, so the book occupied us for several months. We referred to it as our nickel novel.

It was while I was negotiating with the chief across the river for Shamoanna's wife that a native brought in two baby zimba cats, or spotted genets. When full grown, zimba cats are beautiful sinuous little creatures with short legs, long thin bodies, and long, ringed tails. They have rows of dark spots along their backs and sides which show prettily against the grayish-chocolate background. The ears are large, standing out from their heads like delicate petals; their faces are bright and intelligent, and their muzzles, long and narrow. When full grown, a genet may reach eighteen to twenty-two inches in the body, and its tapering tail will add another foot or more to its length.

When the native brought in the genets, they were only about six to seven inches long. Iz fed them, at first with a medicine dropper, but they quickly learned to lap warm milk and then to eat scraped meat. We let them scurry about the house much as they pleased, and at teatime, or when we were at table, the little zimbas would swarm up our legs, get onto the table, examine and taste each dish, and then curl up contentedly against the warmth of the teapot.

Genets easily adapt themselves to household living, and they are magnificent mousers. But they are very quarrelsome little animals and fight furiously among themselves. I believe that genets were the original house cats of the ancient Egyptians, and not, as is commonly believed, the bush cat. Our genets stayed with us for several months, giving us many a laugh with their antics, and much enjoyment, before they wandered off one night and took up life in the open. For a time I used to see them prowling about the kitchen woodpile, searching for insects and lizards, and then they departed.

Christmas came. And passed. For Buncher's sake, for whom I had made a little wooden wagon with solid wooden wheels, we had a tree and it was gaily decorated. We should not have done so, but we allowed the natives to use some of the precious store of grain to brew beer and we slaughtered an ox. Paddy came into the house for Christmas and behaved beautifully, although she was enormous and so tall that standing beside the dining-room table, she could easily lay her lower jaw on the top.

We missed Mr. Thomas dreadfully. Neither Isabella nor I could speak about him without our throats tightening painfully. Fwifwi had left to begin a wilder life and raise a family. Popeye's death had saddened us, and the house seemed empty without her incongruous bumbling presence. The rug before the fire was empty, and outside the locusts beat against the walls and windows and the sound of their rustling wings flowed into the rooms in the house during all the daylight hours.

The physical weariness, the mental exhaustion which we had hoped to shed during our trip to the west, returned. We were bone-tired and without cash. Because of the never-ending swarms of locusts and hoppers it was painfully evident that our crops would not mature. We tried to make the best of things and be gay for Buncher's sake, but as we listened to the tom-toms throbbing in the compound, each of us knew, although we did not say so, that this might well be our last Christmas on Ibamba.

It was in February that Jane Emmeline John met her untimely and unwarranted end. A small flock of about ten wild crested cranes settled on the short grass on the lowland between the compound and the river and beyond the dipping tank. This was unusual, and Iz and I watched the birds. They appeared to be hunting young frogs or insects, and strutted about uttering their mournful calls, *mo-wan, mo-wan.*

Jane also saw and heard the wild birds. Hearing and seeing them was nothing new to Jane, as crested cranes were common on the flats and frequently flew over the house. There was scarcely a day on which we did not hear cranes calling. This was the first time, however, that cranes had come so close to the house and other buildings. Jane suddenly ran across the lawn, took to the air, and flew down to join her wild brethren.

As Iz and I watched Jane fly, I noticed that several natives had come to the edge of the compound and were standing looking at the gathering of crested cranes. They are extremely beautiful and stately birds. Suddenly the wild birds turned on Jane and began to peck savagely at her. Both Isabella and I shouted and started to run to help Jane, and several of the boys raced from the compound.

We were too late. Before Jane could escape or we could reach her, the wild birds had buffeted her to the ground and killed her. Jane was still fluttering feebly when we reached her, but she was badly injured and died immediately.

Why did this happen? It is difficult to arrive at a logical explanation. Jane was in full plumage. Her wings had not been clipped. Standing among wild birds, I doubt that I or anyone else could have singled her out as being in any way different. There must either have been something which told the wild birds Jane was in some way different from themselves, or it might have been that cranes are very clannish and will turn against any outsider endeavoring to join a group.

Mammals, I knew, frequently turned on members of their species which had associated with men and bore, on their coats, the smell of man. I had seen this happen, and I believe it was knowledge of this danger which caused Paddy to scratch dirt at her wild visitors and to run for safety into her brick house. But we did not handle Jane. Even if we had, birds are not believed to have a sense of smell, although they certainly enjoy the sense of taste.

The reason for the sudden and vicious attack on Jane remained a mystery, but we had to accept the hard and saddening fact that we had lost another of our wonderful foster children. A month or two later Garbage flapped heavily out onto the veld to join three other ground hornbills waddling across the grassland in their constant search for food. They accepted him, and he walked with them; the last we saw of him was when he and his three black companions ran clumsily over the ground and rose into the air on huge wide wings and disappeared into the twilight settling over the flats.

Tweetie, our dove, had disappeared while we were in the Home of the Lion. We were left with Paddy, the two little duikers, the lechwe antelope, and the locusts. Always and constantly with the locusts.

Our harvest amounted to only a few miserable bags of grain and fewer of peanuts. We were expecting our second child to be born toward the end of the dry season. The news and advices received from America were discouraging and pessimistic. There were still some tangibles left in the estates of my father and mother, but their values were highly problematical and there was great uncertainty as to when they might be disposed of to make cash available.

Our cattle had steadily been increasing in numbers and the first calf crop was just reaching marketable age and weight. We had about fifty head which could have been sold, and, under normal conditions they would have brought twenty-five to thirty dollars a head. However, the mines which usually took all the cattle produced to feed the native workers were largely closed down. There was no market for copper. Every farmer and rancher was trying to dump what cattle he could at whatever prices he could get. The buyers who, before the coming of the locusts and the disaster of the business depression, had bid excitedly against one another for cattle offered at the periodic auctions, now picked and chose and paid insultingly low prices.

It had never been in our plans to try and make Ibamba pay as a farm. We had always intended to raise only sufficient grain, peanuts, and other products of the soil to feed ourselves and our retainers. Ibamba was essentially a ranch, a place on which to raise cattle, and it was from the sale of cattle that we had expected eventually to derive enough income to carry the establishment and show a profit. Just as we were beginning to reach the point where we could annually offer livestock for sale, the markets were closed to us.

Evening after evening Isabella and I debated what we should do. The Agriculture Department could give no estimate or assurances as to when, if ever, the locusts might leave or die out. From the numbers filling the skies, it looked as if they would be with us for years and years to come. Should we plan to stay or to leave? Which would be the wisest course for Buncher and our unborn child?

If we were to leave, we would have many arrangements to make. Somehow we would have to raise enough money to pay off our boys. That was the first and most important obligation. We would have to negotiate with Mopani about Ibamba, but I expected little difficulty there. Mopani was a fair man. There were the cattle, the other livestock, Paddy, the farm machinery, and all the laboratory equipment to be disposed of in some manner. We would need steamship tickets, which cost money, and railroad fare and eating money so that we would not starve along the way. It would take months to complete all the details if we finally decided that we had to leave.

While we were wrestling with these problems, I wrote an article about the locusts and Ibamba which I called "Chiquiqui." It was probably not the best such piece ever written, but I tried to pour all the agony and terror of our struggles with the locusts into it. Prayerfully we addressed the envelope and mailed the article to the *Saturday Evening Post* in faraway Philadelphia. As the rains ended and the land began to dry, we completed our nickel novel. Iz finished the final typing and we posted the heavy manuscript to our London literary agent.

Unless, during the first months of the dry season, the locusts markedly diminished and it was reasonable to assume that the invasion was petering out, we decided we would leave a few weeks after the baby was born. Iz, after her experience in the hospital in Livingstone, did not want to have her second child there. She said she would rather stay at Kasenga, and John and Florence agreed to have her.

The curse which had hung over Ibamba and kept everyone away from the ranch and the great dark, brooding *saka* at the western end appeared to have been lifted. Ranch and farm life progressed, in so far as the locusts permitted, on Ibamba just as it did on other ranches nearer the railway line. We lived with the, by then, certain knowledge that lions would not attack our cattle. Even the natives had come to this belief.

It was early in the dry season. The grass was still too green to burn and stood mile upon square mile of waving menace all about us. Menace, because when the natives did fire it to get rid of the old dry harsh grass and allow new green shoots to come up for their herds to eat, tremendous fires would sweep the land and run across country with the speed of horses, jumping fire guards and even the broad Kafue River in their rush before the winds. Those terrible fires turned the night red and orange with leaping, crackling flame, and the days were overcast and dark with palls of smoke and clouds of ash.

It happened without warning. Isabella and I had retired and were in that nice cosy doze which anticipates sleep. Buncher was sound asleep in her crib. The duikers were folded up on the veranda. It was peaceful and quiet, and I could occasionally hear one of the hippos sounding off somewhere along the riverbank.

There was a shot from the compound. I allowed Charlie Portuguese to keep a shotgun in his hut. I sat up in bed. Yells and shouts sounded through the night, and then another shot. I scrambled out of bed, lit a lamp, and seizing a rifle, went out onto the back veranda. Pandemonium sounded from the compound. I could hear what I thought were the muffled growls and grunts of lions and could distinctly hear cattle bawl and bellow. Grass torches flared and moved wildly through the night. More shots. Then I heard the hard sound of cattle running on packed earth. They were coming toward the house from the compound.

Lions! Lions had finally attacked us and broken the cattle from the kraals! The herd thundered past the house in the darkness, and as they went, I could hear them bawl and the lions in amongst them growling, grunting, and roaring savagely. Then the turmoil passed and swept down toward the tall grass covering the flatland between us and the mission.

I shouted. Natives' voices answered from the huts and torches came bobbing and flaring through the night. Soon Jam and Mangineera and Charlie Portuguese and Charlie Matabele and all our other natives, laden with spears and carrying flares, were assembled before me.

"What happened?" I asked, although I knew.

"Lions, *N'Kos,*" answered Jam, speaking for all. "Lions. They came from the Namwala flats and stampeded the cattle. This is a bad night for you, Sibyunni'byunni, for the lions have killed at last."

"It is not so," I stated. "Has anyone yet seen a dead beast?"

They shook their heads. "No," admitted Jam, "we have not seen a beast that the lions have killed. But, *N'Kos,* it is night. In the night we cannot see. Tomorrow you will find that the lions have killed."

"How many were there?" I queried.

The natives stared at me. How could anyone count lions while they were running in the middle of a herd of cattle at night! A few shook their heads dubiously.

"Many," said Charlie Portuguese. "More than the fingers on one hand."

The natives stood about uncertainly, staring at me and murmuring one to another.

"Go back," I told them. "In the morning we shall search. We shall find all the cattle. I spoke to the lions as they rushed past. They are strange lions and came from afar and did not know about Ibamba. Return and sleep."

Disbelief and awe were eloquent in the silence in which they all departed. When I entered the bedroom, Isabella looked at me almost angrily.

"Why did you make such an idiotic statement?" she asked. "You know the lions must have killed. How many were there, anyway?"

"The boys couldn't see them well. Charlie Portuguese says somewhere between five and ten. I would guess seven."

"I don't think you were smart," she said as she rolled over and prepared to go back to sleep.

"Maybe not. We'll see in the morning. I was just playing my string out."

The next morning all the natives went out, searching and trying to track down the stampeded cattle. It was a task because when the cattle had run into the long grass they had split and gone dashing off in twos, threes, and small groups.

No dead animals had been found between the kraals and the long grass. I stood for long periods several times during the day, searching the sky for the tell-tale circling of vultures which would indicate that a dead animal lay below, partially hidden in the grass. By evening I had seen no birds. All day the natives kept returning, herding cattle before them. As they came in, we counted. By dark all but nine cattle had been found and returned.

For the next three days we searched for the missing cattle. Jam and Mangineera spent a great deal of time trying to decipher the lion spoor, and followed the spoor to see if the lions might have chased the missing cattle and killed off the ranch. They had no luck and found no signs of kills.

The middle of the following week, when I was about to go into the house for lunch, an elderly native approached me, and clapping hands, sought permission to speak. I granted this, and he squatted before me. Mangineera and one or two others to whom I had been giving orders drew close, and the houseboys watched and listened from the kitchen.

"*Dalumbwa, dalumbwa chinichini,*" the old man greeted me.

"*Dalumbwa,*" I replied, "*kalumma.*"

"I am Shamashoto," he began, "and I live in the village of Marla." He pointed beyond the mission on the far crest of a rise. I nodded. I thought I had seen the old fellow before.

"*N'Kos,* have you lost anything?" he asked, peering up at me from his red-rimmed eyes.

By this time, sensing something afoot, many natives had gathered and stood about us in a circle, listening.

"Yes," I replied, "I have lost something. Why do you ask? Have you found something?"

"I have found something," he told me. It would have been impossible to have hurried him. He was going to tell this in his own manner.

"What have you found, old man?"

Instead of replying directly to my question, he asked again: "Have you lost any cattle, *N'Kos?*"

At that the natives crowded close. Isabella came and joined the circle about the old man and peered at him in the hot sunlight.

"Yes," I told him, "I have lost some cattle. Have you found any cattle?"

"I have found cattle," he answered gravely.

"How many?" I asked eagerly, "and how do you know they belong to me?"

Taking his time, and relishing his audience to the fullest, the old man spoke slowly.

"The cattle are marked as your cattle are marked." He reached to his dirty sweat-stained leather belt and pulled forth a small gourd. Extracting the bit of filthy rag which served as a stopper, he opened the gourd and began to shake out grains of corn. "I have found this many."

One by one the grains of corn tumbled out and Shamashoto laid them in the dust in a row. One, two, three, four, five—the natives gasped, and I could hear them muttering—six, seven, eight, then nine!

The missing cattle had been found. Not one had been touched by a lion! I glanced about the group. The natives were staring at me as if I were a ghost or someone supernatural. Their mouths hung open and an eye rolled and started here and there.

"Jam," I ordered, trying to appear as if this was a perfectly usual matter, "take some boys and fetch the cattle this afternoon." I thanked and paid the old man, and he shuffled off. But the others remained. I spoke to them again. "You should have searched in Marla," I rebuked them. "Did I not tell you I spoke to the lions, and did I not say that all cattle would be found alive?"

Mangineera and Charlie Portuguese turned and started for the compound. As if slightly dazed, the others followed. What could they say? I had prophesied, they had all heard me, and my prophecy had come true. Coming not too long after my struggle with and conquest of the spirit lion of the Kasha Pools, it was too much. Truly the *n'kos* was a *matakatsi* of *matakatsis,* a chief among chiefs. Without a doubt he could indeed talk with lions.

I turned to enter the house, stepping aside at the door to let Isabella precede me. She passed me silently. For once she was utterly flabbergasted.

And so, I must admit, was I. I still am.

chapter seventeen

IT was from Shaluma, Mianje's husband, and Mangineera that I received the accolade which indicated complete acceptance by the natives of my and Ibamba's immunity from attack by lions.

On the day following the return to the ranch of the nine missing cattle, Shaluma and Mangineera came to me and asked permission to bring their stock onto Ibamba. I had known that Shaluma, like all Mashakulumbwe natives, owned a few head, but it was a surprise to find that my carefree, irresponsible gunbearer had used some of his wages to buy and stash away a few cows.

I chided Mangineera about keeping a secret from me, and he hung his head and wiggled his toes in the dust like a small boy being reprimanded by his father. It was a pleasant shock to discover that my swashbuckling, free-spending, devil-may-care gunbearer had, underneath, an eye for his future, although his admission embarrassed him greatly. It was almost as if I had caught him out in some silly act such as stealing candy.

I gave permission, of course, but I had to add that, in honesty, I did not know whether I could protect their cattle as well as my own. I pointed out to them that when Cavadia had had his cattle on Ibamba for a few months shortly after our arrival, the lions had sought out his animals and killed among them.

Both boys agreed that should lions attack and kill their cattle while on Ibamba, they would not hold me responsible or consider me negligent. They were so impressed by what had happened that they would have agreed to any conditions. They were convinced that any cattle which I might take onto Ibamba and place under my supervision would be utterly safe. Sibyunni'byunni's power over lions was no longer a matter for uncertain acceptance. So far as the natives were concerned, it was a fact.

Having reached our decision that we must leave Ibamba before the beginning of the rains, Iz and I then had to decide what, among our possessions, we wanted to take back to the States. Our books were one, and I started Shaluma and the carpenter boys sorting out the softwood boards which we had saved from crates and boxes, and to accumulating mabunga boards and others which could be used to fashion boxes which would not be too heavy.

I catalogued the scientific equipment and wrote to the Department of Agriculture and the Veterinary Department offering to sell the stains, the apparatus, the sterilizer, etc., at whatever figure they might be able and willing to pay. I wrote of our decision to Mopani and detailed our reasons for leaving.

Word got around that we were making ready to depart and that most of our goods and chattels were for sale, and we sold our beds and mattresses, the metal bureaus and other furniture, linens, pots and pans, china and glass. All on the basis of delivery when we left. I kept my rifles and shotguns, although we had practically no ammunition left. The place to sell those would be in Bulawayo on our trip south to catch a steamer.

Toward the end of June, three and a half to four months after we had hopefully posted the article "Chiquiqui" to the *Saturday Evening Post,* a letter arrived, bearing the imprint of the *Post* in the upper lefthand corner of the envelope. Iz and I looked at the envelope for a long time before opening it. When we did, out slid a brief note stating that the article had been accepted, and a check for four hundred dollars. We stared at the check in disbelief. Four hundred dollars! At that time it was a tremendous sum to us and, what was so wonderful, completely unexpected. We mailed the check to the bank for collection and totaled the sum which was gradually accumulating in our account. Receipt of that check helped to diminish some of the aches and unhappiness which filled us every time we walked about the ranch or looked up from our packing to stare out the windows at the lands about us which we had learned to love.

For hours at a time we had talked about what to do with Paddy. We loved her. We could not just drive out somewhere onto the veld and turn her loose. In spite of the fact that I had let her kill her own food now and then, she knew nothing about stalking game and killing it. That was something she would have learned from her natural parents. We had failed to anticipate that we might ever have to turn her out. Paddy knew nothing of life in the open, where she would have to fend for herself. There would be other dangers. Wild lions, which she would be bound to meet, might attack and kill her just as we had seen the cranes attack and kill Jane Emmeline John, and I knew other wild animals killed pets which had wandered away from their homes.

Being so familiar with humans, both native and white, Paddy, if turned loose on the veld, would in all probability follow the first people she found. Trusting in man's kindness, she would expect to be fed and petted and would walk right up to whomever she met. Which could only mean a sticky and painful death from spears or the bullet from an old muzzle-loader.

Transporting Paddy all the way by rail to the coast and then shipping her to the States would be costly. I do not know why we pretended to hesitate about this. Paddy was so much a member of our family, so devoted to Buncher and to Isabella and to me, and such a wonderful animal that there was never a real question in our minds but that, idiotic as this might appear to others, we would take Paddy with us.

I got off letters to the Bronx Zoo and to the Central Park Zoo in New York, asking if they would be willing to board Paddy for a time after our arrival if we paid the costs and had the necessary veterinary certificates to show that Paddy was in good health and free from disease. I wrote also to the veterinary departments of Southern Rhodesia and Portuguese East Africa, inquiring as to what permits would be required to pass Paddy through those territories.

As usual when the land dried, wild lions came to call on Paddy. Three and four times a week we could hear the lions outside in the darkness, moaning and grunting and snarling around her paddock. The wire enclosing her was strained to the limit, and several of the uprights, cracked or broken.

One of the lions started coming every night. From the tracks he left, he was bigger and heavier than any of the others, and he was very bold. Shortly after we remarked on his frequent visits, we noticed that he arrived earlier and earlier each evening. He came down the logging road from the bushveld, crossed the road which led to the compound, pushed his way through the barbed wire which separated the road from the fields on either side, and took up his station in the tomatoes growing just beyond the dip tank. This was, of course, hard on the tomatoes, but we would have borne with it if the lion had not started biting at the wire separating him from Paddy and pulling at it fiercely and strongly with his powerful claws and forelegs.

A lion might possibly bite through a single strand of nine- or eleven-gauge steel wire if it could work the wire back into its mouth to bring it between its strong molars. It would probably break some of its teeth in the process. I was not afraid, however, that the new lion would be able to bite its way into Paddy or break the wire by hauling on it. The danger was that with its great strength, the lion might loosen the wire from its footing in the cement and bricks at the bottom, pull the loosened wire outward, and thus gain an opening.

We did not have any cement left, and I certainly was not going to the expense of making a special trip to the railway line just to buy a couple of bags. We had some left-over barbed wire, and with this we tried to guy the uprights and to form a protective barricade to keep the lion away from the fencing. The lion ignored this. Barbed wire meant nothing to it after the thorns on the veld through which it so frequently had to force its way.

The barbed wire, both along the road and outside the paddock, caught tufts and tufts of mane, and where the lion had pushed its way between the strands the barbs had pulled shorter hairs from its back and sides. These hairs were dark, dark brown, almost black. Paddy's suitor, if he was a suitor and not a marauder intent on killing, had a long black mane and black guard hairs. He was one of the "black" lions so dreaded by the natives!

I never learned when or where the story got its birth, but it was not long before I learned, through Lavison, that Paddy's visitor, the lion which was causing so much trouble at the wire, was believed to be the spirit of the chief who had ruled the last village built on the land which had come to be called Ibamba. This was the chief who, according to the legend, on his deathbed had cursed the land and cursed all those who might try to live upon it.

Every native in the district knew and believed in the legend. With every previous failure of white men to live on and operate Ibamba, the tale had been told again and again about the village fires. Over the course of the years the legend of the curse of Ibamba became a part of native folklore. It was because the natives believed so completely in the chief's reincarnation and in the legend of the curse that it had been so upsetting and so difficult for them to accept the fact of my immunity to attack by lions.

There was only one way by which my position and the acknowledged fact that lions constantly came onto Ibamba but never killed my cattle could be brought to fall acceptably into the framework of the natives' age-old beliefs. That was to install me, in their minds, as a *matakatsi,* a witch doctor, of equal or even greater power than the legendary chief who had cursed Ibamba. This, despite the lip service of my faithful boys, they had been extremely reluctant to do. They knew, from their experiences at missions and in the courts of law, that white men derided and belittled the powers of their witch doctors and had made laws prohibiting many of the ancient practices and customs. It was utterly incongruous that a member of the white race should develop and use powers which, in the native mind, could belong only to accredited witch doctors, or *matakatsis.*

Although acknowledging the power and achievements of whites, the natives refused to allow whites to enter into the world of spirits and gods, of wandering souls and witch-doctoring, which so completely surrounded them during every activity of the day or night. When we whites rebuffed the natives, making a mock of the powers of the witch doctors and laughing at their beliefs in reincarnation and their form of the spirit world, the natives closed ranks against us. They did not abandon their beliefs. They just refused to talk about such things, and cradled the ancient legends, the age-old beliefs, and their wonderful folklore tightly to their bosoms.

My struggle with and conquest of the great spirit lion, Shechambia, of the Kasha Pools, advanced acceptance of my witch-doctoring powers enormously. The final clincher, of course, was the attack by lions and the subsequent recovery of *all* the cattle without injury to a single one.

Now, said Lavison, the spirit of the chief who had cursed Ibamba had come to challenge me. As was fitting, the chief had come in the form of a huge "black" lion. First—Lavison was grave and emphatic as he spoke—the spirit of the chief wished to destroy Paddy because it was not right for men and a lion to live so closely together. When this had been accomplished, the great lion would attack and disperse my cattle.

As I told Isabella, when we discussed the new development in the evening, I supposed that the challenge and the test were inevitable; that the long chain of events which had led to my being installed as a witch doctor of lions just had to lead to such a climax. I had hoped that the spectacular recovery of all our cattle would prove to be that climax, but apparently this was not to be.

The entire affair, as I have tried to make clear, started with a bit of boastful talking on my part in reply to the constant nagging to which I had been subjected in the bars in Livingstone and Choma when it became known that we had purchased Ibamba. I was not drunk when I retorted to those trying to dissuade us that the lions would not run *me* off. I was just sick and tired of being told that they would.

When, during our first days on Ibamba just after the lions had killed one of Pete Cavadia's cattle and I shot one, I stated to my boys that I would talk to the lions and they would understand and would not attack my cattle, I was trying to perk up their morale and have a bit of fun with them. At that time I think the boys took my statement as I intended they should; just as a little braggadocio on the part of their *n'kos.*

As one dry season after another rolled by and the lions did *not* attack our cattle—although they were all over Ibamba—both the natives and I began to ponder things and wonder. What had started as just some boastful talking began to snowball into a serious and disturbing situation.

It was disturbing because there was, so far as Isabella and I were concerned, no logical explanation. There was absolutely no reason which we could discover why the lions did not attack us. The cattle kraals, the compound, and the other buildings were in approximately the same positions and of the same construction and relationship, one to another and to the main house, as they were on other ranches. Other ranches had as many, or more, dogs. True, we pampered the wild lions, particularly after Paddy arrived, but we did shoot and kill two on Ibamba. The fact that ordinarily we did not shoot at the lions would, one would have thought, have made them unusually bold and more prone to attack.

I would not have been normal if I had not taken advantage of the situation and exploited it to the limit. As the months rolled by without attack, I began to think of myself as some sort of witch doctor. Not seriously. But still I wondered. In addition, I suddenly was able to foretell the arrival of lions on the ranch, and this both puzzled me and reinforced my growing belief that maybe I did possess some extraordinary power. The facts certainly indicated that I did.

Nevertheless, I was fed up with the whole matter. So far as I was concerned, the belief that I was a *matakatsi* was getting out of hand. The natives, because of their belief that the new black lion was the reincarnation of the chief who had cursed Ibamba, were pitting me against him. For them it was not a struggle between a white man and a great lion, but a struggle between two mighty witch doctors.

I was tired as I had never been before. The constant strain of battle with the locusts, coupled with the financial strains imposed on us by the business depression, had worn both Isabella and me down to nubbins. I was not in condition, physically or mentally, to engage in any prolonged effort to overcome or kill another spirit lion. However, because of the danger to Paddy, I had to put an end to the visits of the big lion as promptly as possible. If I could do this expeditiously, it would, I hoped, put an end, once and for all, to the witch-doctoring business.

We had very few cartridges of any kind. The batteries for the big electric searchlights were just about burned out. But I still had the great lion traps. The bold visitor came so early and stayed for so long each night that it did not seem he had much time for hunting. I guessed that he might be very hungry. Fresh bloody meat might prove too much of a temptation and bring him, spirit lion though he might be, into the traps. If I could trap him, I should be able to kill him with a single shot.

Jam and Charlie Matabele went off to select a cattlebeast for bait. I told them to pick a fat one. Iz and I would take what we wanted for the house. For bait we would need only the head, shoulders, and the ribs and some of the interior organs. The remainder of the animal the boys could divide among themselves.

Charlie Portuguese, Mangineera, and I talked over what we should do. The lion always had come down the logging road, crossed through the barbed wire into the plowed land near the house, crossed through the wires by the road leading to the compound, and approached the tomato patch by passing along the back of the laboratory building. Fifty yards inside the field I had left a large fig tree standing. We decided to set the traps close to the tree.

While the boys went off to chop four heavy logs to be chained to the traps, Charlie Matabele arrived with the ox. We killed it beneath the fig tree and slaughtered it there so that the blood and juices from the stomach and intestines would seep into the soft ground and give off a tantalizing scent. When the logs were brought, Mangineera and Jam and I set the traps and hid them and then we built a sketchy zareba about the bait. We did not put much effort into the zareba because we figured that too elaborate a construction might make the lion suspicious.

Iz and I had a very early supper, and then, with Mangineera and

Jam, I took up a position sitting in the open door of the office. The moon was early and nearly full.

We hadn't been there an hour when Mangineera pointed silently. Straining my eyes, I made out the dim shape, gliding swiftly and silently down the track along which we dragged firewood logs from the wooded portion of the ranch.

Just as the lion had always acted before, he left the track and started across the plowed land on a short cut to the vegetable garden. Before he reached the fig tree, he stopped suddenly and stood motionless. He *was* big! If I was any judge of animals, he stood at least four feet eight inches to the top of his head.

The great beast, looming a sort of misty silver color in the moonlight, stood absolutely still for perhaps five minutes. We could see him slowly turn his heavy head, with its tuft of mane on top between the ears, and scent the wind. Silently the lion surveyed the scene. He stared toward the house, then the office building, and lastly at the compound, from which low chattering voices could be heard. Everything must have looked normal, for abruptly he moved. Without hesitation he walked toward the bait. Mangineera laid his hand on my arm, and I could feel him straining forward to see.

Although we were tense and expectant, the terrific growling roar of rage made us jump. Chains clanked. I heard Jam suck in his breath, making a hissing sound as if he had been burned. The lion rose straight up in the air in a mighty leap, and came down on his head and chest as the heavy trap and chain yanked him down. Before he became invisible in a cloud of dust, I saw that he was caught by a forepaw, well up on the wrist. Then we could see nothing in a boiling, roaring, raging cloud of dirt, bushes, and dust. Rolling, thrashing on the ground, the lion tore at the chain, at the trap, and yanked the heavy log to which the trap chain was bound in bumps along the ground.

The battle lasted for five, perhaps ten, minutes. Jam and I and Mangineera were out of the door and standing in the open, watching agape as the horrid, savage battle whirled under the tree. We held our rifles ready, because if that lion did get loose and spotted us, he would come for us so fast we would barely have time to raise our guns. A lion can cover seventy-five yards in three or four giant lightning bounds. Even dragging a chain and log.

As abruptly as the uproar had started, it stopped. The dust, glimmering in the moonlight, began to settle. The lion was standing broadside to us, staring about. His mane and the hair on his head stood out stiffly. We could see blood and foam dripping from his mouth.

Silently, moving cautiously and deliberately, I went forward with Jam on one side and Mangineera on the other. The lion turned his head and watched us. Step by slow step we advanced until we came to the barbed wire strung along the edge of the road and only fifty yards from the silent, almost motionless lion.

Quietly we three stood looking at the magnificent animal. His broad chest and flanks were heaving. Otherwise he made no movement. At the far edge of the plowed lands a night bird called out sharply. There was no sound from the compound two hundred yards distant. Probably the people were lined up in the gloom and shadows of the huts, watching. The lion's upper lip curled in a snarl. He made no other sound.

Very slowly Mangineera leaned his rifle against the wire and brought the heavy searchlight up against his chest. Jam and I brought up our rifles. Without a sound, the beam of the light suddenly illuminated the scene. I saw the muscles in the lion's back legs begin to flex. Aiming carefully at a point below the median line of his body and just within the beginning of the mane, I fired. The lion dropped like a stone, without a sound.

Mangineera let out a yell and snapped off the light. Then he climbed through the wire and reached to fetch his rifle after him. I was halfway through the strands when Jam called a warning. I tore my leg getting clear, and straightening on the opposite side, turned to look. The lion was on his feet.

He was facing away from us. Hurriedly I slammed another cartridge into my single shot. Jam laid his hand restrainingly on my arm as I raised the long barrel. "*N'effele,*" he whispered. "He is dead."

The silence was uncanny. Not a sound came from the great beast standing before us. His lower jaw hung a little slack. I would have sworn on a stack of Bibles as to where that bullet had hit. It should have flattened and torn through the lower part of the lungs, the bottom of the heart, and the liver. It was a little low to have hit the great knots of nerves in the upper shoulder, but they still should have been hurt.

The lion moved. Hesitatingly at first. Then he seemed to gain strength. Still without a sound, he started away across the plowed land, dragging his right front paw with the heavy trap and dragging the chain and the log behind. The log, which weighed about sixty pounds, had short lengths of branches sticking out. It plowed a furrow and raised a line of dust as the lion jerked it steadily along.

Again I raised my rifle. Again Jam restrained me. He did not believe another shot, which might spoil the skin, to be necessary. I could see him shake his head as we unbelievingly watched that huge, powerful animal struggle across the field, reach the track, and head for the bush beyond.

The lion did not pause. Steadily he worked and jerked the log along the track and disappeared in the far gloom around a bend.

"*N'effele,*" muttered Jam as we turned away toward the house. "*Kusasa.*"

"Tomorrow," I agreed. It had to be that way. The lion would have to stop and lie down. We were certain he would not rise again.

But Mangineera was not so sure. "*N'ena matakatsi,*" he said as we walked to the back door. "He's a witch doctor."

We found Iz sitting on the back stoop with a shotgun across her lap, slapping at mosquitoes. She had been there from the beginning and had watched the whole affair. I reprimanded her gently—she was seven months pregnant—then we went inside.

Early the next morning Jam and Mangineera came to the kitchen door to ask if I wanted to go along. But I was having my early tea, and declined. They were so certain of what they would find that they had six other natives with them to carry in the lion, an ax to cut a pole, and lengths of rope.

A half hour passed. I began to get restless, wondering what had happened to delay the party so long. Another half hour passed before I saw them coming down the logging track—without the lion!

It was a very solemn group that lined up in front of me. Jam and Mangineera, particularly, wore worried and thunderstruck expressions on their faces. Mutely Jam held out pieces of the trap for my inspection. The heavy, powerful Newhouse trap had been broken and smashed.

Jam told me what they had found. Not far beyond the bend in the logging road the log dragging behind the lion had become fouled in some heavy bushes. Which was why we had left stubs of branches sticking out. The lion had struggled, trying to free the log, and in the course of the struggle had wound the chain around a stout thorn tree. The remains of the trap, Jam said, were lying close against the base as the lion had wound himself right up against it. The uncanny aspect was that the lion had fought in silence. All the natives and Iz and I had been listening for a long time after the lion had disappeared, and none had heard a sound.

What happened was guesswork. Probably, finding himself held tight, the lion had somersaulted, thus bringing his great weight against one of the jaws of the trap, and this had snapped under the strain. What a terrific wrench this must have put on the lion's shoulder.

Free, the lion had staggered off, dragging his right front foot. There was a lot of blood about, Jam said, and the trail of the injured paw was heavy in the loose dirt of the road.

The lion hadn't been able to go far. From Jam's description it sounded about fifty yards. There he had been forced to lie down, and from the impression, the clot of blood, and the bits of mane hair, there was no doubt, both trackers insisted, that the lion had been hit just where we had thought. He had been hit hard, too, because there was quite a lot of blood.

Subsequently the lion had risen, gone on dragging his right paw, and lain down again. All along the track there were drops and small pools of blood, and where he had stopped the second time, there was a large smear full of mane hair where the blood had clotted and pulled the hairs out.

After the second rest he had risen again and succeeded in reaching the edge of the dense *saka*. When the natives had approached, they had heard him growl inside, then, listening, had heard him move. With his injured front paw he couldn't move without making a noise. The lion was far from dead.

When Jam had recounted the story, the two natives stood looking at me with silent questions in their eyes. This was the most dangerous situation a hunter can face. We all knew what we should do. Although we were reasonably brave men, we were also experienced hunters, and not one of us cottoned to the thought of crawling into that long densely matted stretch of *saka* to look for the lion. Yet, as responsible hunters we could not leave a wounded animal to die. Besides, there was a path which cut across the ranch, bordering the two-mile length of the *saka*. Native women and children as well as men used it frequently. If the lion was still alive and lying close to the path, he might kill someone in his fury of pain and rage.

I sent for Charlie Portuguese and Charlie Matabele. Mangineera fetched rifles and my shooting vest, with my few remaining cartridges. I armed each Charlie with a 9.3 Mauser. Jam, as the best shot, had one of my double 500/450s, and Mangineera carried the other for me to use if there was time and my favorite single shot was not enough.

At the tree I examined the remains of the trap and studied the spoor and came to the same conclusions as Jam and Mangineera. We spent a long time at the spots where the lion had lain down. The impressions were not too clear, but there did not seem any question but that that bullet had hit where we all believed it had and where I had aimed to put it.

At the edge of the *saka* we stood listening for some time. There was not a sound. Not even from a bird. Which could have meant anything. Very cautiously, I in the center on the spoor, Charlie Portuguese ahead of me by a few feet, Jam on one side at a little distance, with Charlie Matabele on the other, and Mangineera immediately behind me with the second rifle, we pushed into the *saka*. Within a few feet we found we had to crawl and worm our way. Inch by inch, foot by foot, we advanced. Every yard or so we crouched, listening. Jam lay down with his ear to the ground, then rose silently, shaking his head. Charlie Portuguese did the spooring, his eyes on the ground, the bushes, the leaves and scattered sticks and vines. It was my part of the job to peer constantly ahead, seeking any slight movement which might betray the position of the lion which, we were certain, either lay dead or was waiting, listening to us come on. It is impossible for one man to both track and watch.

How much time passed before we came to the spot where the lion had been lying when the natives had heard him growl, I don't know. One loses all sense of time in such a place and under such tension. Probably about half an hour. We were not moving faster than five or six yards every fifteen minutes.

The spot where the lion had lain was clear enough. He must have rested there for hours. The body impression showed clearly, and there was quite a lot of blood, both from his paw, which he had stretched out, probably to lick it, and from his chest. There were no bubbles which we could see in the dried blood, so apparently the bullet had not hit the lungs.

When the natives had approached, the lion had risen and gone off, heading deeper into the *saka* and quartering down its length northward.

We backed out and made our way out of the *saka*. Sweat streamed off us. The natives' dark bodies shone as if polished. Leaves clung to us, and Mangineera had a twig caught in his fuzzy mop of hair.

We decided to wait until the beginning of the afternoon before going into the *saka* again. It was incredible that the lion was still able to move. He was still losing blood, although the wounds were clotting and the bleeding was not so profuse as at first.

If we waited, he might die from loss of blood. If he did not die, his wounds and the fearful wrench he must have sustained when he broke the trap should stiffen, and halt his travel and cause him to lie down, when his muscles would stiffen even more. Thirst should take its toll in the heat of the *saka* and bring further exhaustion.

I ordered a guard posted at each end of the footpath which followed the edge of the *saka,* so that no natives would attempt to pass. We posted four other natives at points along the western edge of the *saka,* in the short grass and burned-over area where the *saka* ended and the wide level flat at the back of the ranch began. Should the lion appear, they could try to drive it back into the *saka* or notify us as to which way it had gone if it crossed the flat. Contrary to general belief, lions, even when wounded, will usually give ground unless they feel cornered. We didn't think the lion would try to exit on that side, as there was no water close by. The river with its fresh, cool water was on the eastern side and came nearest to the *saka* at the northern end. We posted another native there, on a ridge, to watch and report. The ground was bare, as a fire had swept across the week before.

That afternoon, bare-headed—any kind of head covering which might be pushed down by a branch or vine and hide my view was out—wearing a pair of shorts and light crepe rubber-soled *veldtshoen,* I stood with my four hunters at the spot where the lion had entered the *saka* the first time. I had discarded my shooting vest, and my chest and back were bare.

Then we went in. Within a few feet sweat streamed off us and gathered in our eyebrows and trickled down into the corners of our eyes, making them smart. Traveling chiefly on all fours, inching our way over fallen logs, and flattening to get under trailing vines armed with hooks like cats' claws, we moved forward, each man conscious of the other four and watching for any hint that something had been seen or heard. Charlie Portuguese carried a little gourd from which he dribbled a fine stream of bone-dry meal to test the wind. The meal dropped plumb to the ground. Crouching, sliding on our bellies, bitten by mosquitoes and ants, lying motionless to listen, sniffing the air, we worked our way along. We reached the point where the lion had lain down the first time, and went on even more slowly than before. For short stretches the lion had tried to hold the injured paw off the ground, but then he had let it drag. Where bushes had scraped against his right side there were flecks and an occasional blob of dried blood.

Moving behind Charlie Portuguese as he advanced foot by slow foot, my eyes stabbed into the cluttered tangle ahead. Except through occasional peepholes in the crisscross and jumble of vegetation, it was impossible to see farther than two or three yards in any direction. There were times when I couldn't see either Jam or Charlie Matabele, although I knew they were not more than ten feet away. I noticed the fragments of leaves stuck to Charlie Portuguese's back, and watched an ant run up a wrinkle in his skin as he twisted to get over an obstruction.

One would have thought that it would have been relatively easy to follow so large an animal as that great lion. But it was as if he had melted through the tangled mass. There was an occasional broken vine, a bent twig with fine mane hairs trailing from it, an overturned leaf, to show the way. The jumbled tangle had closed behind the lion as though conspiring to help him.

An hour and a half dragged by. The muscles of my arms and legs ached from the strain of slow, deliberate movement. I kept rubbing my palms into the dirt to keep my hands dry enough to handle the rifle without slipping.

Since we had entered the *saka,* not a word had been spoken. The strain was terrific. Never was I in a proper position from which to make a shot. The silence was unnerving. Had the lion growled or broken a stick or rustled the bushes, it would have been an enormous relief, for we would then have known where he was. At least for a moment. As it was, we sneaked and inched along, never knowing what might erupt within the next foot or two.

The sun was beginning to sink. We could tell because the sharp, dark, thin shadows cast by the branches entwined over our heads were lengthening like crooked fingers reaching for the trunks of the trees and the dark pools under the denser clumps of matted bushes. The light was growing uncertain.

We left the flattened area and crept and crawled farther into the *saka*. In the more than two hours that we had been inside, we had covered perhaps two hundred or two hundred and fifty yards. It doesn't sound like much, but it was more tiring and exhausting than if we had trekked thirty miles across the open veld.

Another twenty minutes, maybe it was half an hour, and we converged again. Charlie Portuguese, squatting under a cluster of vines like some dirty sweat-streaked black gnome, extended his arm before him to indicate the angle of the sun. Although it was probably still very light outside, inside the *saka* it was getting much too dim to risk seeing a rifle sight or to locate the slow, slinking movement of an animal. I nodded my head, and after a look all about to locate our position, we turned and began the laborious task of crawling and creeping out of the *saka*. Not knowing where the lion might be, we proceeded nearly as cautiously and slowly as when coming to that point along the spoor. It was not, fortunately, far to the edge of the dense bush. The *saka* was long but narrow. We got out within three-quarters of an hour.

Mangineera let out a long piercing whistle. Within a few minutes the natives we had left at the spot where we went into the *saka* came up and we sent them to recall the men we had posted as watchers. Within an hour it would be too dark for them to distinguish a lion bellying along the ground.

Stretching to get the kinks out of our backs and legs, we stood talking in low voices. One of the natives massaged the calves of my legs to loosen them.

The lion had been without water almost twenty-four hours. Wounded as he was, his thirst must be demanding. If we could keep him from water, we might be able to enhance our chances of meeting with him on the morrow, because it never occurred to any of us, in spite of our weariness and what we had been through in tension and strain, that we should not go back into the *saka* again. Having gone as far as we had, we intended to finish the job.

On reaching the compound, Charlie Portuguese was to send out parties of men to build a series of fires along the road which cut through the bush from the house to the river at the northern end of the ranch. Others were to patrol up and down in gangs of five or six. I would have a wash, some supper, and then would get out the truck and drive up and down the road throughout most of the night. We thought that the sound of the motor and the sight of the sweeping headlights might keep the lion from coming down to the river.

About nine o'clock that night I climbed into the truck. Behind, we had fastened a bunch of branches to act as a sweep. Dragging this down the road would leave a clean stretch, and on the return we could see whether any animals had crossed after our passing. Shaluma rode with me for the first part of the night.

On the first return trip we picked up the watchers by the various fires and dropped them at the compound. There they loaded the back of the truck with firewood, and as we returned down the road, we replenished the fires as necessary.

I kept the vigil until a little after two. I hoped that by then the lion, if he had had any ideas about trying to reach the river, might have abandoned them and returned to the *saka*. If I was to hunt the next morning, I had to get some sleep.

chapter eighteen

IT was a little before five and the sun was just poking its rim over the Luiri Mountains far away across the Kafue River when I got up after less than three hours of sleep. The four hunters and the natives who were to act as lookouts were ready. We talked in low voices in the kitchen as I drank my early tea.

With Mangineera on one side of the cab, Charlie Portuguese on the other, and Jam and Charlie Matabele standing in the back, I drove the truck slowly along the road. Although we found a few antelope tracks, one leopard track, and the tracks of many small cats, we found no sign that the lion had crossed the brush-swept trail which I had left behind on the last trip of the night.

We posted guards, as on the previous day, and then sent natives around the western edge of the *saka* to meet us at the point where we had come out the day before.

We had stripped down even more than on the previous day. The natives had discarded their khaki shorts and reverted to the traditional loincloth. I also changed to a breechclout. Sticks and twigs made very little noise scraping against flesh, and the thorns and catnails were less likely to stick in skin than in cloth. They scratched, but that did not really matter. We were so bitten by insects that a few more tears in our skin would not matter. Shorts can be dangerous if one has to move very quickly. Even though it is very exceptional that such a thing happens, short broken-off branches do sometimes get up inside a pair of shorts and hamper a man's movement.

Why did we persist? We knew, each one of us, that the odds were against us. We five had hunted together for years, in Northern Rhodesia, Southern Rhodesia, and Portuguese East Africa.

Maybe it was pride which drove us back into the *saka*. More likely it was the terrible fascination of that kind of hunting. It is the ultimate in the chase. Facing a charging animal is as nothing compared to the hours of tension, of terrific nervous excitement, experienced while crawling through dense, matted bush after such an animal as a wounded lion or a wounded buffalo.

We went in. Slowly. Back-tracking our own spoor, we reached the point where we had abandoned the stalk the evening before. Silently each man rechecked his rifle and we resumed the positions we held the previous day. Down on all fours, creeping, edging under low branches or trailing vines, stopping to test the wind, to listen and stare into the bush, we inched along the spoor of the lion, now twelve hours old. We moved even more cautiously than the day before. The *saka* did not extend indefinitely. Somewhere in that square mile of matted bush the wounded lion was either waiting for us or lying dead. He might well have gone to the northern end, seen or heard the truck, and retreated to lie up on either side of his own spoor. He might even have come all the way back down the *saka* and be behind us as we painfully and cautiously moved forward.

The pace slowed, and we felt every bit of ground before we put pressure on a knee, or hand, so that we would not break a stick, roll a bit of wood, or rustle the occasional piles of leaves drifted under a bush or against a tangle of vines. Twigs and branches we bent gently, and allowed them to scrape against our bodies as we passed. We parted the vines as though they were the most valuable laces, and eased and flowed our way between the strands. Once during the morning we passed beneath a wild orange tree. The ground beneath was clear of obstructions. Eland antelope and pigs and kudu had come to feed on the fruit, which they stamped open to break the hard shells, and they had cleared the ground. We stretched out for a rest, to ease our aching muscles and to quiet the pumping of our hearts, and to allow the sweat to dry. Rubbing my forehead and shoulders, I could feel the granules of salt which had formed from the evaporation of sweat. I itched where the insects had bitten me, and my eyes smarted from the sweat which had trickled into them.

With a glance at me, Charlie Portuguese tugged at his loincloth and got to his feet, and we started again. Just within the thick stuff we found where the lion had rested. There was not so much blood as previously. What there was had run down among the bits of leaves and soaked the ground. Charlie dug at the caked mass and rolled a pellet between his fingers. It was still a trifle sticky. The lion must have lain there a long time. It was a strategic spot. From the place where he had been lying, he could see the clearing under the orange tree. Anyone following would have had to cross that, exposing themselves, as we had.

On and on. Stooping, crawling, bending, twisting, we made our way. Hours passed. The shadows were shortening and the heat increasing. Sunlight, driving almost straight down through holes in the canopy of vegetation overhead, bounced off evergreen leaves, making them shine spectacularly in the general gloom. Our throats were dry and parched, partly from the heat, partly from the dust, and largely from the dryness of excitement. We carried no water. I thought of the wounded lion and marveled that it had been able to go so long without liquid. What measure of an animal was it that we were spooring, which could bear up under such a dreadful wound, such an injured paw, and such lack of moisture? The strength and will of the lion was incredible and indomitable.

Another yard. Another two. Abruptly, a harsh, threatening growl rolled out of the nearly impenetrable bush ahead. Charlie Portuguese froze, his left leg partly raised to pass a fallen branch. Immobile, on all fours, with my rifle stretched before me, I crouched, listening. I glanced along the smooth barrel to see that no branches lay across it, and then my eyes stabbed and searched the bush. Again that warning growl, throatier and more powerful than the first. Afterward, each man told me that they had experienced the same momentary feeling of relief that I did. At last we knew where the lion was. Dangerous as our position was, it was a relief to know, if even for a brief slice of time, where the danger waited.

Neither Charlie Portuguese nor I had raised our rifles. There was no sound to indicate that the lion had moved or was moving. Slowly, twisting his head so that he could see ahead, Charlie lowered his ear to the ground to try and pick up any sound of footfalls. He shook his head slightly.

Motionless, we waited. I could feel the muscles in my arms and legs tightening toward cramps as I strained to hold my position. Another growl. The lion was about twenty yards from us. A branch snapped. The muscles in Charlie's arm and shoulder bunched as he started to raise his rifle. I could feel the sweat running in a rivulet between my eyebrows and my nose. There was a rustling sound, and then the sound of a heavy body moving clumsily and fairly fast.

Silently, Charlie Portuguese straightened up. I heard Mangineera, immediately behind, let out his breath in a long, soft *woof*. The lion was giving ground. It was moving away, down the *saka*.

Jam and Charlie Matabele joined us. The dark, rather cruel face of the lanky Matabele was split in a crooked grin which showed his white but broken teeth.

In a group we went forward, not bothering to stoop and crawl, but pushing through the bush. Ten, fifteen yards, and our nostrils were filled with a dreadful, nauseating stench. For a moment we hesitated. Such an overwhelming stench of lion could mean that the lion was still close by.

Charlie Portuguese took a few steps, and then he pointed. The matted tangle of brush and vines through which we had just come ended suddenly. Three tallish spreading mabunga trees stood in a group, and beneath them the ground was bare except for a few tufts of short dry yellow grass. The stench came from under the trees. Scanning the scene, I could see where the lion had been lying, and scuffed patches showed where it had struggled to get its feet under it and rise. The stench rose from a watery spreading mass on the farther side. The lion had defecated. Not once, but twice. He must have remained in that place for many hours, as one mass was obviously much older than the other.

We examined the mess. There was no blood. But Charlie and Mangineera, searching the spot where the lion had left the little clearing, found fresh blood wiped against a twig and, a yard farther, a small drop of bright red on a broken leaf. The bullet wound had clotted over while the lion had lain down and broken open with his movements. We followed the trail ten yards into the dense bush, and found two more drops of blood. Only too evidently the wound was closing and the lion had stopped losing blood. We returned to the clearing and stood for a long moment, staring at one another. Not a word had been spoken since we had entered the *saka* hours before. With one accord we turned and made our way slowly, and as quietly as possible, out of the *saka.* Back at the house, I took a quick bath and had some lunch and a short rest while the four natives bathed in the river and also ate their food.

By about two-thirty we five stood once again in the evil-smelling clearing. After the brief respite of fresh air, the stink hung in our throat so that we could almost taste it. The sweltering, debilitating heat inside that green-brown oven of crisscrossed tangled bush enveloped us oppressively.

For a few yards we followed the spoor quickly. Then Charlie Portuguese sank down and we melted into the old hurting, exhausting routine. Crawl, ease over fallen branches, slide, naked belly to the ground, under catclaw vines. Sweat jumped out in beads on our bodies and insects inflicted stinging, itching bites on our exposed bodies.

After threatening us, the lion had traveled in a sweeping curve. Our progress, becoming steadily slower and more cautious as we followed farther and farther along the trail, led us toward the western edge of the *saka* and a possible exit by the lion onto the open flat which bordered the long, dense patch. Toward mid-afternoon we came so close to the edge that we could see the thinning of the bush, and we halted while Jam slipped away to find and question the nearest native posted to watch for the lion's possible appearance in the open. He returned, sliding silently through the bush, and shook his head. The lion was still inside.

Another long hour dragged past. We were returning down the *saka* toward the south, paralleling the way we had come, and moving steadily, however slowly, farther and farther away from the river.

Just as I was deciding to call a halt and leave the *saka,* the lion growled again. He was close, very close. Suddenly I could smell him. It was a rotten, sour, putrid smell. The faint breeze changed and the stink was gone.

The lion growled once more. He was so close that we could tell, from the position of the sound, that he was standing. Then again he gave way, and we heard him moving back into the *saka*.

As I started to follow Charlie Portuguese, Mangineera grabbed my leg. I reached forward and held Charlie's foot, and he stopped instantly. I turned my head and looked back. Mangineera stared at me earnestly and shook his head and motioned sideways with it to show that he thought we should get out.

Within half an hour the light would be very poor. The lion was letting us get closer, which meant that he was feeling bolder, and probably stronger, although it was impossible to explain how that could be.

So we eased our way out to the western side and set our faces toward home, two miles away around the southern end of the *saka*. Out in the open we had difficulty walking. Our muscles were so tight and taut and cramped that it was painful to walk normally. I felt as if someone had beaten me across the small of the back with a knotted club. I craved a drink, and picked up a small pebble and popped it into my mouth to bring saliva.

As we trudged homeward, picking up the guards posted along the *saka's* edge and giving them our guns to carry, we talked of the lion. He now had been in the *saka* for forty-four hours. How could he go so long without water? It was obvious now that my bullet had not passed through the lion where we had thought. It could not have missed by more than a fraction, however, and the fever in the lion must have been raging hot. He had lost a lot of blood that first day, and his paw was giving him much trouble and pain. That he was big and powerful and in the prime of life, we had seen with our own eyes when he had stood revealed in the beam of the searchlight. How powerful, how tough, how indestructible could a lion be? Mangineera insisted, simply but with complete conviction, that we would never kill him. I could see the same thought written on the faces of my other companions. Indeed, I was coming to the same conclusion myself.

That night we followed the same routine as previously. I didn't think I could stay awake to drive the truck, but somehow I managed, although my eyelids drooped; once I almost drove off the track and into a small tree.

As we assembled the next morning, we realized that the lion was besting us. He hadn't come out, so far as we or the watchers and hunters could determine. Instead of being up most of the night, he had lain quietly in some spot in the *saka,* resting, controlling his thirst, and waiting for strength to return and for the fever in his body to ease. While we exhausted ourselves with nervous tension and physical punishment following the lion's spoor, he had lain quietly waiting for us to come close. Then, either because he was more seriously wounded than we realized, or because, as lions often do, he decided that discretion was the better part of valor, he backed away, warning us with growls, and sought another place to rest again.

As we stood in a tight group on the bare burned-over ground on the western edge of the *saka* preparatory to going in, tightening our belts and adjusting our loincloths, the quickening light revealed our physical deterioration. I knew that black circles surrounded my eyes and that the eyeballs seemed to have sunk into my head. I had seen them when I had shaved that morning. I needed a haircut badly, but what was most disturbing was the slight twitch at the outside corners of my eyes, from fatigue and the strain of constant anxious peering, and the tremulous feeling in my hand and leg muscles.

Looking at the natives, I could see that their eyes, too, were sunken in their heads, and that there seemed to be loose baggy flesh beneath their eyes. They had bathed, yet somehow their usually shiny skins lacked luster and looked dead and tired.

All of us were covered with long scratches and welts from bites. There was a dark, bluish bruise on my left forearm, collected how I did not know. I hadn't felt it at the time. Jam's right shin boasted a three-inch, red scrape at which some flies were already nibbling. A nest of hard, round lumps showed where army ants had bitten Charlie Portuguese on the forearm.

We went in. Again the rotting smell of humid vegetation surrounded and enveloped us. Our bodies grew wet and slick and we moved, each in his own aura of acrid body odor. We picked up the spoor where we had left it the evening before, and again sank down to the ground and began the ceaseless crawling, wriggling, listening, crouching series of motions which was our method of progression.

The morning wore on. The intensity of the heat swelled and pressed on our flat bare backs like a great weight holding us to the earth beneath. Our pauses to rest and listen, to test the eddies of the vagrant breeze, became more frequent. With every wriggling movement forward, the tension increased. We stared for long, long moments at the dark shadows beneath the massed tangles of vines and bush. Our eyes were beginning to play tricks on us. We saw movement where there was none, and shapes which at first glance looked menacing and fearful slowly dissolved into stumps or an accumulation of leaves bunched and whirled into a bush by a heat devil thrashing its life out in the *saka.*

And what of the lion? What was he doing and where was he? Somewhere ahead, or to one side? Hidden in that dense *saka,* he was lying, listening to us. Quiet and silent as we thought we were, the lion undoubtedly heard us from afar. His hearing was a hundred times more acute than ours.

While we expended our energies and frayed our nerves to nubbins, he lay waiting, having chosen his spot. We couldn't get to him without his being long aware of our approach. Yet we went on. Our only chance would come if he finally decided to make a fight of it. Should the lion elect to do so, there would be one lightning flash of the great body, and then he would be among us. Weary and strung almost to the breaking point as we were, the odds in favor of the lion mounted minute by minute. He was miraculously growing stronger. We were weakening with every sweating, nervous, dragging quarter hour.

The tell-tale stench once again flooded into our nostrils. The lion grunted. Lord, he was close! Another coughing grunt, and then a rush. In a single movement Charlie flowed up from the ground and crouched, his rifle at his shoulder. I, too, was up on one knee and aiming at the sound, over Charlie's shoulder. Had I fired, he would have been deaf in his left ear for many a day.

The rush passed to the side. We could see the bushes sway and hear the vines snap with a squeaky tearing sound. Brush scraped against a heavy body, and then the lion was gone and was around behind us.

Slowly the stricture in my throat relaxed. I swallowed and set my gun butt down. Charlie Portuguese turned to face me. His upper lip was twitching peculiarly. Mangineera straightened and let his breath out in a long whistling sigh. We waited while Jam and Charlie Matabele closed in. My questioning look at Jam brought a shake of the head. The lion had passed on his side but he had not seen him.

Although that brief rush had been expected for hours, it left us shaking and washed out. For a moment it was terrifying, but as we realized it had been more bluff and warning than charge, our spirits sank and we felt deflated. It was frightening, when we found the spoor the lion had left in his rush, to realize that he had passed less than ten yards from Jam and twelve from Charlie Portuguese, Mangineera, and me, and that not one of us had caught even a glimpse of the long tawny body. It brought home, hard, how quickly and how suddenly the lion could be upon us in that matted mass.

We picked up the new trail and hurried along it for thirty yards or so. Then, as the tracks showed the lion had slowed, so did we. He headed north, up the eastern side and not far from the more open country at the edge. Cautiously we followed for a time, and then left the *saka* and quit to rest and eat and wash some of the filth off our sore and twitchy bodies, at home and in the river.

It was a terrible afternoon when we went back in. We hadn't

gone far along the trail when the lion growled and grunted and then broke, going north and along the length of the *saka*. Within an hour and a half we caught up with him again. And again nerves stretched and seemed to break as the lion snarled and growled at us, then broke away. He was moving more reluctantly each time we came up, and when he did give way, he moved a shorter and shorter distance. The game was drawing to a close. He might not growl the next time, but come hurtling at us, appearing suddenly, almost at the muzzles of our rifles. If he did, could we stop him? Would the heavy bullets, hitting with practically muzzle energy, kill him and cause him to slide and roll over us as we hit the dirt before his rush?

We reached the lion once more before we gave it up. That last time he stood a long time before breaking back. As we crouched motionless in the heat and gloom and stench, we could hear the rumblings in his throat as he brought up his throaty growl. It was followed by a savage snarl. After the lion had given way, we made our way out of the *saka* and trudged home. I don't believe that any one of us could have stood another thirty minutes in the *saka*. The cheekbones of the natives stood out hard and sharp, and there were hollows in their cheeks. The corners of their eyes and mouths twitched spasmodically. My nerves were close to the breaking point.

It was that evening that Isabella handed me a note she had received from John Price.

"Kasenga Mission—N. Rhodesia
"July 12, '34

"Dear Mrs. Hubbard:

"The boys have told me about the big lion your husband is chasing. A wounded lion is very, very dangerous. I understand why he doesn't want to leave a wounded lion, but his life is more precious than prestige.

"The word has gone out and all natives are staying away from IBAMBA. So there is no need to worry that one might be caught.

"I know that you must be terribly worried yourself, but try again and see if you can't get him to stop this insane pursuit. We *must* avoid a tragedy.

"God Bless
"John Price"

Wearily I read the note, hand-written on cheap lined paper. There wasn't anything I could say. I dropped the note on the low table in the living room and stared silently at Iz. The thought flashed through my mind that it wasn't fair that she should have to stay in the house while I spent days and nights tracking, hunting, crawling in the thick bush, trying to come to final grips with a tremendous lion. The strain of waiting, especially as she was carrying our second child, must have been nearly unbearable. What my old friend John Price had written was quite true. Only a crazy man would do what I was doing—had been doing for the past three days. For some reason I grinned crookedly.

Part of the trouble was that this was all happening close to the house. Iz had sat and watched the beginning of it all. She had seen the great lion in the glare of the searchlight and heard the bullet hit. She knew how big he was and understood how great must be his pain and rage and fear.

It was all happening right in the front yard, so to speak. If I had encountered the lion while out on a hunting trip, neither Iz nor John would have known anything about it until I returned and, maybe, related the story.

I sighed and started to rise. I needed a wash. My body reeked with the acrid, bitter stink of nervous sweat. My arms and legs and face were blotched with bloody streaks from the thorns and prickly vines and the bites of insects, and I was covered with dust and bits of leaves. My hair was matted like that of some Neanderthal man.

"I'll quit if you say so." I forced what I hoped was a smile.

Iz stared at me earnestly before replying. I felt her gaze run over the dark circles under my eyes, and saw that she noticed the slight twitching which was bothering me around the corners.

"How much longer?"

"Twenty-four hours," I answered. "He either gets away then or he dies."

"Or . . ." her throat moved as though she were swallowing.

I shook my head. "He's terribly hurt. He hasn't had any water for more than fifty hours now. He must be nearly finished. And don't forget, I have four magnificent hunters with me all the time. He won't get me."

Iz sighed, and I thought for a moment her eyes misted over. I wondered if she had learned anything from her questioning of the natives when we had returned. They were a tight-lipped lot. I didn't think they would have told her the truth, that actually the wounded lion seemed to be getting stronger and stronger the longer the hunt wore on.

"Well, it's your fight," she spoke bravely. "I only hope you know what you are doing."

We maintained the patrol again that third night, I in the truck until two in the morning and the natives with the line of fires. We might have saved ourselves the trouble.

Early in the morning the native who had the post at the far end of the *saka* came running in. He had seen the lion! It had gone down to the river to drink and returned across the burned ground which lay between the river and the *saka*. A herd boy from the little village just off the ranch had a small herd of cattle on the burned ground searching for the new grass which follows a fire. The lion had chased a cattlebeast and then made a rush toward the herdsman, who had shouted and waved to try to scare it. The native had fled, and the lion, either to conserve its strength, because its belly was full of water, or because it was just being cautious, stopped its rush and returned into the *saka*.

Hurriedly we piled into the truck and drove to the north end. It was easy to read the story in the dust and ashes. We followed the trail into the *saka*. In the face of the fact that the lion had come out and secured water, which could only mean he had regained a portion of his strength from some miraculous source, we moved, if that were possible, even more slowly and cautiously than before.

The spoor led straight through the *saka*. We emerged at the western edge and stood staring silently, filled with reluctant admiration and, I must admit, relief, at the tracks leading across the wide bare flat beyond, toward the miles of wild and uninhabited veld stretching unbroken to the Home of the Lion seventy miles away.

The spoor was large and clear and firm. The lion was placing all four feet upon the ground. There was no sign of hurt or hesitation.

We stood for a long time, staring along that line of pug marks.

Mangineera spoke for the five of us.

"*N'dio nena matakatsi. Tao y n'kos.* Truly he is a witch doctor. A chief of lions."

chapter nineteen

AT first thought it might seem that the ending of that terrible hunt for the animal we came to think and speak of as the "Mighty Lion" was an unsatisfactory stalemate. On the contrary, except for the frightful suffering endured by the lion, the end was, I believe, the most satisfactory one which could have happened. Although neither the Mighty Lion nor I won a clear-cut victory—a victory which could, in the final analysis, have only been secured either by my killing him or his killing me—neither of us really was defeated.

The boys, whose emotions had been far more deeply involved than mine, felt, I am sure, enormous relief. The conflict which had raged in them between their ancient belief in the sagacity and strength of a spirit lion and Sibyunni'byunni, their great chief who could talk to lions, had been resolved. I had not, despite terrific efforts, been able to kill the lion which they believed was the reincarnation of the last chief to rule Ibamba. On the other hand the spirit lion had failed in his purpose to kill Paddy and to drive me from Ibamba by destroying my cattle.

The fact, which they had witnessed, that I had been able to trap the Mighty Lion and wound him fearfully and, after strenuous effort, had repelled his attempt to take over Ibamba and forced him to return to the bushveld supported and confirmed the position of witch doctor in which the natives had installed me.

Sensitive and intelligent, the boys gave the Mighty Lion full credit for tremendous courage, a tenacious determination to live, and incredible strength and recuperative powers. The Mighty Lion left only glory and huge respect for him when he stalked from the *saka* that morning and, as the sun chased away the darkness of night, paced majestically toward the west.

Two great chiefs, two witch doctors, one of whom had once ruled

Ibamba and the other who presently ruled Ibamba, had met, struggled, and parted. There would never be another meeting.

About this time we received word by mail from the Central Park Zoo in New York that, provided all necessary and quarantine regulations were complied with, the zoo would be happy to board Paddy for a reasonable time. We also received a quantity of official forms from the veterinary departments in Southern Rhodesia and Portuguese East Africa, to be filled out by ourselves and a Northern Rhodesia veterinary officer, certifying to Paddy's physical condition and freedom from disease or exposure to certain diseases.

For a year or so we had had a veterinary officer, a chap named Frost, stationed at the Namwala *boma*. He and his wife had often stopped off at the ranch for a meal, and he had helped me with inoculations of my cattle. In response to a note, Frost came to Ibamba; we filled out the papers together and he stamped them with his official seal.

Frost did not examine Paddy. He was afraid of her and she knew it and teased him, thus making the situation worse. The important point, so far as securing export and transit permits was concerned, was not, however, the actual physical condition of Paddy. Pleuropneumonia was prevalent in Barotseland, the border of which was, in places, less than a hundred miles distant. There had been occasional outbreaks of foot-and-mouth disease, although none had occurred within recent years. The Veterinary Department wanted to be assured by a responsible officer that any animal transiting its territories had not been exposed to any contagious disease, and to be even more certain that any bedding in the shipment crate was free of contamination. Frost could, and did, enter such assurances on the papers, and after we had signed them, he took them to the *boma* and mailed them.

Isabella was in the eighth month of her pregnancy. It was not easy for her to attend both to Buncher's wants and needs and to help with the sorting and packing. Mianje, for whom childbearing was, can I say, an everyday affair, and a birth, easy and quick—as, of course, this was planned to be until humans insisted upon walking upright—was a trifle contemptuous of the solicitude shown to Maseccasecca. But the boys, Lavison in particular, were most concerned, and did all they could to make life easier for their mistress.

When, one morning early, one of the water boys came rushing to the house to tell us that there was a big angry lion lying on an anthill near the river and close to the spot at which we drew our water, excitement buzzed and we all hurried to the front lawn to look.

We could not, of course, see the lion. The anthill was covered with a fairly thick growth of brush and grass, and if it was there, the lion was well concealed.

Somewhat to my surprise, Isabella announced that she thought this would be a good opportunity for her to shoot a lion. When I protested that she was in no condition to risk walking across the rough veld for even so short a distance as a couple of hundred yards, she countered by appealing to Mangineera and Charlie Portuguese, who had joined us, asking if they would help her. They, of course, said they would.

Iz said that she had long wanted to have a pair of lion collarbones such as I wore around my left wrist. A pair of lion collarbones are supposed to bring the wearer very good luck, but to be effective they must be bones taken from a lion killed by the wearer.

Few persons seem to know that lions have collarbones. Light and fragile and only some two inches long, they lie in the massive muscles between the shoulders and the neck of a lion, one on each side. These collarbones appear to be rudimentary. They are not attached to any other bones, but rest embedded in muscle and flesh. They are very light, slightly curved, and knobby at each end. When dried, they feel like chicken bones.

I was surprised at Iz's announcement mainly because she had never wanted to do much shooting until then. She was a good shot, and she had her own 8 mm. rifle which had been lightened and cut down to fit her, but she did not like to kill animals. However, if she wanted to have a last try for a lion, she had certainly more than earned the right to do so.

Jam and Charlie Matabele and Shaluma arrived and we discussed the Maseccasecca's wish. From where we stood, we could see that the anthill on which the lion was reported to be hiding was surrounded on all sides by grass which had either been trodden down by men and cattle or cut for thatching or bed-making. The river-bank was only about twenty yards from the anthill, but at that point the bank was steep and rocky, and the papyrus, which grew so plentifully elsewhere, was almost entirely missing. On the north, or upriver, side of the anthill the ground was bare due to the constant passage of the watercart, oxen, and people going to draw water; just beyond this lay the dusty once-plowed land where we had tried, abortively, to grow the onion crop.

If men approached the anthill from three sides, in a semicircle, we thought we could drive the lion into the open on the bare ground fronting the watering spot. Should we be able to do this, Iz would have an opportunity for at least one good shot, unless the lion moved too fast.

Mangineera and Jam went into the house and brought Iz's rifle, my single-shot 500/450, and the pair of double rifles of the same caliber. Mangineera would carry Maseccasecca's gun and stay close by her. Jam and Charlie Portuguese, each with a double rifle, were to be on either side. Charlie Matabele, who insisted upon fetching a Mauser for himself, and Shaluma, together with several other natives, would go with me to drive the lion off the anthill.

Word of what was afoot had spread like wildfire. The cook and houseboys and all the women and children and men from the compound lined up as a gallery to watch from the lawn.

Very slowly we walked down the path toward the river. Lavison and Mangineera strode on each side of Isabella, offering their strong black forearms or their shoulders to steady her if she needed assistance. As we moved toward the river, I could not help but think of what a strange hunting expedition this was. At the same time I studied the lay of the land and the anthill and decided how we should proceed.

We stopped at the corner of the old onion field. Between Iz and the river lay some fifty yards of clear ground. It was as good a place as any for her to wait. Mangineera handed her her rifle, after making sure the safety was off and that there was a cartridge in the chamber —actions which caused Isabella to smile because she had loaded the gun herself and was cooler and more relaxed than anyone—and then stood near her.

Assured that she was as fully protected as possible, I started toward the anthill. Shaluma and Charlie Matabele went ahead and circled and formed a cordon about the western and southern sides. Up until then there had been no signs that there actually was a lion about, but as the men closed the semicircle, a lion suddenly growled loudly and the bushes on the anthill shook and trembled.

I was some thirty yards from the anthill, halfway between it and Isabella. When the lion growled, the boys let out terrific yells and beat on the ground with spears and sticks. They began to close in, and the lion growled more fiercely.

Abruptly the lion burst in a rush from the bushes and raced in tremendous bounds onto the clear ground between Iz and the river. I do not know where it thought it was going, except that it was escaping the shouting natives closing in from the opposite side. The speed with which a lion can cover ground is almost incredible until one stops to realize that a lion can catch a madly stampeding antelope and that antelope can run at forty miles an hour or better in an emergency. This means, if you figure it out, that a lion can cover fifty-eight to sixty feet in one second!

Iz had her rifle up, but the lion was going too fast for a decent shot. As the lion burst from the bushes, my rifle had flown, almost automatically, to my shoulder. I snapped a shot at it as it raced into the onion field, and hit it far back and just in front of the powerful muscles in its hindquarters. The blow spun the lion around in a cloud of dust. It faced Isabella.

For a fleeting moment it stood, its tail thrashing and deep savage growls pouring from its throat. I knew it was going to charge straight at Iz, and yelled at Jam while I feverishly levered my rifle and rammed home a fresh cartridge.

Just as the lion started its charge, a shot rang out. The lion stood absolutely still for a fraction of a second and then collapsed like a pricked balloon. As coolly as if facing a lion was something she did every day, Iz had aimed and shot it dead.

As the lion fell, a tremendous shout went up from the natives gathered on the lawn, and the boys taking part in the hunt rushed toward the fallen animal. Quickly, as I hurried to Iz to congratulate her, the boys examined the lion and rolled it over to see where it had been hit.

They found the holes where my bullet had passed through the lion but could find no other. Puzzled and excited, they parted to let their mistress approach and gazed at her with awe and admiration.

It was Jam who found Iz's bullet hole. She had shot the lion squarely in the left eye, and the bullet had entered the lion's skull without leaving a mark except for the destruction of the eyeball. When Jam pulled back the lion's eyelid and showed Isabella the bullet hole, she nodded her head.

"I didn't want to spoil the skin," she told the hunter. I saw his jaw drop and his eyes widen, and the other boys gasped in disbelief.

Their astonishment and admiration were as nothing compared to mine. I learned right then and there that I was not the only member of our family who could make extraordinary statements regarding lions. And make them stick.

Our return to the house, preceded by natives carrying the lion, was a triumphal procession. The gathering on the lawn cheered and clapped as Isabella slowly approached, and the women started their shrill keening and singing. Attended by the hunters, Iz walked like a queen between the excited, shouting natives. Slowly and carefully she mounted the steps of the front veranda and turned to thank the hunters and remind Charlie Portuguese that she wanted the collar bones of *her* lion. Then she disappeared inside.

The locusts were as numerous as ever. The enormous swarms swirled and hovered, settled, and later rose again over the vast expanse of the flats stretching to the horizon south and eastward of the ranch. Every so often clouds of the reddish-appearing insects blotted the white buildings of the Kasenga Mission from view as they settled on the rise on which the station had been built or passed over the flat which lay between the mission and Ibamba.

We paid them little attention. The locusts had won the battle and we were leaving. Their depredations could no longer hurt us. The locusts, aided greatly by the world-wide depression, had accomplished what the famed Ibamba lions had failed to achieve. It was, however, heartbreaking and discouraging to see and to hear the devastation the swarms had wrought throughout the district and the entire territory. Whenever I drove a load of goods to the railway line, we rode through swarm after swarm after swarm. Flying insects were everywhere, and hoppers covered the ground for hundreds of yards along the sandy track. The fluttering locusts mashed themselves against the windshield and clogged the radiator so that we had to stop and clean them off. They flew into the cab and beat against my face and crawled on my bare legs and thighs and arms.

As Iz's time drew near, I worked over the old truck to be sure that it would start quickly if needed in a hurry. Mangineera, Jam, and Charlie Matabele, with a compound native to keep them company, took turns sleeping for a night on the kitchen floor in case I might need their help in a hurry. Mianje was warned to be ready to come on a moment's notice to carry Buncher when we left for the mission.

The night of the thirteenth day after Isabella had shot her lion, she woke me not long after we had retired to tell me that her child was on its way. Quickly lamps were lit. A native ran to the compound to summon Mianje. I started up the truck and let the engine warm. Iz had thoughtfully packed a bag with things she thought she might need and this was placed in the truck. We wrapped Buncher warmly in her blankets, and Mianje carried her.

Lavison and I helped Iz through the house and then to climb awkwardly and painfully into the high cab. Mangineera and Lavison and some others clambered to the back of the truck to ride with us in case anything went wrong on the short four-mile journey across the flat to the mission. Two natives had been sent running on ahead to warn the Prices that we were coming.

Although I had had gangs on the road trying to keep it in some state of repair and passability, it was rough and full of potholes. Where we had to cross dips on the flat, the track was gooey and the mud, heavy and sticky. I drove as slowly and as carefully as I could, but still could not avoid all the holes. The truck, its headlights throwing streams of light ahead, lurched and swung from side to side. In the darkness which enveloped the veld stretching endlessly on every side, we were a minuscule dot of light striving to reach the assistance we would shortly need so very much.

Iz did not talk during the trip. She was, I am sure, gritting her teeth against the labor pains already pulling and contracting in her body. Her thoughts were on the ordeal which lay ahead that she could not now avoid. If she was frightened—and if she was, who could blame her?—she gave no sign. Outwardly, at least, I was the one most apprehensive and upset.

When we reached the long avenue planted with silver-leaf pines, the track became sandier but smoother. I drove more quickly, and within minutes drew up before the front veranda of the Prices' house. Light streamed from the windows, and as I left the cab, John and Florence, followed by the trained nurse, hurried out. John and I helped Iz descend, and then helped her to mount the veranda steps and walk to the bedroom which had been prepared. Florence took Buncher from Mianje. The child was only half awake, and soon was asleep in another bedroom.

Then the women shooed me out. For hours I paced in the darkness beneath the fig and jacaranda trees, listening, listening. John came out and walked with me for a while and put his arm around my shoulders. Together, at his gentle suggestion, we recited the Lord's Prayer.

At long last it was over. Standing shaken with anxiety in the gloom near the window of the room in which Isabella lay, I heard the first whimpering cry of a tiny child. Within moments John came hurrying out to tell me that the child was a boy and that Isabella was exhausted but all right. I was glad of the darkness because John, although he might suspect, could not see the tears streaming down my face.

In a little while Florence called me and I went into the bedroom. Iz, with her dark hair spread over the pillow, looked very white and tired. Her face was pinched, and there were dark circles beneath her eyes. But she smiled and pointed proudly to the little bundle lying wrapped in a blanket beside her, and I knew that she was happy that she had a boy.

There was nothing that I could do. Fathers are only a nuisance at such times. Taking Florence's advice, I collected Mianje and the boys who had come with us and drove back to Ibamba. Before departing for the compound, each of the boys shook my hand and congratulated me on having a son. I walked to the paddock and spoke to Paddy and stroked her, and then, back in the house, fell on the bed and sank into a deep sleep. Drowsily, as I drifted into slumber, I heard a tom-tom pulse, and knew that Mangineera was drumming in honor of the child which had come to Maseccasecca and Sibyunni'byunni.

It was several days before I brought Isabella and Buncher and Bubbles back to Ibamba. The boy's name was really Wynant Davis Hubbard, Jr., but we named him Bubbles because of his habit of blowing little bubbles all the time.

John and Florence gave us a letter confirming Bubbles' birth, and as we had done previously with Buncher, we forwarded the information to the American Consulate General in Johannesburg, so that our child would be registered properly as an American citizen. Incidentally, for children born overseas to American parents the State Department issues elaborate birth certificates complete with a big red seal of the Department and a bit of red silk ribbon. Very posh indeed.

It was six to eight weeks before the first rains could be expected. We had accumulated enough cash by then to be able to pay the boys and pick up the I.O.U.'s we had given them. We had completed most of our arrangements to leave except for steamship tickets. Cavadia and Frost, the stock inspector, had agreed between them to take over the cattle, although the prices they paid were considerably below what we ought to have received. The veterinary department had returned transit permits allowing us to take Paddy with us to the coast.

As a result of a rather angry and demanding letter to the executor of my parents' estate, in which I laid our situation out in detail, we received sufficient money to pay for rail travel, the steamship tickets, freight, and incidentals. The executor had never either approved of or, far less, understood what it was that I had wanted to accomplish in Africa.

We planned to return on the steamship line which had brought us to Africa. Accommodations were limited on those combination freight-passenger vessels, and we learned that we could not secure passage until late in November. We decided to stay on Ibamba until the last moment before the rains would make traveling difficult, and then to take the rail trip south to Beira in easy stages. This would give Iz the maximum time in which to regain her strength, and it would be better for Bubbles.

Frost had applied for retirement, and he made arrangements with Mopani Clarke to move into our house and to run a few head of cattle on Ibamba after we left. This helped to resolve the problem of what to do about all the building material on Ibamba. I had bought and paid for and erected a considerable number of casement windows and interior doors, sheets and sheets of galvanized roofing, wire netting, stock fencing and barbed wire. There was the bathroom with its, for Rhodesia, unique equipment.

In theory, of course, in as much as I had erected these on land which belonged to Mopani Clarke—because I had not been able to complete the payments to purchase Ibamba—the building materials and the buildings belonged to Mopani. He came out to the ranch and we went over all these things together and inspected and appraised the farm machinery which I had not been able either to return to North and Company or to sell. Mopani was very generous and paid a decent sum for what he called the "improvements." This helped financially quite a lot.

During September I took the two duiker antelope out to the big *saka* and left them. They were fully adult, knew how to graze, and would be able to care for themselves. Their greatest danger lay in the fact that having been raised in association with a civet cat and a lioness and having mingled freely with dogs, they might not dash for safety as promptly as might be necessary.

Frost had taken a fancy to the lechwe and asked if we would leave the antelope on Ibamba for him and his wife. I was only too happy to agree. I had never learned to care much for the lechwe, but I did not want to shoot it. The only other thing I could have done would have been to take the truck and carry the antelope far out onto the main flats and release it near some wild lechwe. But I had neither the time nor the gasoline to do so.

Both Isabella and I wanted to do something for our special boys which would, at least, indicate how fond we were of them and how greatly we appreciated their loyalty and the advice and help they had given us so consistently. Although we had some funds by then, we dared not run ourselves short by giving each man a monetary present. Our future was far more problematical than theirs.

I knew that my hunters and trackers and gunbearers, Jam, Mangineera, Charlie Portuguese, and Charlie Matabele had long been casting envious eyes upon my traps. Should I give the traps to them, I knew that they would not use them, as I had, to trap lions, leopards, hyenas, and small cats. In their own way they would use the traps to catch antelope and buffalo, which would be cruel. Nevertheless, I divided the traps and gave each man his share. This was perhaps wrong, but I justified my actions by telling myself that the boys were not getting any younger, and that after we left, they would face a difficult problem securing food because of the locusts. The traps would help them to secure meat, and meat could be traded for many things as well as being used as food for themselves.

We gave Shaluma a very decent assortment of carpenters' tools so that he could set himself up in business, and to Mianje we gave a small single-furrow plow. Shaluma said he had a pair of oxen trained to the yoke and he would teach his wife how to handle the plow, which would mean much less back-breaking work for her and, if Mianje paid attention to what she was doing when plowing, a far larger return in grain than she could expect otherwise.

Although they were too large for him, Lavison gleefully accepted all the shorts and short-sleeved shirts for which I would no longer have use, and such socks, shoes, old jackets, and other clothing as I could spare. Iz, too, went through the remains of her wardrobe and found many items to give away. These we distributed so that everyone received at least a small gift of sorts. We divided the salt remaining in the storeroom and the small quantity of weevil-infested grain and gave away the last tins of jam and the few pounds of flour and sugar and tea.

By the end of September we were about ready to leave. Paddy's shipping crate had been completed and stood waiting for her. The Frosts had packed their belongings at the *boma* and were ready to move onto Ibamba the day after we left.

Then came the final crushing blow. An outbreak of foot-and-mouth disease was discovered near the Barotse border. Immediately all permits for the movement of livestock of any sort were canceled. In the mail we received notification of the cancellation of our transit permits and the export permit for Paddy. There was no possibility of securing a special permit or a reprieve.

Stunned and disbelieving, we read and reread the letter from the Veterinary Department. Frantically we debated what to do. Our steamship passages were booked. There was very little time in which to try and make other arrangements for Paddy. No other white man I knew of wanted so large a lioness or would know how to care for her if I could find someone who would take her. Actually, until the first blanket restrictions on the movement of livestock were amended, we were not supposed to move any animals off Ibamba.

If I had thought that Paddy would have been able to survive, I would have taken the truck and driven her to the Home of the Lion and released her and taken a chance on being caught and fined. But although Paddy had killed a few times when in her paddock, she knew nothing about how to stalk and kill wild game on the open veld.

There was the very real danger that the wild lions which she was bound to meet would turn on her and kill her. Having been raised with humans, she, of course, had no fear of men. If I released her in the Home of the Lion, Paddy would trot right up to the first hunters she encountered, seeking to make friends. In such an event she would die beneath their spears or from wounds from their muzzle-loading guns.

There was also the possibility, remote but still there, that because of her association with people Paddy might develop into a fear-some man-killer. If I released her and she was unable to kill her natural food of antelope and pigs, she might, in desperation and hunger, turn to killing humans.

There was only one possible answer. I put the awful decision away from me for as long as possible. But it was inevitable. I would trust no one except myself to carry it out.

One morning, with tears streaming down my face, I called Paddy to me and shot her through the head between her great luminous, trusting eyes. With that shot something went out of me that has never returned. That was twenty-six years ago, but as I write, my throat tightens, I find myself swallowing, and my glasses do not seem as clear as they were.

We buried Paddy very deep so that no one would dig up the body to take the skin. Over her grave I cast a slab of cement which I obtained from the mission, and in the wet surface I wrote a curse, in native, with my finger, so that no man would dare to disturb her as she slept.

When the final day came and we left Ibamba, we drove continuously through a swarm of locusts which were flying at right angles to the track. We did not know where the swarm began or ended, but at a minimum it was one hundred and twenty-five miles wide and the Lord only knew how lengthy. The trip took eight hours. I drove slowly so that Iz and I could savor the country for the last time and so that the children would not be bounced about too much. During those hours we were never out of the locust swarm.

We stayed a few days in Choma, during which time we disposed of the long-suffering truck and made arrangements to join the ship we were to take in Cape Town instead of Beira. By journeying to Cape Town, I would have an opportunity to show Isabella another part of Southern Rhodesia; the red sand edges of the Kalahari Desert, Johannesburg, and the great sheep-raising country of the Karroo.

All the way south to just outside De Aar, in the Cape Province, the train ran through swarms of locusts which swirled up with the passage of the heavy engine and the cars. As we stared out the windows, the land looked desolate and bare. At the end of the dry season the country always had a bone-dry abandoned appearance, but it seemed to us that this time it looked worse than ever; forlorn, eaten out, and weary unto death.

To cross the level land of the high Karroo, with its almost limitless desert and salt bush, two powerful Mallet type locomotives were necessary. So many hoppers were crossing the tracks that one engine could not grip the rails with sufficient traction to pull the train. The driving wheels slipped and whirled and jerked the cars along, shaking all of us aboard and keeping the children awake in their bunk.

We indulged ourselves in Cape Town with a sitting-room suite at the beautiful Mount Nelson Hotel. The windows looked out over the lovely gardens, the city as it sloped down to the harbor, and the wide blue bay. In the distance we could see the dark mounds of cliffs which were the Cape of Good Hope.

Our little splurge in Cape Town while waiting for the ship to come down the east coast from Beira was taken care of unexpectedly by a bonanza from England. A letter came from our agent in London informing us that our nickel novel, *The Thousandth Frog,* had been sold for publication to Blackie and Sons. Enclosed was a check for one hundred pounds as advance against royalties.

Such a disastrous, heartbreaking four years would, one would think, cure anyone of what is known as the African sickness. But there was something about that great wild country, with the friendly natives, the even friendlier animals, the enormous sweep of territory, the storms and the gigantic fires, the towering mountains, that dug into a person and secured a grip which never slackened. Perhaps it was the challenge of the land, so brooding, so huge, so quiet.

Far out on the veld, with the stretching canopy of the sky overhead, surrounded by trees and grass, rivers, mountains, animals, and birds, there was peace and quietness and time to think and ponder; to study, to play with children, and to plant seeds and watch them grow. The things by which we moderns set so much store—money, clothes, the latest automobile—shrank in importance and in value. There was time on the veld to think of God and what He means. Out on the veld there was time to practice patience and forbearance, to see the other fellow's side of things.

Having animals live with you is an enormously satisfying, demanding, and broadening experience. It is impossible to live with animals and not come to realize that we humans are not so unique after all. Living with animals teaches any but the most stupid that animals also experience love and fear, hatred and jealousy, and that they will make sacrifices for their companions and their loved ones equal to any that man will make.

One comes to know, living far away and alone, that there is some Supreme Being who put the spark of life in all of us animals, four-legged and two-legged, winged and crawling and swimming. Deep underneath, the same basic principles motivate each and every one of God's creatures.

Living with animals, above all, teaches one that it ill becomes a human to look down upon others of the great animal family. In these hectic days we seem to have forgotten the golden rule by which all animals should live. We humans, supposedly the most civilized of all animals, are the only species which consistently breaks every rule of God and of man.

Shalla gushi. Rest in peace.